The Travels of Dean Mahomet

The Travels of Dean Mahomet

An Eighteenth-Century Journey through India

Edited with an introduction
and biographical essay by

Michael H. Fisher

UNIVERSITY OF CALIFORNIA PRESS

Berkeley   Los Angeles   London

University of California Press
Berkeley and Los Angeles, California

University of California Press, Ltd.
London, England

© 1997 by the Regents of the University of California

An expanded version of this book is being published as *The First Indian Author in English: Dean Mahomed (1759–1851) in India, Ireland, and England* (Delhi: Oxford University Press).

Library of Congress Cataloging-in-Publication Data

Mahomet, Sake Deen, 1759–1851.
    The travels of Dean Mahomet : an eighteenth-century
journey through India / edited with an introduction and
biographical essay by Michael H. Fisher.
        p.   cm.
    Includes bibliographical references and index.
    ISBN 0-520-20716-5 (alk. paper). — ISBN 0-520-20717-
3 (pbk. : alk. paper)
    1. Mahomet, Sake Deen, 1759–1851—Biography.
2. Mahomet, Sake Deen, 1759–1851—Journeys—Europe.
3. Immigrants—Great Britain—History 18th century.   4.
East Indians—Great Britain—Social conditions.   5. East
India Company.   Army—History.   6. India—Politics and
government—1765–1947.   I. Fisher, Michael Herbert,
1950–   .   II. Title.
DS412.M25A3   1997
915.404'29
[B]—DC21   96-19700
                                                   CIP

Manufactured in the United States of America
9   8   7   6   5   4   3   2

To Nathan and Doris,
also the children of immigrants

CONTENTS

Contents / ix

ILLUSTRATIONS

MAP

FIGURES

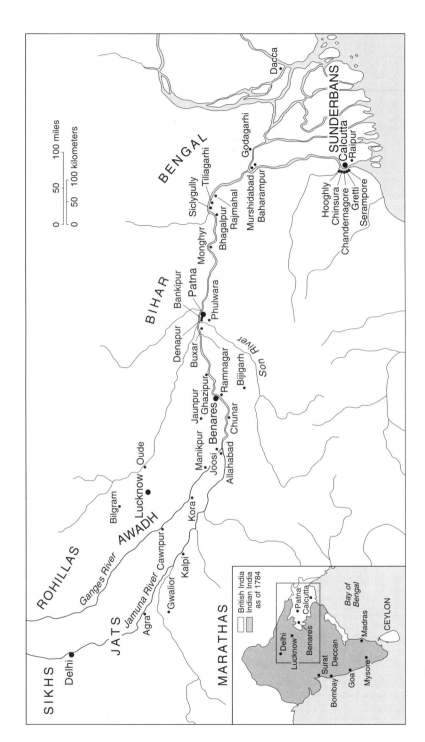

India in the time of Dean Mahomet.

PREFACE

A TEXT AND A LIFE

[W]e have never been as aware as we are now of how oddly
hybrid historical and cultural experiences are, of how they
partake of many often contradictory experiences and domains,
cross national boundaries, defy the *police* action of simple
dogma and loud patriotism. Far from being unitary or mono-
lithic or autonomous things, cultures actually assume more
"foreign" elements, alterities, differences, than they con-
sciously exclude.

Edward W. Said, *Culture and Imperialism* (1993)

Dean Mahomet composed his book *Travels* in 1793–94 as "a series of letters to a friend," recounting to the Europeans among whom he lived the
world of India from which he came.[1] He began his autobiographical travel
narrative with his wrenching departure in 1769 from his childhood home
among the Muslim elite of north India. He concluded it with his voyage
of immigration to colonial Ireland in 1784. Through *Travels*, he presented
his personal account of the multitude of peoples and customs he encountered while marching across north India as part of the English East
India Company's military conquest of his homeland. His *Travels* thus rep-

resents a fascinating perspective on these peoples, these customs, and this colonial conquest: the first book ever written and published by an Indian in English.[2]

Dean Mahomet grew up during the tumultuous late eighteenth century, as the largely Muslim rulers of north India—whom his family had served for generations—succumbed to the expanding English East India Company. The Company rapidly shifted from a commercial corporation to the assertive ruler over vast Indian territories—two hundred and fifty thousand square miles by 1800, a million by 1856, with another half million under its indirect control. While the English Company continued to trade (especially in cotton cloth and opium), its extraction of taxes and loot from Indian lands under its sway garnered even larger sums. In this environment, Muslim families such as Dean Mahomet's had to make difficult and potentially dangerous choices about their future and their allegiances. Many chose service to the English: Dean Mahomet recounted the entry of his father, his elder brother, and then himself into the English Company's army.

During Dean Mahomet's twenty-five years in India, he moved among multiple roles. The premature death of his father, and his elder brother's inheritance of their late father's position, left him at age eleven to make his own fortune. In 1769, he attached himself as a camp follower to a teenage Protestant Anglo-Irish officer, Godfrey Evan Baker; the two men remained together until Baker's death eighteen years later. Over the course of their respective careers in the English Company's army (1769–83), Dean Mahomet rose to become a subaltern officer, as Baker rose from cadet to captain and independent command. During these years with the Company's army, Dean Mahomet's relationship with other Indians remained ambivalent. While his Muslim relatives accepted him as an honored guest at their domestic rituals, he nevertheless stood as an outsider to their world by virtue of his attachment to the British. Some Indians in the countryside assaulted him as part of their resistance to British control; others rescued him and gave him shelter. In his life and writings, he revealed the social and cultural tensions inherent within that substantial class of Indians which fostered British colonial expansion over India.[3]

Through Dean Mahomet's own words and surviving British records, we can retrace his eventful journeys with the English Company's army as it passed up and down the Ganges River, forcing the many peoples and states of north India under British rule. His dramatic narrative of his travels though diverse cities (including Calcutta and Benares) and rural environments (including dense jungles, arid plains, and rich agricultural regions), and his range of interactions with the varied peoples living in each, enables us to understand the complexity and internal divisions within Indian society. We can note the specificity with which he described his natal community's internal social organization and domestic customs, in contrast to his more limited knowledge of those of other Indian castes—for example, Brahmin Hindus. His marches with the English Company's army took him perhaps as far west as Delhi and certainly as far east as Dhaka (today Bangladesh); later he sailed to Madras in south India (see Map). As he traveled, the multiplicity of Indian society meant that each city and region which he encountered struck him as novel. He described each vividly to his British audience.

As we examine Dean Mahomet's life and words, we can see the vital roles taken by many different classes of Indians in the colonial process. The English Company used remarkably few Europeans to conquer and rule India. For example, in 1771 the Company had only 187 British civil officials in Bengal to govern some thirty million people; thousands of Indian subordinate officials at many levels carried out the actual work of administration.[4] Similarly, the Company's armies which extended and enforced British rule consisted of many times more Indians (officers, soldiers, servants, camp followers, and their families) than Europeans (mainly Protestant English, Anglo-Irish, Irish, Scottish, or Welsh officers, men, and—less frequently—their families). Dean Mahomet brings alive for us this colonial world in which an array of ethnicities and social and economic classes interacted, sometimes in hostility, sometimes in cooperation, always in cross-cultural exchange.

Travels exposes the complex and often alienating attitudes Dean Mahomet—and tens of thousands of other Indians in service of the English Company—held toward the British conquest. Many felt distanced from cultures of the old regimes which their ancestors had served. All remained apart from the Europeans who hired them. Like Dean Mahomet, each worked in distinct ways to create new social spaces for themselves between these cultures.

DEAN MAHOMET IN EUROPE (1784–1851)

In crossing boundaries, Dean Mahomet went further than most of his class. Following the abrupt and disgraceful end of his patron Baker's military career in 1783, Dean Mahomet began yet a more distant journey: as an immigrant to colonial Ireland. After marrying Jane Daly, a young Protestant Anglo-Irish gentry woman, he published in Cork his two-volume memoir of his Indian travels. In this 1794 work, he retained a strikingly accurate command of detail long after the events he described. He also demonstrated his elegant command over high English literary conventions.

Modern readers of his *Travels* can note the ways in which he appropriated the English travel narrative genre—the only Indian to do so in the eighteenth century. His generally sympathetic representations of Indian peoples and beliefs distinguished his work from those of Europeans in revealing ways. He, after all, wrote as someone from India for an audience of Europeans, representing himself and his background for their approval. Their images of India stemmed from their position as the colonizer not the colonized. Yet, Dean Mahomet too had fought to support the English Company's colonial regime in India.

While Dean Mahomet's book apparently bolstered his stature in the eyes of Irish society, it also highlighted his alien origins from the Europeans whom he had served and among whom he lived, married, and wrote. Further, his presentation of India had little lasting effect on prevalent British colonial attitudes toward the land of his birth or its cultures. After over two decades in Cork, he left Ireland, looking elsewhere for a place for himself and his family.

Dean Mahomet and his growing Anglo-Irish-Indian family emigrated to London around 1807. The increasingly cosmopolitan world of the British capital presented both opportunities and constraints for immigrants from India, Ireland, or elsewhere in the burgeoning British empire. In London, Dean Mahomet served for a time as a medical practitioner in the fashionable mansion of a rich Scottish nobleman and veteran of the East Indies. Then he started an Indian coffeehouse catering to members of the British elite with "Oriental" tastes. By 1812, however, he had exhausted his financial resources. Searching around for yet another way to market his Indian attributes to the British public, he moved to the resort town of Brighton, on England's south coast.

Starting over again at age fifty-five, Dean Mahomet struck upon a profession, combining Indian and British medical practices, that would bring him fame if not fortune. In Brighton, he created appreciation for his medical arts as an Indian therapeutic masseur. Through skillful practice and publicity that elicited the patronage of the British elite including the English royal family, he rose to the top of the professional world of medical bathhouse keepers. Claiming exclusive access to "Oriental" medicinal arts, Dean Mahomet negotiated for himself a distinguished place in British society. He left for us carefully crafted newspaper advertisements, his second autobiographical book (about Oriental and Western scientific medicine), evidence of the architecture of his bathhouses, and his medical innovations. From these, we can explore the ways that he created images of himself, combining Asian and English elements in ways that for two decades proved highly attractive to British society.

Dean Mahomet lived, however, during a time of expanding British imperialism. As the Victorian era proceeded, British attitudes toward Indians, Muslims, and the Orient generally, hardened into doctrines of British racial superiority. These English ideologies of an essential "difference" between English and Indians diminished the space available for his own representations of India to the British.[5] In the years before his death in 1851, he lost control over his career and reverted to the margins of British society.

THE SIGNIFICANCE OF
DEAN MAHOMET'S WORK

Dean Mahomet's act of writing *Travels*, including his selections of content and genre, have powerful implications for the ongoing scholarly debate about the relationship between literature and colonialism. Edward Said, in his highly influential work, *Orientalism* (1978), asserted that Westerners enforced—and largely still enforce—exclusively unilateral cultural representations of Asia: "The power to narrate, or to block other narratives from forming and emerging, . . . constitutes one of the main connections between . . . culture and imperialism. . . . From the beginning of Western speculation about the Orient, the one thing the Orient could not do was to represent itself."[6] As Pratt demonstrates, European travel writers consistently objectified colonized peoples and localities through the "imperial gaze," constructing them for the West.[7]

Despite the unquestionable fact of Dean Mahomet's authorship of his *Travels*, many Westerners of his day believed Asians incapable of authoring such a polished work of English literature. Even today, some readers may cling to similar doubts and look for a British hand behind Dean Mahomet's pen. While he clearly borrowed—in today's terms, plagiarized—brief sections of his descriptions from European authors (as I analyze in Chapter Three), he nonetheless clearly retained his own voice throughout. Further, unlike some of his British contemporaries, Dean Mahomet's book presented Indians as human beings worthy of respect in their own terms. They had virtues, superior in some ways to—albeit different from—those of Europeans. Few European works of his day took his position. Thus, Dean Mahomet's book stands as an important counterexample to any one-sided view of English literature during the age of imperialism as the sole preserve of Europeans.

Homi Bhabha, Henry Louis Gates, Edward Said, and other scholars have shown that Asians and Africans regarded their power to narrate and represent their own experiences in their own terms as powerful modes of resistance to European cultural domination.[8] For example, former slave Olaudah Equiano (and other antislavery activists of Dean Mahomet's day) explicitly argued that his autobiographical book, *The Interesting Narrative of the Life of Olaudah Equiano . . . The African, Written by Himself* (1789), proved the humanity of Africans and hence the immorality in trafficking in such humans as if they were mere property. Indeed, Equiano toured Ireland, including Cork, publicizing his autobiography in 1791, just three years before Dean Mahomet published his *Travels*.[9] The existence of such non-European perspectives on, and participation in, the imperial process exposes the multilaterality of that process. Nevertheless, while Dean Mahomet's book demonstrates the existence of long-neglected Indian voices in the colonial process, the limited impact of his book on British attitudes toward India suggests European lack of openness to his narrative.

Some modern readers may expect that, because Dean Mahomet was ethnically Indian, he would have produced an account radically—instead of subtly—different from his contemporary European writers. Such an anachronistic expectation of an Indian nationalist stance misinterprets his position and circumstances. We must move beyond the stark dichotomies of identity between colonized and colonizer, Orientals and Westerners, "us" and "them" that have become the hallmark of both imperialist and nationalist/anti-imperialist discourse.[10] Rather, each person embodied a range of positions, as Dean Mahomet and Equiano demonstrated in their writing and their lives.[11] Dean Mahomet wrote for the British elite, on whom he depended and among whom he married and lived as an immigrant, about his years of service as an Indian camp follower and then subaltern officer in the English Company's army as it conquered India. In his *Travels*, he assessed the virtues and flaws of both British and Indian cultures, each of which did much to shape his identity. He stood between them, rather than as wholly part of either.

Dean Mahomet chose the fashionable English genre of the epistolary travel narrative for his presentation of his life in India. Constructed letters, addressed to a fictive European friend, enabled him to establish a personal relationship with his British readers. He further identified with his intended audience by publishing at the head of his book the list of his three hundred and twenty prominent British patrons. He dedicated his book to a colonel in the English Company's Bengal Army, W. A. Bailie. The sophisticated genre he chose also allowed him scope for allusions to high English literature and Latin quotations (which he did not translate into English, thus presupposing the erudition of both his readers and himself). Since this literary genre held great popularity in Britain at the time, but was unknown in his natal culture, his choice recapitulated his self-location as an intermediary, drawing upon an English form to represent his Indian background for an elite anglophone audience. Pratt uses "transculturation" to describe how subordinated or marginal groups select and invent from materials transmitted to them by a dominant or metropolitan culture. While subjugated peoples cannot readily control what emanates from the dominant culture, they do determine to varying extents what they absorb into their own, and the uses to which they put it.[12]

Dean Mahomet's deliberate use of an autobiographical voice in *Travels*, especially in his early chapters, bears on the current debate over differences between conceptions of the self in Asia as opposed to Europe.[13] Some scholars argue that the concept of the individual as a historically minded being, and hence autobiography as a literary genre, emerged only in post-Enlightenment Europe; more recent scholarship has questioned this assertion as ethnocentric.[14] Although the term "autobiography" would first appear in English print only years later in 1809, Dean Mahomet clearly presented himself as an individual, with passages (particularly in his first chapter) which show his self-awareness—imagining how others perceived him. Each of the engravings which he published in *Travels* represented an aspect of his identity: an European-dressed Indian Gentleman, an Indian army officer, and an Indian courtier in an Indian ruler's procession (figures 1–3 of this book).[15] His decade living in Ireland prior to writing *Travels* distinguished his account from those of Muslims and Asians who visited Europe but did not remain as immigrants.[16] Indeed,

Dean Mahomet lived continuously in Europe for the last sixty-six years of his life.

Dean Mahomet's marriage to an elite European woman, as well as his use of literary (and later medical) accomplishments to enhance his honored place in British society, suggest the diversity of experiences among Indian immigrants to Britain. British society relegated the vast bulk of Asians in Britain at this time to the lowest social classes.[17] Nevertheless, many of the elite in Ireland subscribed to Dean Mahomet's book and accorded respect to his marriage with a woman of their class. Later, large numbers of the English elite submitted their bodies and health to his hands as a medical surgeon and masseur. These attitudes remind us that British society during his lifetime did not demand racial segregation or condemn (what would later be called) interracial sexuality, including sexuality involving White women and Black men. Indeed, a number of other Asian and African men married or moved freely through society with European women during this period.[18] Thus, Dean Mahomet's marriage and his degree of success as a professional medical man stand as warnings against simple projections backward of later English racial categories or attitudes.

Overall, Dean Mahomet's life and his writings reveal much about cultural interactions within the imperial process, a process which created what Pratt terms "contact zones": "social spaces where disparate cultures meet, clash, and grapple with each other, often in highly asymmetrical relations of domination and subordination."[19] Dean Mahomet lived for decades in colonial India and Ireland, where the dominant English used force of arms to try to impose their rule and culture on the indigenous peoples. Yet these English impositions proved far from hegemonic, as his own self-expressions indicate. Throughout his life in these colonies, he made himself a man transculturated: neither assimilated into the dominant English colonizing culture nor integrated with the subordinated, colonized one. By examining his life and writings, and those of other such intermediaries, we can move toward an understanding of the hybridity of the imperial process.

The neglect his *Travels* has endured for two centuries among literary critics and historians indicates the marginality of its position and his. Like other books published in Cork, *Travels* received little attention in the metropolis. As an Indian author, Dean Mahomet did not fit European conceptions of India. Thus while elite journals in London knew of his book, they did not accord it a review (although they did review many travel narratives about India by Europeans, even ones they considered inferior).[20] Further, when Irish nationalism ended the Anglo-Irish Protestant Ascendancy, few of the more than four hundred and fifty copies of Dean Mahomet's book survived. Thus, this republication of *Travels* brings his book and role in the imperial process to our attention.

A GUIDE TO THIS VOLUME

This book reproduces many of the words of Dean Mahomet and sets them and his deeds in their historical context. In order to understand the world in which he moved in India, Chapter One surveys his life to 1784, when he emigrated. Readers who wish to go directly to his original account of his life in India might begin with Chapter Two: a republication of his entire book, *Travels*. To present his work as directly as possible, I have made no changes in his organization. I have, however, left out the list of subscribers and also placed in square brackets the modern form of place names for which he simply made up his own phonetic spellings as no standard transliteration system existed in his day. I have also translated, in brackets, his Latin quotations. The Glossary contains brief definitions of key words he used and the index includes the full names of people he mentioned. Chapter Three traces his eventful later life, from when he concluded his narrative in *Travels* at age twenty-five until his death at ninety-one.

ACKNOWLEDGMENTS

I would like to thank Paula Richman, Roswita Fisher, James Fisher, Dane Kennedy, and Lynne Withey in particular for their careful suggestions for revision of drafts of this book. Rozina Visram, J. Stewart Cameron, and Prabhu Guptara were especially generous in sharing their knowledge of, and enthusiasm for, Dean Mahomet.

I am grateful to the staffs of the following libraries for graciously allowing me access to their collections: Brighton Reference Library, British Library, Cork Public Reference Library, East Sussex Record Office (Lewes), Family History Centre (Chancery Lane), Greater London Record Office, Guildhall Library, Marylebone Public Library, National Army Museum, National Archives of India, National Library of Ireland, India Office Library (British Museum), Pavilion Art Gallery and Museum (Brighton), Public Record Office of England (Chancery Lane, Kew), Public Record Office of Ireland, School of Oriental and African Studies Library, Society of Genealogists Library, Office of Population Censuses and Surveys (St. Catherine's House, London), Principle Registry of the Family Division (Somerset House, London), Trinity College (Dublin) Library, University College Cork Library, Wellcome Institute, Westminster Public Library.

Finally, I thank Oberlin College for awarding me Research Status for this project. I am, of course, responsible for the material in this book, including any errors.

ONE

The World of Eighteenth-Century India

THE MUGHAL EMPIRE AND THE REGIONAL STATES

During the eighteenth century, the Mughal Empire, which for two centuries had provided political and cultural leadership for virtually all of India, fragmented as a variety of regionally based rulers seized power. As these regional states clashed with each other and with the Emperor, little sense of a unified Indian nation existed. The expanding presence of rival European trading companies inserted further levels of discord into this contentious mix. Conflicting loyalties cut across each other, each demanding a different set of allegiances from the diverse peoples of India. Thus, over the generations preceding Dean Mahomet's birth in 1759, his family—among others—had to make fundamental and potentially dangerous choices about their commitments: to the nominally sovereign Mughal Emperor, to their Muslim community, to their distant relative who ruled the provinces of Bengal and Bihar, to their fellow elite of Patna city, or to one of the European East India Companies which increasingly offered employment.

The Mughal imperial dynasty drew its initial support from a band of central Asian and Iranian adventurers but over the sixteenth and seventeenth centuries it managed to command the submission and service of virtually all the peoples of India. The Mughals had invaded India from central Asia in 1526, justifying this conquest as their inheritance from their two world-conquering ancestors: Changiz Khan and Timur (Tamerlane). The great wealth and prestige of the Mughal imperial court continued to attract ambitious warriors, scholars, and merchants from west and central Asia. Dean Mahomet asserted that he descended from Arab and Turk immigrants drawn to India via Iran in the seventeenth century by the lure of honorable service to the Mughal Empire. Eventually, the Mughals coerced or enticed India's many regional rulers into subordination. Thus, the Mughal Emperors had woven together Muslim immigrants and members of India's regionally distinct local populations into a relatively centralized state; hitherto, this much of India had never been unified under one ruler.

Many factors held each of the many distinct regions of India together as a political, cultural, and economic entity. Every region—including Bihar, where Dean Mahomet's family lived—had long traditions as an autonomous state or, under the Mughal Empire, as a separate province. The majority of the people in each region had a distinctive language or dialect (although Persian had become the language of administration and high culture, linking the elites of each region to the Mughal imperial court). Much of the agricultural and craft production within each region circulated internally, yet the regions were linked commercially by interprovincial and international trade and fiscally by the Mughal land-revenue administration.

At the Mughal Empire's peak, its extensive land-revenue collection system drew from the Indian countryside sufficient wealth to support its elaborate centralized superstructure. The ornate Mughal imperial court and household, and the households of its upper officials which were nearly as grand, lavishly expended these vast resources. The dress, music, and literary compositions of the Mughal imperial court inspired imitation in a range of elite households of both Muslims and Hindus across the subcontinent. In turn, these households gave employment to cascades of subordinate families, including that of Dean Mahomet, providing as well cultural models for them to emulate in consumption patterns and norms of comportment. The Mughal Empire thus offered honorable and lucrative employment for large numbers of both indigenous Indians and immigrants. It created an expansive service elite of administrators and military who continued to dominate Indian life for centuries.

The Mughal imperial armies in particular had provided regular or occasional employment for literally millions of officers and soldiers each year. One authoritative account from the end of the sixteenth century listed 343,696 cavalry and 4,039,097 infantry as the military manpower base within the Mughal Empire.[1] The Mughal armies, in turn, comprised vast markets for a variety of clothing, weapons, foodstuffs, and other necessities and luxury goods. They employed many times their number of provisioners, artisans, and other camp followers. These armies remained almost constantly deployed in extending the Empire, in enforcing imperial rule over resisting peoples within it, and in succession struggles among contending Mughal princes. Thus, their consumption of men and other resources continued to be insatiable. Indeed, one major factor in the eventual decline of the Mughal Empire from the end of the seventeenth century onward stemmed from its overexpenditure on the imperial court and army, given its declining income from an overtaxed agricultural and manufacturing resource base.[2]

During the eighteenth century, each province in the Mughal Empire broke away from the effective control of the Emperor. A number of imperial governors entrenched themselves in their provinces and transformed their appointments into hereditary possessions. One such dynasty, prominent in *Travels*, was the Shiite Muslim family ruling (1722–1856) Awadh, in the central Gangetic plain. Dean Mahomet claimed kinship with another such dynasty: the Nawabs (Governors) ruling (1740–1854) Bengal and Bihar provinces, in eastern north India.

As the imperial center weakened, indigenous peoples in several regions produced their own leaders who fought to reestablish regional autonomy. Such peoples included the Marathas (from west-central India), the Sikhs (in central Punjab), and the Rohilla Afghans (in the upper Ganges plain)—who all appeared in *Travels* as threats to English rule. The rulers of such states had strong cultural bonds with the dominant people of their home region, unlike the Nawabs of Bengal and Awadh. Nevertheless, virtually all regional rulers continued to submit symbolic and monetary offerings and promises of revenues to the Mughal court in order to legitimate their power with imperial-sanctioned authority. Such rulers then fought to extend their control over their neighbors, with varying degrees of success. Since each region had its own local culture, the conquered people often regarded these rulers as outsiders. For example, the people of Bihar, who spoke a local dialect of Hindi, became subordinated to the Bengali-speaking province of Bengal, under a Persian-speaking Nawab, who boasted family origins from outside of India but defended the province from Marathi-speaking conquerors from the southwest. In short, political identity proved highly diffuse and many loyalties remained divided. During Dean Mahomet's youth, service to one or another of the European trading companies seemed an attractive opportunity for families such as his.

THE EUROPEAN EAST INDIA COMPANIES

The European presence in India had become quite diverse by the time of Dean Mahomet's youth, with a variety of implications for the shape of Indian society and politics. European travelers and merchants had been journeying overland to India, or via the established Indian Ocean trading networks, for centuries. The Portuguese had discovered a direct sea route to India in 1497, three decades before the Mughal Empire established itself. As the cosmopolitan Mughal Empire grew, it simply accommodated the burgeoning European presence without radical dislocations: in Mughal eyes, Europeans were just another set of peoples, having different values and strengths, but ones with whom they could deal.

During the seventeenth century, northern European states chartered national trading companies: England (1600), Holland (1602), Denmark (1616), and France (1664). Each European company built warehouse bases (called "factories") on the Indian coast with dependent factories inland. In Patna where Dean Mahomet grew up, satellite factories were erected by the English (c. 1650), Dutch (c. 1650), and French (c. 1720). Patna's production of saltpeter (essential for manufacturing gunpowder), indigo (a powerful dye for cloth), and opium (vital for the European trade with China) proved particularly attractive to these European merchants. To Dean Mahomet's family and others like them in Patna, the various European companies may not have seemed threatening to their order at first. By the mid-eighteenth century, however, the expanding presence and aggressive policies of the competing European companies had began to dislocate and reorient trade and culture at all levels in India.

European companies vied with each other, and with private European merchants, for control over production, trade, and—increasingly—political influence. The English East India Company proved the most successful of the European powers but it felt continually threatened by French operations in Europe, Africa, and Asia, especially by the French diplomatic and military presence in the courts of many of the Indian rulers. Napoleon's invasion of Egypt in 1798 had as one major objective a threat to the British in India. Indeed, the French and the British remained almost continuously at war until 1815 (when Dean Mahomet was fifty-six years old and had been living in Europe for over thirty years).

While other European companies in India at times proved annoying to the English, they did not present the same military threat as did the French. The English fought one brief war with the Dutch in 1759, the year of Dean Mahomet's birth, and subsequently reduced the Dutch Company to a limited role in India. In *Travels*, Dean Mahomet blamed the Dutch Company's remaining factory in Bengal for the extensive and—in his view—immoral trade in opium from India to China. Dean Mahomet did not explain that the English Company monopolized opium production, collection, and sale in India or that the importation of opium into China remained mostly in British hands. Even the English Company's Directors in London recognized the stigma of this trade, writing in 1781: "Under any circumstances it is beneath the Company to be engaged in such a clandestine trade; we therefore, hereby positively prohibit any more opium being sent to China on the Company's account."[3] The English Company's officials in India, however, responded that the economics of purchasing tea in China made this "not a matter of choice but necessity," since they had little else the Chinese would buy.[4] The Company's face-saving solution was to auction its opium in India to other merchants, including Dutch and private English traders, who then exported it to China.

The Danish Company, with a factory near Calcutta (the English capital in India), also remained an irritating commercial rival—but not a substantial danger—to the English. Indeed, the Danes in India remained in an uneasy state of dependence, relying on purchases of cotton cloth, saltpeter, and other goods controlled by the English. Therefore, a variety of European companies and private merchants interacted, always in competitive—and often in hostile—ways.

From the mid-eighteenth century on, the English Company sought enhanced political influence with India's regional rulers (including the Nawab of Bengal) so as to extend both its own special exemptions from their judiciary and also tariff privileges for its trade—and for the private trade of its European employees. This led eventually to a transformation in the commerce in Bengal and Bihar, at the cost of established Indian merchants. In particular, the English Company reshaped the region's extensive cotton hand-weaving industry around its demands and requirements, a major factor in the English Industrial Revolution.

In Patna and elsewhere in north India, many prominent families declined under these trying circumstances and their own infelicitous choices of allegiance and commitment. Other families, such as that of Dean Mahomet, managed to take advantage of the unstable situation. Over time, the most successful families were those which oriented themselves toward commercial, administrative, or military service to the English Company, acting as intermediaries between the British and the other peoples of India. Since Dean Mahomet and his family chose to serve the English Company's Bengal Army, and since *Travels* tells us so much about life within that army from an Indian perspective, it will be useful to examine this army's origins and early development.

THE DIVERSE ORIGINS OF THE BENGAL ARMY

A significant shift for Indian society—and for Dean Mahomet's family in particular—came as the English gradually transformed the role and form of the military in India from the late eighteenth century onward. During the years that Dean Mahomet's father, his elder brother, and he himself served the Company's Bengal Army, what it meant to be a soldier in India changed markedly. The amalgamation of European military science with various military patterns traditional in India proceeded sporadically, in the Company's armies as well as in those of its allies and enemies.

During the first half of the eighteenth century, the Company had maintained only a limited military component: a few European officers, drawn either from the Royal Army or from the Company's commercial branch, serving to supervise European or part-European "sentinels" and Indian "peons" who had guarded the Company's factories.[5] As the English Company involved itself in regional politics and in anti-French maneuverings, its armed forces grew. Indians with martial experience provided the only viable source—in terms of cost, quantity, and quality—for such expansion.

The English Company gradually developed a separate army in each of its three bases ("Presidencies"): Bengal, Madras, and Bombay. Although the youngest of the three, the Bengal Army developed into the largest. It arose directly out of the conflicts between the English Company and the Nawabs of Bengal. By the 1750s, the Company had five hundred soldiers (including Europeans and Indians) and ten to twenty British officers in Calcutta.[6] In June 1756, the newly installed Nawab of Bengal, Siraj al-Daula (r. 1756–57), expelled the English from Calcutta in retaliation for English repudiation of his authority, and seized the Company's reputedly large treasury. His capture of Calcutta caused the ignominious flight of most of the Company's British officials and officers there, a flight which abandoned most of the Company's Indian employees and soldiers to his mercy. Many of the captured Europeans died, giving rise to the "Black Hole" legend. On receiving word in Madras of this disaster for the Company, Robert Clive undertook a hurried expedition north by sea to Bengal with what forces could be spared from the Company's Madras Army.

On his arrival in Bengal, Clive rapidly recaptured Calcutta (January 1757) and began local recruitment of three to four hundred Indians—professional and semiprofessional soldiers and officers, most originally from Bihar.[7] Further armed confrontations led to the decisive battle at Plassey (June 1757), during which the English Company arranged the defection of much of the Nawab's army and defeated the rest. Indeed, Persian-language histories of the day explained the English Company's conquest as resulting from the internal factionalism and moral decline of the ruling Indian families of the region, rather than from English military superiority.[8] After the English drove the incumbent Nawab out of office, the Company installed a series of Nawabs, each more tightly under its control than the last. In addition, the high officials of the Company extracted vast personal fortunes—totaling some £2,600,000—as gifts from successive Nawabs in exchange for their elevation.[9]

Given the velocity of his military recruitment drives, Clive must have hired men from the extant Indian military labor market of professional and semiprofessional soldiers, many with experience serving in other armies. For most of these recruits, therefore, military service to the English Company would have been a job opportunity, rather than a career or an ideological cause. Only gradually did the Company shift military employment from more traditional and indigenous forms to a new model which reflected both Indian and European patterns.

THE NEW MODEL: THE SEPOY

Indian soldiers, including Dean Mahomet and others of his family and class, developed new roles under the command of European officers. With Clive as commander, the English Company started to train and equip Indian recruits uniformly along the lines of an innovative and distinctive military type: the sepoy. This Persian term (*sipahi*) had been long current in India to mean a cavalryman. From the mid-eighteenth century onward, however, the French and English Companies adapted it into their prime model for an Indian infantryman, trained, dressed, and armed in a semi-European manner.[10]

The military science of Europe, which had developed over decades of costly war on that continent, brought to India a pattern of military discipline and supply that would prove decisive in the English Company's conquest of India. The quality of European weaponry was not then superior to the best that India could produce by hand. Nevertheless, England's system of mass manufacture meant that large numbers of identical weapons of reasonable quality could be supplied at a relatively low cost. Instead of groups of Indian soldiers, often recently hired by their Indian commander, wearing a variety of clothing and bearing nonstandard weapons and requiring custom-made ammunition, the Bengal Army began to substitute the regular training of standing military units in disciplined field maneuvers, supplied with uniform equipment. Such European models of "rational-bureaucratic" organization of indigenous soldiers gradually made the difference in India—and elsewhere in the European colonies in Asia and Africa.[11]

In Europe, military scientists had discovered empirically that rigorous close-order drill of a standing, professional army enabled trained officers to reposition orderly bodies of troops even while under heavy fire or cavalry attack. In India, this meant that companies of sepoys with European or European-trained officers could stand up to—and maneuver while under attack by—the artillery and heavy cavalry that formed the core of many Indian armies. Further, the larger groups of less drilled foot soldiers that filled out the forces of Indian rulers and landholders had to give way before the sometimes smaller but frequently more disciplined and uniformly armed units of Company sepoys. As a contemporary of Dean Mahomet recognized in his Persian-language commentary, so long as the British-commanded soldiers "maintain their formations, which they call 'lines,' they are like an immovable volcano spewing artillery and rifle fire like unrelenting hail on the enemy, and they are seldom defeated."[12] The sepoy thus formed the dominant model for soldiers within the Indian component of what would become the Company's new armies.

During the second half of the eighteenth century, many Indian states also followed this model. Across India, sepoys became increasingly a factor in war and in the enforcement of land-revenue demands, but such units proved relatively expensive. Individual European officers claiming the expertise to train sepoy units demanded from their Indian employers large salaries and often autonomy as well. The European-model weapons and training of sepoy units became a constant drain on the treasury of all who deployed them.

The English Company itself only just managed to sustain the cost of such European-pattern Indian armies. The Company's Bengal Army consumed a high percentage of its budget: over the decade prior to 1770, the Company spent about £8,000,000 directly on the Bengal Army (in addition to the costs of building and maintaining the army's bases), over 50 percent more than it spent on the purchase of trade goods.[13] In the eyes of the Company's Directors and shareholders in London, the army was a largely unproductive expense; indeed, the army's activities seemed only to generate further costly political and military entanglements with India's regional rulers. Nevertheless, the Company recognized the growing necessity for an army for the defense and subjugation of territories under its control.

To support the expense of this army, the Company drew upon an extensive and effective revenue-collection administration, unprecedented financial support and subsidies from the English Government, and unsurpassed borrowing credit in India and England. Rival European companies and the regional rulers of India could not command such a range and scale of resources. Thus, they could not sustain the continuous employment of the tens of thousands of European-trained Indian officers and men—like those of Dean Mahomet's family—who composed the English Company's armies.[14]

For many regional rulers, alliance with the Company, and hence access to the services of its sepoy armies, proved a superficially attractive but ultimately even more costly strategy. The Company subsidized large portions of its army by essentially renting its troops to its Indian allies. These troops went on the payroll of the Indian ruler, but remained under British command. Military dependency on the Company, however, meant that these rulers gradually lost much of their treasuries, sources of revenue, and finally their independence. Over the course of the period described in *Travels*, for example, the ruler of Awadh slipped from command over the most powerful military force in north India to almost complete military dependence on the Company's army and therefore on the Company's will. By the mid-nineteenth century all Indian rulers had succumbed either to annexation or to indirect control at the hands of the Company.[15]

SEPOY BATTALIONS

Throughout the period of Dean Mahomet's *Travels*, the boundaries of the Bengal Army remained ill-defined. Sepoys and Indian officers moved relatively easily from one army to another, including into or out of the Company's army and that of its opponents of the day. For example, Clive raised his third battalion of sepoys (eight hundred to a thousand men) at Patna in April 1758, mainly out of men who had seen military service in other armies. Dean Mahomet's father most probably entered the Company's army in this recruitment drive, between the births of his first and second sons.

Not until 1764 did the Bengal Army formally start to institutionalize its sepoy model. The Company found that the existing relatively informal organization and discipline of the Bengal Army had led to mutinies variously by its European officers, European soldiers, and Indian officers and sepoys. Following the suppression of a mutiny by sepoys near Patna in 1764, the Army established a regularized body of rules and systematic set of maneuvers, based on the code of standing orders then in force in the Royal Army.[16]

This code of standing orders sought to bring further uniformity to the military conduct of the Bengal Army. Traditionally in India, a military labor contractor bargained for the best deal for himself and his professional or peasant-soldiers from any one of a number of possible military employers; soldiers felt free to shift from army to army as opportunity offered.[17] Many sepoys continued to regard service with the Company's army as a temporary situation, to be entered into or left at their pleasure. In 1781, for example, the Company complained that whenever one of its sepoy battalions relocated to a different region, locally recruited sepoys regularly deserted it and reenlisted in the new battalion transferring into their region, rather than accept relocation.[18] The English Company sought to reorient sepoys until they saw themselves as individuals bound professionally and by "honor" to the Company's army.[19]

British commanders used a semi-European uniform and drill to try to professionalize sepoys and minimize individuality and visible ethnic or community differences. Hindu and Muslim sepoys—indeed sepoys from all religions and regions—had to dress and act uniformly, at least while on duty. The sepoy uniform reflected European elements mixed with British interpretations of Indian traditions. The standard-issue military coat and flintlock "Tower musket" (one stamped as tested at the Tower of London) were European in pattern. The necklace of beads—the relative quality of the glass, conch shell, or precious metal beads respectively denoting rank—was apparently a British adaptation of the gorget used in European uniforms to denote military rank.[20] The Company's official specifications for a sepoy's uniform required: "1 turban, 1 cummerbund and caross [waist-shawl and crossed bands], 1 linen jacket, 1 pair of junghiers [military shorts], 1 coxcomb or turah [ornament], 1 silver regimental device for ditto," plus a round shield (target) suspended at the back of the left shoulder of both sepoys and Indian officers;[21] Dean Mahomet supplied figure 2 to depict a sepoy and Indian officer in uniform.

For the Company, profit remained an intrinsic organizational principle in its army as well as its commercial operations. Each sepoy had to purchase his own uniform for Rupees 6, which gave a generous profit to his British commanding officers, who arranged to supply it. In addition, each sepoy had a fixed sum withheld from his monthly salary to pay for the new uniform coat he received each December. Yet the sepoy did not own the coat he so purchased; a discharged or promoted soldier had to give his used coat to his replacement. Thus, Indians inducted into the Company's Bengal Army increasingly found a vocation with professionalized characteristics growing ever more distinct from earlier military service patterns.

The Company continued to recruit Indians by the thousands annually for its Bengal Army from the 1760s onward. By 1765, Clive reorganized it into 3 Brigades (each consisting of 7 battalions of sepoys plus 1 regiment of European troops, 1 company of European artillery, and 1 troop of cavalry), totaling some 14,000–15,000 Indian soldiers and some 3,000 European officers and men.[22] When Dean Mahomet attached himself to the Bengal Army (in 1769), it totaled 27,277 active Indian officers and men, in addition to about 522 European officers and 2,722 European soldiers.[23] By the time Dean Mahomet resigned from the Bengal Army (in 1782), some 52,500 Indians were currently serving in it, and over 115,000 in the Company's three Presidency armies combined.[24] In addition, many more Indians entered and then left the Company's armies over the years through resignation (as did Dean Mahomet), death, or disability. Thus, a substantial number of Indians enlisted in the Company's armies and submitted to the training and discipline that made them sepoys, then conveyed their experiences serving the British with them back into Indian society.

Further, a broad variety of Indian official servants and informal camp followers enveloped the European and Indian officers and soldiers.

Camp servants formally employed by the Company worked under the command of Quartermasters to set up and move the camp, transport its baggage and equipment, and handle the distribution of its supplies. Additionally, individual soldiers, officers, and units had a variety of personal servants and camp followers, according to their rank and purse. Indian mistresses or families of soldiers or officers, both European and Indian, often accompanied the army—even in the field. The ratio of official servants and unofficial camp followers to soldiers varied but generally averaged two or three of each per soldier: some 35,000 per brigade. Feeding, clothing, and defending such a large concourse of people proved a continual logistical problem of enormous proportions. Arthur Wellesley (later famous as the Duke of Wellington) maintained that his experience organizing the logistics of his campaigns in India (1799–1804) prepared him for his successful contest with Napoleon in the Iberian Peninsula. Dean Mahomet would himself number among the unofficial camp followers until he was twenty-three years old. In these ways, large numbers of Indians chose to enter the Company's military structure, either formally as sepoys or informally as camp followers; their collective participation in, and shaping of, British rule over India should not be overshadowed by the largely European accounts that have survived from this period.

THE BENGAL ARMY'S EUROPEAN REGIMENTS

Alongside Indian sepoys, European troops served in the Company's armies, but under quite different conditions. Unlike sepoys, European troops remained perennially in short supply and expensive; nevertheless, the Company believed them to be the heart of its army. The long English wars in Europe created a chronic shortage of able-bodied European males—even for the Royal Army which, by law, held precedence in recruiting over the Company. Consequently, the Company engaged contractors ("crimps") to supply Europeans—of any nationality, including

French, German, and Swiss prisoners of war—at a rate of up to £5 per man.[25] Indeed, London newspapers reported that the Court of Directors illegally arranged for European men to be kidnapped and forcibly impressed into its armies.[26]

During this period, Company officers in India constantly complained, and London regularly made excuses, about the low quality and inadequate quantity of these European recruits. Mortality rates on those transport ships that reached India sometimes approached 50 percent. In addition, the high rates of deaths in India from disease—and occasionally from wounds—created a constant, and largely unmet, demand for European soldiers. Despite nominal requirements for age, size, and health, many of the recruits who finally reached India proved unfit for duty.[27] In 1768, the Commander-in-Chief wrote about the latest crop of European recruits: "they are exceedingly bad . . . the refuse of our metropolis. . . . The Company are at a great expence to send abroad annually a number of soldiers when in fact, instead of recruiting our army, they only serve to increase our Hospitals. . . . [A]t present our European Regiments compared to a Battalion of Sepoys appear like a Regiment of Dwarfs."[28]

Despite the difficulties in recruiting such European soldiers, and the relatively abundant supply of Indian soldiers, the Company saw these European infantry regiments as its moral core—although they comprised only about 15 percent of the Company's army in India. At this time European officers and European troops "mutinied" about as frequently as Indian troops. Nonetheless, many Britons in the Company believed that sepoys would only stand firm in battle if European regiments provided "stiffening."

DEAN MAHOMET'S YOUTH IN BIHAR
(1759–69)

From the time of Dean Mahomet's birth onward, the English Company proved the most consistent patron for his family and many others like it. Muslim families like his comprised an important component of the Company's army and administration, particularly in the upper ranks of Indians, but always below Europeans. In the Bengal Army over the period that Dean Mahomet chronicled, Muslims consistently composed nearly half of the higher Indian officer corps, about two-fifths of the lower Indian officers, and about one-third of the sepoys, far in excess of their minority proportion of the general population (roughly one-quarter).[29] As the power of the Nawab of Bengal and the other mainly Muslim regional rulers of India declined, many members of the Muslim service elite decided to attach themselves to the rapidly expanding English East India Company's armies or administration. Additionally, Clive and others in the Company sought to retain an even balance between Hindus and Muslims in the army. The Company throughout this period devalued Bengalis as soldiers, preferring to recruit non-Bengalis for its Bengal Army: "the fighting Tribes of the Hindoos and Musselmen [Muslims], and as many of the latter as can be procured."[30]

For the Company, as for the Mughals, strong class distinctions separated high Indian officers from lower officers and sepoys. The elite background of Dean Mahomet's father apparently led the Company to put him directly into one of the officer ranks in the Company's Bengal Army. His father reached the rank of *subadar* (lieutenant), the second highest that an Indian could attain at that time in the Company's army (after *komidan*, "commandant").

Dean Mahomet grew up in a context where the English East India Company increasingly forced and precipitated changes in virtually all aspects of life in India. These were years when the Company began to assert increasingly broader authority over the administration of Bengal and Bihar. By installing a series of their clients as Nawabs of Bengal, the English Company had gained political supremacy over the incumbent officials in Bihar as well. From 1757 to 1765, the English Company largely attempted to use the Nawab of Bengal's existing administration to extract revenues from the Bihar countryside. Dissatisfied with the results, the Company thereafter created an ever more British-controlled administration. In particular, the Company appointed Thomas Rumbold in 1766 to head the Patna Revenue Council, supervising the Nawab of Bengal's Deputy Governor for Bihar, Raja Shitab Rai.

To remain in his position of power over Bihar, Shitab Rai had to please Rumbold and other British officials of the Company. He lavishly entertained British officers and officials. Further, he collected ever increasing land revenues for the Company from Bihar, backed up by the force of Company troops—including those under the command of Dean Mahomet's father. Both landholders and villagers frequently engaged in armed resistance to such revenue exaction. Only when hard-pressed would they negotiate payment of that year's revenue. Dean Mahomet's father died in 1769 while enforcing Shitab Rai's revenue demand during a time of famine. Nevertheless, the Rajas who killed Dean Mahomet's father subsequently negotiated an adequate revenue payment and thus soon obtained their release from prison.[31] Thus, the British and Shitab Rai may have regarded the death of Dean Mahomet's father as only an unfortunate but minor incident in their annual campaign to force landholders to pay their taxes; Dean Mahomet's family clearly regarded his sudden and premature death as a tragedy.

DEAN MAHOMET AS CAMP FOLLOWER (1769–81)

As the second son of a distinguished, but deceased, father, Dean Mahomet had to establish a career for himself. In earlier generations, he might have drawn on the traditional ties between his family and their relatives and patrons, the Nawabs of Bengal, for an opportunity for military service. By 1769, however, the Nawab's service promised little, at just the time a career in the Company's service seemed especially inviting.

The eleven-year-old Dean Mahomet reported his fascination with the colorful uniforms and confident bearing of the Company's British officers, as he watched them participate in the convivial life of Patna's high society. At a British tennis party, Dean Mahomet caught the eye of his future patron, Godfrey Evan Baker of Cork, Ireland. Baker, a newly appointed cadet at the beginning of his career, had just been assigned to the Third European Regiment of the Third Brigade in the Bengal Army. In a European regiment, little place existed for Dean Mahomet except as a camp follower. Although Dean Mahomet dressed and drilled in the regimental style, until age twenty-three he nevertheless remained attached to the Bengal Army only as a member of Baker's entourage.

Over Baker's years in India, his entourage would grow significantly. A Captain (the rank at which Baker retired) would ordinarily have thirty-five to forty servants and attendants; a Lieutenant Colonel over a hundred.[32] As Dean Mahomet matured and gained experience, he probably took charge as majordomo of Baker's expanding household.

For the first dozen years of Baker's military service, he chose the lucrative career track of a Quartermaster commanding Regimental *lascars* (laborers) and other official uniformed camp servants, rather than a line officer commanding a regular infantry company. Quartermasters had to extract provisions for their regiment from the countryside, ensuring that Baker had far more contact with Indian society than most British officers. Further, he had continual opportunities to profit from provisioning his regiment, as well as to conduct his own personal trade. Since the Company spared its European regiments the most dangerous or onerous duties (relegating such duties to sepoy units), neither Baker nor Dean Mahomet engaged in combat during their first dozen years in the Bengal Army.

The complex political situation in India, however, meant that Baker's Brigade, with Dean Mahomet in his entourage, ranged across north India. Early in 1771, a threatening advance by the Marathas from the west toward Company territory determined the Company to dispatch the Third Brigade from Denapur cantonment (near Patna) to the Karamnasa River at Buxar.[33] This expedition drew Dean Mahomet away from his mother in Patna; indeed, the entire life of the Brigade was disrupted. The existing stores in the cantonment—including tents, clothing, weapons, ammunition, and a panoply of other goods—had to be packed up or sold off and new stocks purchased for the campaign. The families of soldiers, servants, and camp followers all had to be left behind or brought along. Financial arrangements with local businessmen or moneylenders had to be wound up. For the transport of stores, the Brigade's Quartermasters had to obtain a thousand or more bullocks from reluctant villagers.

Once into the countryside, the Brigade's foraging and looting soldiers and their servants disrupted life in all the villages and towns they passed. Villagers who encountered this march in 1771 identified the damage from the Brigade with that of a devastating hailstorm; one district complained of Rupees 15,000 worth of losses.[34] In addition, this journey to the western edge of Bihar apparently took Dean Mahomet on his first trip outside the Patna area, into territory clearly alien to him. The people of these territories were not reconciled to English rule as their sporadic raids on the regiment's camp, and their kidnapping of Dean Mahomet, demonstrated. On the banks of the Karamnasa River, which marked the western border of Bihar, the Brigade poised ready to advance further against the Marathas, whom Dean Mahomet later characterized as "disturbers of the public tranquility" (Letter XXXI).

When this latest Maratha threat receded and the hot season of 1771 intensified, the Company ordered the Brigade to withdraw in stages down the Ganges River toward Calcutta in order to repulse a dreaded French invasion.[35] As the Brigade left Bihar, Dean Mahomet passed through countryside particularly resistant to Company rule. The narrow passes through the hills into Bengal had long been a much contested route as Paharis ("hill people") fought off outside control. Part of the Bengal Army's assignment was to suppress such resistance, a process that Dean Mahomet described in gory detail. Emerging from these passes, the Brigade moved slowly down to Calcutta, where it arrived in May 1772. For the next six months, Dean Mahomet lived in the Company's military headquarters, Fort William, at the center of Calcutta.

Calcutta, as the major center for the English Company's commerce and administration in India, had become a prosperous and entrepreneurial city. As the "City of Palaces," Calcutta stood second only to London in the British empire. Dean Mahomet described in impressed tones the city's

bustling markets for local and international trade and the Company's expanding administrative structures. New—largely Hindu—commercial
and administrative elites evolved and prospered in Calcutta; during the
early nineteenth century these classes would begin the vibrant cultural
movement known as the "Bengal Renaissance." For Dean Mahomet,
however, these new elites seemed pretentious, filled with "supercilious
disdain," and alien to men of his background (Letter XXXVII).

Some hundred and twenty miles to the north of Calcutta at Baharampur, the English Company had just constructed an expensive new
base for its troops, adjacent to the Nawab of Bengal's capital of Murshidabad. Dean Mahomet and Baker shifted to these cantonments, where
they remained for two years (1773–74). Here, Dean Mahomet rediscov-
ered the culture from which his family came, but toward which he had
become an outsider.

In contrast to Calcutta, the Nawab of Bengal's Murshidabad continued as a capital in decline from its former glory. The Company's peri-
odic cuts in its pension to the Nawab, its forced reductions in his army,
and its diversion of the administration from his officials into its own hands
all meant that Murshidabad and the—largely Muslim—elite of the old
regime had lost their sources of income. Even the main channel of the
river had shifted away, making Murshidabad a literal backwater. Dean
Mahomet's poignant depiction of himself as spectator to the passing of
the Nawab's court suggested his own position on the outside of that fad-
ing world of his ancestors.

When the Third Brigade marched back up the Ganges in 1775, the
journey brought Dean Mahomet into contact with the world of the central Gangetic plain—further west than he had ever been before.[36] His
fresh description of the people, countryside, and cities through which he
passed reminds us of the cultural and ecological variety of the Indian subcontinent which made everything so new and striking to him. Each region evoked a different set of associations for him, and each was part of
a different political entity. Benares, under a subordinate ally of the Company, Raja Chayt Singh, reminded Dean Mahomet of the sacred element

in Indian culture and of its ancient accomplishments, which he proudly described without communal distinctions between Hindu and Muslim. The cities of Allahabad and Delhi—the Mughal imperial capital—led him to describe in rich detail the faded glories of the Mughals; at that time, the Emperor remained a palace prisoner of the Marathas.[37] The Third Brigade camped near Bilgram in Awadh for two years, as part of the English Company's lease of its troops to the Awadh rulers.

The English Company sought to decrease its military expenses and simultaneously gain influence over its Indian allies by renting them parts of its Bengal Army. This sometimes left the Army vulnerable to dangerous entanglements in those allies' affairs. In 1774, parts of the English Company's Bengal Army had fought on behalf of the Awadh ruler Shuja al-Daula (r. 1754–75) against his neighbors, the Rohilla Afghans. Dean Mahomet, and many British officers, complained that the Bengal Army bore the burden of the fighting but the Awadh ruler received the spoils—including captured Rohilla princesses. Although Dean Mahomet remained in the Baharampur cantonments during this war, he recounted the Awadh ruler's mortal wound at the hand of the Rohilla princess whom he sexually violated—an event widely rumored at the time but unsubstantiated.

At the end of 1775, Dean Mahomet and the Third Brigade bivouacked in Bilgram, taking their turn on the Awadh ruler's payroll.[38] In June 1776, while Baker's European Regiment remained safely in garrison, sepoy battalions of their Brigade bloodily suppressed a mutiny by the Awadh army against the new Awadh ruler, Asaf al-Daula (r. 1775–97). The Brigade incurred in the process substantial casualties—and the consternation of the Company's government against this unauthorized intervention in the domestic affairs of Awadh. The Third Brigade finally abandoned Bilgram in October 1777, burning that base to deny it to the Awadh ruler. The Brigade's withdrawal reflected the Company's effort to pull back from such deep involvement in Awadh. In his account of Awadh and its capitals of Lucknow and Faizabad, Dean Mahomet emphasized the immorality of its rulers and also their splendor (see figure 3).

Over the next three months (November 1777–January 1778), Dean Mahomet marched with the Third Brigade some eight hundred miles down the Ganges River to Calcutta.[39] News of the declaration of renewed war between France and England reached Calcutta in July 1778, mobilizing massive preparations for the defense of that city from the expected French invasion. For nearly three years, the Third Brigade stood ready to defend Calcutta: in cantonment at Calcutta (January 1778–September 1779), then Baharampur (September 1779–December 1780). Meanwhile, other parts of the Company's armies won and lost against its enemies elsewhere in India. From a distance, Dean Mahomet took pride in the Company's daring capture of the supposedly impregnable fortress of Gwalior during the First Anglo-Maratha War (1775–82).[40] He also highlighted a "victory" by Colonel Baillie in the Second Anglo-Mysore War (1780–84) against Haydar Ali, a Muslim military entrepreneur who had subordinated the Hindu dynasty of Mysore state and then challenged the Company for control over peninsular India. In fact, the Mysore army defeated Baillie and killed or captured his entire detachment of 3,720 men (September 10, 1780). Dean Mahomet wrote little about his own life during these years in garrison.

DEAN MAHOMET
AS BENGAL ARMY OFFICER (1781–82)

With the promotion of his patron, Baker, Dean Mahomet entered a new phase of his career, as an official provisioner and then subaltern officer in the Bengal Army. In January 1781, Baker's seniority garnered him a promotion to Captain and command of one of the two sepoy battalions in Major William Roberts's Thirtieth Infantry Regiment in the Second Brigade, then stationed up the Ganges at Cawnpur.[41] This promotion came despite Baker's recent conviction by court-martial for insubordination, brought against him by his commanding officer—an event which Dean Mahomet refrained from mentioning in *Travels*.[42] As Baker marched to Cawnpur, he took command of a detachment of two companies of sepoys and two companies of Europeans (some four hundred men) also going in the same direction. He used his newly acquired patronage to appoint Dean Mahomet as market master to supply this detachment by collecting provisions from the territories through which they passed. Local resistance to the depredations of Bengal Army sepoys led to Dean Mahomet's narrow escape from death at the hands of a hostile peasantry.

After taking command of his new battalion at Cawnpur, Baker again exercised his patronage by arranging to have Dean Mahomet appointed *jemadar* (ensign) in one of its elite grenadier companies under his command. This appointment, however, violated the Bengal Army's formal regulations for such appointments, since Dean Mahomet lacked the necessary seniority. The irregularity of his appointment may have made Dean Mahomet feel reticent about command of this grenadier company. Further, he was much shorter (about five feet tall) than the men he commanded, who were selected for their imposing height (closer to six feet). Nonetheless, Dean Mahomet took command, although he never mentioned any of his men or other Indian officers in *Travels*. As was customary, Dean Mahomet had personally to pay a gratuity of half a month's salary to Major Roberts, commanding the Regiment, for confirmation of his appointment.

As officers in a sepoy regiment, Dean Mahomet and Baker engaged in far more combat than they had during their dozen years with a European regiment. Further, by 1781, the Company's financial situation had become particularly precarious. Its military expansion and extremely costly wars against the Marathas and Mysore had drained its treasury. Governor-General Hastings (1772–85) sought to extract money from the Company's enemies and thus prevent bankruptcy and placate the British Parliament and Company's Directors.

Almost immediately after Dean Mahomet's appointment as officer, his Regiment joined the expedition under Colonel Morgan to drive the Marathas out of the Kalpi region, just south of the Jamuna River, and collect the region's revenues for the Company.[43] In April 1781, Morgan attacked Kalpi fort and expelled the Maratha garrison. He then demanded that the local administration pay the Company the tribute it had previously submitted to the Marathas. When the Maratha negotiator sought to prevaricate until his force could fully collect that season's harvest, Morgan launched a preemptive strike (including Dean Mahomet's company) against the Maratha force of some two thousand cavalry. The Marathas withdrew with no loss on either side.

In addition to using the Bengal Army for fiscal and territorial gains at the expense of its enemies, Hastings also used military threats to extract money from its allies: the rulers of Benares and Awadh. In the fall of 1781, Hastings ordered Dean Mahomet's battalion to the Awadh capital, Lucknow, where he intended to visit and thus put pressure on the Awadh ruler for more funds. Meantime, Hastings personally visited Benares to force that Raja to contribute more to the Company. Immediately after having reached Lucknow, however, Dean Mahomet's battalion received a desperate message from Hastings ordering it to rush to Benares and rescue him.

Raja Chayt Singh (r. 1770–81, d. 1810) of Benares had been a subsidiary ally of the Company since 1775. By treaty, the Raja promised to pay Rupees 2,340,249 annually to the Company, and to maintain troops ready to assist its army. In 1778–79, the Company unilaterally increased its demands, asserting that the Raja, as the Company's "feudal vassal," was obliged to provide as much cash and military support as his overlord needed. For some time, Chayt Singh had argued that these enhanced demands exceeded what the extant treaties required, and that he could not afford to meet them in any case. After Hastings arrived at Benares in August 1781, he had upped the pressure on Chayt Singh by ordering two companies of sepoys to arrest him. Chayt Singh's loyal troops assembled to release him and slaughtered the Company's sepoys. By an oversight on the part of their British officers, these sepoys had not been issued ammunition; 174 sepoys and their British officers were killed or severely wounded.[44] When open warfare broke out, Hastings himself nearly fell into Chayt Singh's hands and had to retreat while issuing frantic orders for all the Company's troops in the region to assemble for his rescue. Another ill-conceived Company attack led to another massacre of sepoys, French "Rangers" in the Company's service, and their officers. This second defeat forced Hastings to flee for his life. Dean Mahomet's battalion marched rapidly from Lucknow, while other Company troops escorted Rupees 50,000 (borrowed from the Awadh ruler) in order to pay the Company's troops their long overdue salaries.

After Dean Mahomet's company arrived at Benares on September 13, he took a leading part in the attack on Patita fort. Hastings described this fort as: "much stronger, and the approach more hazardous, than he had expected . . . a small square house of stone, itself fortified with four round towers, and enclosed with a high rampart, and a ditch, which is in most parts broad and deep."[45] Grenadier companies of the Thirty-Fifth and Thirtieth Regiments—including Dean Mahomet's company—assembled into a shock force which successfully stormed the fortress, at their loss of twenty-one casualties.[46] In his report, Hastings especially commended the grenadiers and their British commander, Captain Lane. Dean Mahomet modestly highlighted Baker's service in this battle rather than his own.

Following this action, Dean Mahomet and Baker took on the task of commandeering much needed supplies from the hostile countryside for the Company forces pursuing Chayt Singh's remaining army. After Major Popham drove Chayt Singh into exile, he negotiated a surrender of the virtually impregnable fortress of Bijigarh in November. When this fortress fell, Popham interpreted a private letter from Hastings to mean that he could divide Chayt Singh's vast treasure among his troops "on the drum-head" (i.e., immediately, on the spot). Since this treasure amounted to some Rupees 4,000,000 (£400,000) cash plus much jewelry, and since the whole purpose of Hastings's journey was to extract funds from Chayt Singh for the Company's official use, this summary distribution led to considerable acrimony within the Company. Popham himself took Rupees 294,000 while each British Captain received Rupees 22,478 and even sepoys received Rupees 50 each.[47] Despite their protests, neither Dean Mahomet nor Baker received anything since their units were not present at the time Bijigarh surrendered.[48] The Company, on its part, demanded that all the prize money be returned, and instituted court-martial proceedings and civil suits against those officers who refused to comply.[49]

In Dean Mahomet's final series of operations as part of the Bengal Army, he helped suppress insurrection in the Benares countryside. After expelling Raja Chayt Singh, the Company installed his infant nephew in his place under the guidance of a Regent, but with the reduced status of *zamindar* (landholder) rather than ruler. The Company also raised its demand on Benares to Rupees 4,000,000 annually. It further placed the civil and judicial administration under the supervision of its Resident political agent.[50] This divided authority led to tension and mutual recriminations. Baker and Dean Mahomet's battalion had orders to impose this new government's authority on the villagers in the region, who resisted it. In particular, Baker and Dean Mahomet's battalion undertook punitive expeditions into the countryside around Ghazipur and Jaunpur. Dean Mahomet mentioned his promotion to *subadar* during this service in Benares.[51] Nevertheless, the brutality of these expeditions seems to have inspired him to elegiac poetry about the tragic waste of war.

Subsequently, Dean Mahomet abruptly recorded that he and Baker decided to resign from the Army and move to Ireland. Behind this cryptic statement lies much that illuminates both Dean Mahomet's own possible divided loyalties and also the hostility between the Bengal Army and the Indian countryside. Although Dean Mahomet did not mention it, Baker's resignation eventuated from accusations against him by villagers that he had extorted money from them. Governor-General Hastings had ordered Baker to arrest three alleged murderers of a Brahmin named Dharma Dube, early in 1782. The Benares Regent complained to Governor-General Hastings that, instead, Baker had seized an entire village and held it for ransom.[52] Hastings thus ordered Baker recalled from active duty in disgrace in July 1782. Although the Company's Resident in Benares investigated and declared Baker not guilty of these accusations, Baker resigned from his command of a battalion in the Thirtieth Regiment in October 1782. He may also have given notice that he intended formally to resign from the Army; the rules of service required a year's advance notice.

On his part, Dean Mahomet had come to find his career in the Bengal Army disagreeable, particularly in contrast to accompanying Baker into a new life in Ireland. Dean Mahomet's defense of the deposed Raja Chayt Singh and his obvious pain at the destruction and suffering inflicted by the Bengal Army on the Indian countryside—necessary to impose order as they might have been in his eyes—may suggest his mixed feelings about his position in that army. His explicit reasons for resigning his commission were his own "desire of seeing that part of the world" and conviction "that I should suffer much uneasiness of mind, in the absence of my best friend," Baker (Letter XXXV).

DEAN MAHOMET IN TRANSIT (1782–84)

Following Baker's dishonorable recall and Dean Mahomet's resignation, they took time to visit Dhaka city and explore the Sunderbans jungle on their way to Calcutta. Even for ordinary transfers between postings, the Bengal Army allowed British officers a generous amount of time: six weeks for this trip to Calcutta.[53] If he followed the usual practice, Baker hired at least three boats: a twelve-oared vessel for comfortable travel during the day and for sleeping at night, an attendant baggage boat for luggage and servants, and a separate cookboat. Dhaka remained famous at that time for the court of its Nawab, its urbane culture, and the quality of its fine muslin cloth and other products. Thus, Baker and Dean Mahomet may have been attracted to Dhaka to indulge in tourism and/or in private trade, purchasing goods for later sale in Calcutta or Ireland. Their subsequent voyage through the deltaic Sunderbans brought them into a densely jungled maze of low islands. British officers customarily took with them an escort of sepoys, since gang robbers lurked in fast boats among the islands.

The year that Baker and Dean Mahomet spent in Calcutta (January 1783–January 1784) must have been somewhat painful for them both.

Dean Mahomet, having resigned from his prestigious appointment as *subadar*, apparently returned to the status of majordomo or dependent companion in Baker's household. Baker, also having effectively terminated his career in the Army, marked time as a supernumerary officer with no specific command. While in Calcutta, Baker may also have been winding up his business affairs, or passing them on to his younger brother, Lieutenant William Massey Baker, before leaving India permanently.

Baker officially resigned on November 27, 1783, citing pressing family responsibilities.[54] In deciding to end his career after some fifteen years in India, Baker was not unusual. In the more prestigious civil service, less than half the inductees of his age set still remained in service.[55] Further, prospects for promotion in the Army's officer corps (even for someone without Baker's tainted record of service) were in decline, as looming peace in Europe and India brought reductions in the Company's army. Cutting their ties to the English Company, Dean Mahomet and Baker left India on a Danish ship, rather than an English East India Company vessel.

The Danish and English Companies remained commercial rivals. The English Company tried to control the export of capital from India, desiring to harness it for the Company's own use. The Danish Company also tried to tap this capital for its purchases of Indian goods and thus offered better interest rates than the English.

On a more personal level, Dean Mahomet's emigration may not have been legal. The English Company had long worked to prevent the creation of an indigent community of Indians in London—mostly dismissed or runaway sailors or servants—since, by law, the Company was ultimately responsible for their passage back to India. Thus, the Company required all Europeans bringing an Indian servant with them to post a bond of £50 pounds as surety for the return passage of that Indian.[56] The English Company also repeatedly warned the Danish Company to respect this requirement.[57] Although the Danish Company assured the English that they would comply with this request, it is quite likely that the Danes circumvented this, as they did other English restrictions on them.[58] We do not know Dean Mahomet's legal status since he was not a simple servant, but sailing on a nominally Danish ship, and boarding it outside Calcutta, might have avoided the necessity for Baker to post such a bond, one he never would have recovered since Dean Mahomet never returned to India.

The very ship on which Baker and Dean Mahomet sailed added to the tension between the English and Danish Companies. This ship (originally named *Fortitude*), some seven hundred tons, had been part of the fleet built for the English East India Company. A French frigate, *La Fine* (thirty-six guns), had captured *Fortitude* off the Madras coast.[59] The French then sold the captured ship to Portuguese merchants in Calcutta. These Portuguese merchants, however, failed to raise sufficient capital to fill *Fortitude* for a return voyage to Europe. Eventually a British consortium in Calcutta bought *Fortitude*. In the summer of 1783, as peace between the English and French approached, merchants knew the first ships to reach Europe with Indian goods would reap a huge profit. To avoid English Company control, the new owners reflagged and renamed the ship as a Danish vessel, *Christiansborg*, with Ole Bie (head of the Danish factory) as the pro forma shipowner and Captain Adam Doack in command.[60]

After a year in Calcutta, Baker and Dean Mahomet sailed downriver to board *Christiansborg*, as the ship was loading a secret cargo. Bie sent a load of cloth from the Danish factory, officially consigned for other ships, seeking to evade English Company duties.[61] Baker and Dean Mahomet sailed with a cargo costing £102,656—what Bie called the "richest cargo that any Danish ship has ever brought from India to Denmark."[62]

The trip to Madras often took only the week Dean Mahomet mentions; in a less favorable season, this trip could take up to three months. *Christiansborg* touched on the Coromandal Coast near Madras to load more piece goods.[63] As with many other such nominally Danish vessels, it probably also loaded cloth diverted from the English Company's stocks by profiteering English Company officials.

During his brief visit to Madras, Dean Mahomet noted both the European and the Indian parts of the city. His military training led him to assess the strengths and foibles of Fort St. George, at the heart of the European presence. He also remarked upon the pomp of the procession of the Governor of Madras, George Macartney. For someone like Dean Mahomet, the indigenous language, culture, and people of Madras appeared quite different from those of his own Bihar, a thousand miles to the north. He particularly described the "female choristers," by which he probably meant *devadasi*s (women trained in dance and music who were nominally married to a Hindu divinity). Following a tempestuous voyage, *Christiansborg* finally reached its next port of call, St. Helena in the south Atlantic, where it refitted and reprovisioned for ten days (June 13–23, 1784).

Dean Mahomet's brief mention of his arrival in southwest England, at Dartmouth, may conceal much. This region remained a center for smuggling of goods into and out of England. It is possible that some of *Christiansborg*'s cargo made its way ashore to England in this small port or was transshipped to a coastal trader bound for Cork where Baker's father held charge of shipping, in the powerful office of Water Bailiff (harbormaster).

Although thousands of Indians made the trip to Europe over these years, apparently no one else had exactly Dean Mahomet's status. Most were sailors, servants, wives, or mistresses of Europeans. A few were travelers or visiting dignitaries. Dean Mahomet clearly fit into none of these categories. In his decisions to remain in Britain as an immigrant, to create a distinct identity there, and to record his life in his own words, he remained unique during his lifetime. His own account, reproduced in the next chapter, reveals his perspectives on the peoples of India and their changing relationship to British rule. The final chapter traces Dean Mahomet's life in colonial Ireland and Georgian and Victorian England (1784–1851).

TWO

The Travels of Dean Mahomet, A Native of Patna in Bengal, Through Several Parts of India, While in the Service of The Honourable The East India Company Written by Himself, In a Series of Letters to a Friend

DEDICATION

To William A. Bailie, Esq., Colonel in the Service of
The Honourable the East India Company

Sir,

Your distinguished character both in public and private life, is a powerful incitement for soliciting your patronage; and your condescension in permitting me to honour my humble production with your name, claims my best acknowledgements.

Though praise is a kind of tribute due to shining merit and abilities; yet, Sir, even envy must confess, that your well-earned laurels, the meed of military virtues, obtained in the service of the Honourable the East

India Company, have been too eminently conspicuous, to receive any additional lustre from the language of Encomium.

Your respectable name prefixed to these pages, cannot fail to shield them with the armour of security, as the judicious must be highly gratified with the peculiar propriety of inscribing them to a Gentleman so perfectly conversant with scenes, which I have attempted to describe.

Allow me to request, Sir, your indulgence for any inaccuracies of style, or other imperfections, that may arrest your judgment in glancing over this Work, as my situation in life, and want of the literary attainments, that refine and polish the European, preclude me from embellishing it, with that elegance of expression, and those fine touches of the imagination, which always animate the performance of cultivated genius.

However, Sir, I have endeavoured, at least, to please; and the sincerity of my intention, will, I trust, in some degree, make even an inadequate compensation for my deficiency in learning and refinement. I have the Honor to remain,

Sir, with the most profound veneration, your much obliged, and devoted, humble servant, Dean Mahomet, *Cork, South-Mall*, Jan. 15, 1794.

[List of subscribers omitted]

Figure 1.   Dean Mahomet, an East Indian (Mahomet, *Travels*, frontispiece).

LETTER I

Dear Sir,

Since my arrival in this country, I find you have been very anxious to be made acquainted with the early part of my Life, and the History of my Travels: I shall be happy to gratify you; and must ingenuously confess, when I first came to Ireland, I found the face of every thing about me so contrasted to those *striking scenes* in India, which we are wont to survey with a kind of sublime delight, that I felt some timid inclination, even in the consciousness of incapacity, to describe the manners of my country-men, who, I am proud to think, have still more of the innocence of our ancestors, than some of the boasting philosophers of Europe.

Though I acknowledge myself incapable of doing justice to the merits of men, whose happy manners are worthy the imitation of civilized nations, yet, you will do me the justice to believe, that the gratification of your wishes, is the *principal* incitement that engages me to undertake a work of this nature: the earnest entreaties of some friends, and the liberal encouragement of others, to whom I express my acknowledgements, I allow, are *secondary* motives.

The people of India, in general, are peculiarly favoured by Providence in the possession of all that can cheer the mind and allure the eye, and tho' the situation of Eden is only traced in the Poet's creative fancy, the traveller beholds with admiration the face of this delightful country, on which he discovers tracts that resemble those so finely drawn by the animated pencil of Milton. You will here behold the generous soil crowned with various plenty; the garden beautifully diversified with the gayest flowers diffusing their fragrance on the bosom of the air; and the very bowels of the earth enriched with inestimable mines of gold and diamonds.

Possessed of all that is enviable in life, we are still more happy in the exercise of benevolence and good-will to each other, devoid of every species of fraud or low cunning. In our convivial enjoyments, we are never without our neighbours; as it is usual for an individual, when he gives an entertainment, to invite all those of his own profession to partake of it. That profligacy of manners too conspicuous in other parts of the world, meets here with public indignation, and our women, though not so accomplished as those of Europe, are still very engaging for many virtues that exalt the sex.

As I have now given you a sketch of the manners of my country; I shall proceed to give you some account of myself.

I was born in the year 1759, in Patna, a famous city on the north [south] side of the Ganges, about 400 miles from Calcutta, the capital of Bengal and seat of the English Government in that country. I was too young when my father died, to learn any great account of his family; all I have been able to know respecting him, is, that he was descended from the same race as the Nabobs of Moorshadabad [Murshidabad]. He was appointed Subadar in a battalion of Seapoys commanded by Captain Adams, a company of which under his command was quartered at a small district not many miles from Patna, called Tarchpoor [Tajpur], an inconsiderable fort, built on the side of a little river that takes its rise a few miles up the country. Here he was stationed in order to keep this fort.

In the year 1769, a great dearth overspread the country about Tarchpoor, where the Rajas' Boudmal [Budhmal], and his brother Corexin [Kora Singh] resided, which they took an advantage of by pretending it was impossible for them to remit the stipulated supplies to the Raja Sataproy [Shitab Rai], who finding himself disappointed in his expectations, sent some of his people to compel them to pay: but the others retired within their forts, determined on making an obstinate defence. My father having received orders to lead out his men to the scene of dispute, which lay about twelve miles from the fort he was quartered in, marched accordingly, and soon after his arrival at Taharah [Telarha], took the Raja Boudmal prisoner, and sent him under a strong guard to Patna, where he was obliged to account for his conduct. My father remained in the field, giving the enemy some striking proofs of the courage of their adversary; which drove them to such measures, that they strengthened their posts and redoubled their attacks with such ardour, that many of our men fell, and my lamented father among the rest; but not till he had entirely exhausted the forces of the Raja, who, at length, submitted. The soldiers, animated by his example, made Corexin a prisoner, and took possession of the fort.

Thus have I been deprived of a gallant father, whose firmness and resolution was manifested in his military conduct on several occasions.

My brother, then about sixteen years old, and the only child my mother had besides me, was present at the engagement, and having returned home, made an application to Capt. Adams who, in gratitude to the memory of my father, whose services he failed not to represent to the Governor, speedily promoted him to his post. My mother and I suffered exceedingly by his sudden yet honourable fate in the field: for my Brother was then too young and thoughtless, to pay any great attention to our situation.

I was about eleven years old when deprived of my father, and though children are seldom possessed of much sensibility or reflection at such immature years, yet I recollect well no incident of my life ever made so deep an impression on my mind. Nothing could wear from my memory the remembrance of his tender regard. As he was a Mahometan, he was interred with all the pomp and ceremony usual on the occasion. I remained with my mother some time after, and acquired a little education at a school in Patna.

LETTER II

Dear Sir,

In a few months after my father's fate, my mother and I went to Patna to reside: she lived pretty comfortable on some of the property she was entitled to in right of her husband: the rest of his substance, with his commission, came into the hands of my brother: our support was made better by the liberality of the Begum and Nabob, to whom my Father was related: the Begum was remarkably affectionate and attentive to us.

The Raja Sataproy had a very magnificent palace in the centre of the city of Patna, where he was accustomed to entertain many of the most distinguished European Gentlemen, with brilliant balls and costly suppers. My mother's house was not far from the Raja's palace; and the number of Officers passing by our door in their way thither, attracted my notice, and excited the ambition I already had of entering on a military life. With this notion, I was always on the watch, and impatiently waited for the moment of their passing by our door; when, one evening in particular, as they went along, I seized the happy opportunity, and followed them directly to the palace, at the outward gates of which there are sentinels placed, to keep off the people and clear the passage for the Gentlemen; I however got admittance, on account of the respect the guards paid my father's family. The Gentlemen go to the palace between seven and eight o'clock in the evening, take tea and coffee, and frequently amuse themselves by forming a party to dance; when they find themselves warm, they retire to the palace yard, where there are marquees pitched for their reception; here they seat themselves in a circular form, under a semiana, a sort of canopy made of various coloured double muslin, supported by eight poles, and on the ground is spread a beautiful carpet; the Raja sits in the centre; the European Gentlemen on each side; and the Music in the front. The Raja, on this occasion, is attended by his Aid-du-Camps and Servants of rank. Dancing girls are now introduced, affording, at one time, extreme delight, by singing in concert with the Music, the softest and most lively airs; at another time, displaying such loose and fascinating attitudes in their various dances, as would warm the bosom of an Anchoret: while the servants of the Raja are employed in letting off the fireworks, displaying, in the most astonishing variety, the forms of birds, beasts, and other animals, and far surpassing any thing of the kind I ever beheld in Europe: and to give additional brilliancy to the splendor of the scene, lighted branches blaze around, and exhibit one general illumination. Extremely pleased with such various entertainment, the Gentlemen sit down to an elegant supper, prepared with the utmost skill, by an Officer of the Raja, whose sole employ is to provide the most delicious viands on such an occasion: ice-cream, fowl of all kinds, and the finest fruit in the world, compose but a part of the repast to which the guests are invited. The Raja was very happy with his convivial friends; and though his religion forbids him to touch many things handled by persons of a different profession, yet he accepted a little fruit from them; supper was over about twelve o'clock, and the company retired, the Raja to his palace, and the Officers to their quarters.

I was highly pleased with the appearance of the military Gentlemen, among whom I first beheld Mr. Baker, who particularly drew my attention: I followed him without any restraint through every part of the palace and tents, and remained a spectator of the entire scene of pleasure, till the company broke up; and then returned home to my mother, who felt some anxiety in my absence. When I described the gaiety and splendor I beheld at the entertainment, she seemed very much dissatisfied, and expressed, from maternal tenderness, her apprehensions of losing me.

Nothing could exceed my ambition of leading a soldier's life: the notion of carrying arms, and living in a camp, could not be easily removed: my fond mother's entreaties were of no avail: I grew anxious for the moment that would bring the military Officers by our door. Whenever I perceived their route, I instantly followed them; sometimes to the Raja's palace, where I had free access; and sometimes to a fine tennis court, generally frequented by them in the evenings, which was built by Col. Champion, at the back of his house, in a large open square, called Merseville-keebaug [Mir Afzal ka Bagh]: here, among other Gentlemen, I one day, discovered Mr. Baker, and often passed by him, in order to attract his attention: he, at last, took particular notice of me, observing that I surveyed him with a kind of secret satisfaction; and in a very friendly manner, asked me how I would like living with the Europeans: this unexpected encouragement, as it flattered my hopes beyond expression, occasioned a very sudden reply: I therefore told him with eager joy, how happy he could make me, by taking me with him. He seemed very much pleased with me, and assuring me of his future kindness, hoped I would merit it. Major Herd [Heard] was in company with him at the same time: and both these Gentlemen appeared with distinguished eclat in the first assemblies in India. I was decently clad in the dress worn by children of my age: and though my mother was materially affected in her circumstances, by the precipitate death of my father, she had still the means left of living in a comfortable manner, and providing both for her own wants and mine.

LETTER III

Dear Sir,

My mother observing some alteration in my conduct, since I first saw Mr. Baker, naturally supposed that I was meditating a separation from her. She knew I spoke to him; and apprehensive that I would go with him, she did everything in her power to frustrate my intentions. Notwithstanding all her vigilance, I found means to join my new master, with whom I went early the next morning to Bankeepore [Bankipur], leaving my mother to lament my departure. As Bankeepore is but a few miles from Patna, we shortly arrived there, that morning. It is a wide plain, near the banks of the Ganges, on which we encamped in the year of 1769. It commands a most beautiful prospect of the surrounding country. Our camp consisted of four regiments of Seapoys, one of Europeans, two companies of Cavalry, and one of European Artillery: the Commander in Chief was Col. Leslie; and next to him in military rank was Major Morrison; Capt. Lundick [Landeg] had the direction of the Cavalry; and Capt. Duff of the Artillery. The camp extended in two direct lines, at Patna side, along the river, on the banks of which, for the convenience of water, were built the Europeans' bangaloes: at one extremity of the line, was Col. Leslie's; at the other, Major Morrison's. The second line was drawn in a parallel direction with the first, at a about a quarter of a mile from the river; the front was the residence of the Officers; the rere a barrack for the soldiers; and the intermediate space was left open for the purpose of exercising the men, a duty which was, every day, performed with punctuality. Near a mile farther off, was the Seapoys' chaumnies; and a short space from them, the horse barrack. Thus was the situation of the camp at Bankeepore.

The Officers' bangaloes were constructed on a plan peculiar to the taste of the natives. They were quite square; the sides were made of mats, and the roof, which was supported by pillars, thatched with bamboes and straw, much after the manner of the farmer's houses in this country [Ireland]: their entrance was wide, and opened to a spacious hall that contained on each wing, the servants' apartments, inside which, were the gentlemen's dining-rooms and bed-chambers, with large frames in the partitions, and purdoes, that answered the same end as our doors and windows fastened to those frames.

Purdoes' are a contrivance made of coarse muslin, ornamented with fancy stripes and variegated colours, and so well quilted that they render the coolest situations agreeably warm: they are let up and down occasionally, to invite the refreshing breeze, or repel the sickly sunbeam. Inside is a kind of screen called cheeque, made of bamboes as small as wire, and interwoven in a curious manner, with various coloured thread, that keeps them together: it is let up and down like the purdoe, when occasion requires, and, admirable to conceive! precludes the prying eye outside from piercing through it, though it kindly permits the happy person within to gaze on every passing object.

The Colonel and Major had larger and more commodious bangaloes, than the other Officers, with adjacent out-houses, and stables. On the left angle, fronting the road, was the Colonel's guard-house, and stood diametrically opposite to his bangaloe; between which and those of the Officers, is situate an ever-verdant grove inclosed with a brick wall: overshadowed by the spreading trees inside, a few grand edifices built by the Nabobs, made a fine appearance; among which was the Bank of Messieurs Herbert and Halambury [Hollingberry], the dwelling of Mr. Barry [Berrie], Contract Agent, and a powder magazine.

The barrack of the European soldiers, was a range of apartments, whose partitions were made of mats and bamboes, and roofs thatched with straw. The chaumnies of the Seapoys were on the same plan; and such of them as had families, built dwellings near the chaumnies.

There are but few public buildings at Bankeepore: the only remarkable one that appeared in its environs, was the house of Mr. Goolden [Golding], who lived about a mile from the camp: it was a fine spacious building, finished in the English style; and as it stood on a rising ground, it seemed to rear its dome in stately pride, over the aromatic plains and spicy groves that adorned the landscape below, commanding an extensive prospect of all the fertile vales along the winding Ganges flowery banks. The happy possessor of this finely situated mansion, was in high esteem among the Officers, for his politeness and hospitality.

At some distance from Mr. Goolden's, lived Mr. Rumble [Rumbold], a Gentleman who received the Contracts of the Company, for the supply of Boats and other small craft. Mr. Baker had the utmost esteem for this Gentleman, for his many good qualities, and frequently visited him. For the honour of my country, I cannot help observing here, that no people on earth can be more attentive or respectful to the European Ladies residing among them, than the natives of all descriptions in India.

In gratitude to the revered memory of the best of characters, I am obliged to acknowledge that I never found myself so happy as with Mr. Baker: insensible of the authority of a superior, I experience the indulgence of a friend; and the want of a tender parent was entirely forgotten in the humanity and affection of a benevolent stranger.

I remember to have seen numbers perish by famine this year: the excessive heat of the climate, and want of rain, dried up the land; and all the fruits of the earth decayed without moisture.

Numbers of people have dropped down in the streets and highways: none fared so well as those whose plantations were watered by wells. The proprietors, some of whom were Nabobs, and other European Officers, distributed as much rice and other food as they could possibly spare, among the crowds that thronged into their court-yards and houses: but the poor creatures, quite spent and unable to bear it, fell down and expired in their presence: some endeavoured to crawl out and perished in the open air. Little did the treasures of their country avail them on this occasion: a small portion of rice, timely administered to their wants, would have been of more real importance than their mines of gold and diamonds.

LETTER IV

Dear Sir,

When six or seven months had elapsed from the time I was first received by Mr. Baker, my mother unhappy at the idea of parting with me, and resigning her child to the care of a European, came to him, requesting, in the language of supplication, that I might be given up to her: moved by her entreaties, he had me brought before her, at the same time observing, that it was so remote from his intentions to keep me from her, he was perfectly reconciled to part with me, were it my inclination. I was extremely affected at her presence; yet my deep sense of gratitude to a sincere friend conquered my duty to an affectionate parent, and made me determine in favour of the former: I would not go, I told her—I would stay in the camp; her disappointment smote my soul—she stood silent— yet I could perceive some tears succeed each other, stealing down her cheeks—my heart was wrung—at length, seeing my resolution fixed as fate, she dragged herself away, and returned home in a state of mind beyond my power to describe. Mr. Baker was much affected, and with his brother Officers, endeavoured to find amusement for me. I was taken out, every morning, to see the different military evolutions of the men in the field, and on such occasions, I was clad myself in suitable regimentals. Capt. Gravely in particular, was very fond of me, and never passed by without calling to know how I was. This kind attention gradually dispelled the gloom which, in some pensive moments, hung over my mind since the last tender interview. My poor mother under all the affliction of parental anxiety, and trembling hope for my return, sent my brother as an advocate for her to Mr. Baker, to whom he offered four hundred rupees, conceiving it would be a means of inducing him to send me back: but Mr. Baker had a soul superior to such sordid purposes, and far from accepting them, he gave me such a sum to bestow my mother. Having given his people the necessary directions to conduct me to her, he provided for me his own palankeen, on which I was borne by his domestics.

When I arrived at my mother's, I offered her the four hundred rupees given me by my disinterested friend to present to her; but could not, with all my persuasion, prevail on her to receive them, until I told her she should never see me again, if she refused this generous donation. Thus, by working on her fears, I, at length, gained my point, and assured her that I would embrace every opportunity of coming to see her: after taking my leave of her, I returned on the palankeen to the camp.

We lay in Bankeepore about six months, when we received orders from Col. Leslie to march to Denapore [Denapur], where we arrived in the year of 1770, and found the remaining companies of the Europeans and Seapoys, that were quartered there for some time before. Our camp here, consisted of eight regiments; two of Europeans, and six of Seapoys. Denapore is eight miles from Bankeepore, and has nothing to recommend it but a small mud fort, on which some cannon are planted, fronting the water. Inside the fort is a very fine barrack, perhaps the first in India; and when it was ready to receive the number of men destined to serve in that quarter, we marched into it. 'Tis a fine square building, made entirely of brick, on the margin of the Ganges, and covers both sides of the road; on the east side, opposite the river, were the Captain's apartments, consisting of two bed chambers and a dining room, with convenient out-offices, stables, and kitchen, at the back of the barrack: a little distance farther out on the line, was the General's residence, an elegant and stately building, commanding a full view of the country many miles round. It was finished in the greatest style, and furnished in a superb manner: the ascent to it was by several flights of marble steps, and the servants about it were very numerous. In the north angle, on the same line, was the hospital, at a convenient distance from the barrack. In the other angles were planted some cannon, which were regularly discharged every morning and evening, as the flag was hoist up or pulled down. At one end of the fourth side, was the Artillery barrack; at the other, their stores: on the west, lay the companies of the brigade; on the north, the Doctors and inferior Officers had their apartments. About a mile thence, were the chaumnies of the Seapoys.

No situation in the world could be more delightful than that of the

General's mansion; at the front and back of which, were gravel walks, where the soldiers and servants, at leisure hours, were accustomed to take recreation. A mud battery is drawn round the whole; and from north to south is a public road for travellers, which is intersected by another from east to west. Country seats and villas were dispersed through the neighbouring country, which was highly cultivated with fertile plantations and beautiful gardens. At one end of the avenue leading to the barrack, stood the markets or bazars of the Europeans; at the other, near their chaumnies, were those of the natives. Colonels Morgan, Goddard, and Tottingham, commanded here this year; and the army was mostly employed in going through the different manoeuvres in the field, as there happened no disturbances of any consequence in the country, that interfered with this duty. I called now and then to see my mother, who, at last, became more reconciled to my absence; and received some visits from my brother while I was in camp.

LETTER V

Dear Sir,

I felt great satisfaction in having procured the esteem of my friend, and the other Officers, and acquired the military exercise, to which I was very attentive. We lay about eight months in Denapore, when Col. Morgan having received intelligence of the depredations committed by some of the Morattoes [Marathas], gave orders to the army to make the necessary preparations for marching to Chrimnasa [Karamnasa], at a moment's warning. The baggage was immediately drawn out, and the cattle tackled with the utmost expedition. The Quarter Masters provided every necessary accommodation for the march: some of the stores they sent before them by water; the rest was drawn in hackeries and wagons, by bullocks. Mr. Baker, who was also Quarter Master, and his brother Officers in the same line, had each a company of Seapoys, as a piquet guard along the road, and about seven hundred attendants, who were occasionally employed, as the army moved their camp, in pitching and striking the tents, composed of the lowest order of the people residing in the country, and forming many distinct tribes, according to their various occupations. We had a certain number of these men appointed to attend the garrison, which was usually augmented on a march, and distinguished under the various appellations of Lascars, Cooleys, Besties, and Charwalleys. They set out with us, a day before the main body of the army, accompanied by several classes of tradesmen, such as shoe-makers, carpenters, smiths, sail-makers, and others capable of supplying the camp; and were ranged into four departments, in order to perform the laborious business of the expedition without confusion. To each department was assigned its respective duty: the employment of the Lascars, who wore mostly a blue jacket, turban, sash, and trousers, was to pitch and strike the tents and marquees; load and unload the elephants, camels, bullocks, waggons &c. The Cooleys were divided into two distinct bodies for different purposes; to carry burthens, and to open and clear the roads through the country, for the free passage of the army and baggage: The Besties were appointed to supply the men and cattle with water: and the Charwalleys, who are the meanest class of all, were employed to clean the apartments, and do other servile offices. Thus equipped, we marched in regular order from Denapore, early in the morning, in the month of February and the year of 1771. We enjoyed a pleasant cool breeze the entire day; while the trees, ever blooming and overshadowing the road, afforded a friendly shelter and an agreeable view along the country. The road was broad and smooth, and in places contiguous to it, we found several refreshing wells to allay the thirst of the weary traveller. In a few hours we reached Fulwherea [Phulwari], a spacious plain adapted for our purpose, where the Quarter Masters ordered out the Lascars to pitch the tents and marquees on the lines formed by them. Our camp, which made a grand military appearance, extended two miles in length: it was ranged into nine separate divisions, composed of two battalions of Europeans, six regiments of Seapoys, and one company of European Artillery. On the front line, the standards of the different regiments were flying: it consisted of a number of small tents called beltons [bell-tents], where they kept their fire arms: the central ones belonged to the Europeans; near them, were those of the Artillery; and on each wing, the Seapoys. The several corps were encamped behind their respective beltons, close to which, were first the tents of the privates; about twenty feet from their situation, were the larger and more commodious ones of the Ensigns and Lieutenants; next to them the Captains' marquees; a little farther back, the Major's; at some distance behind the two battalions, and in a middle direction between them, was the Colonel's, which lay diametrically opposite the main guard, situate outside the front line in the centre: a small space from the Colonels' marquees was the stop line, where the Quarter Masters, Adjutants, Doctors and Surgeons, were lodged: and between the stop line and bazars, was the line for the cattle. Every company of European privates occupied six tents and one belton: an Ensign, Lieutenant, and Captain, each a tent: such Officers as had jenanas or wives, erected tomboos, a kind of Indian marquees, for them, at their own expence. A Major had two marquees, one store, one guard tent, and one belton; a Colonel, three marquees, two store, two guard tents, and one belton; the Quarter Masters, Adjutants, Doctors and Surgeons, had each one marquee. On account of their peculiar duty in furnishing the camp, the Quarter Masters had, besides their own, other tents for their Serjeants, Artificers, and stores. The Seapoys lay behind their beltons, in the same position as the Europeans, and their Officers, according to rank, were accommodated much in the same manner. The hospital was in a pleasant grove not remote from the camp, about half a mile from which were the magazine and other stores for ammunition and military accoutrements; and on an eminence, at some distance, over the wide plain, where we encamped, arose in military grandeur, the superb marquees of the general Officers. In the rere of the entire scene, were the bazars or markets, belonging to the different regiments, on a direct line with each, and distinguished from one another, by various flags and streamers that wantoned in the breeze. Our camp, notwithstanding its extent, number of men, equipage, and arrangements, was completely formed in the course of the evening we arrived at Fulwherea, which is about twelve miles from Denapore.

LETTER VI

Dear Sir,

We had scarcely been one night at Fulwherea, when some straggling villagers of the neighbouring country, stole unperceived into our camp, and plundered our tents and marquees, which they stripped of every thing valuable belonging to Officers and privates. It happened, at the same time, that they entered a store tent, next to Mr. Baker's marquee, where I lay on a palankeen, a kind of travelling canopy-bed, resembling a camp bed, the upper part was arched over with curved bamboo, and embellished with rich furniture, the top was hung with beautiful tassels and adorned with gay trappings; and the sides, head, and foot were decorated with valuable silver ornaments. In short, it was elegantly finished, and worth, at least six hundred rupees; for which reason, such vehicles are seldom kept but by people of condition. Every palankeen is attended by eight servants, four of whom, alternately, carry it, much in the same manner as our sedan chairs are carried in this country [Ireland]. But to return—the villagers having entered the store-tent above mentioned, bore me suddenly away to a field about half a mile from the camp, on the conveyance I have just described to you, which they soon disrobed of its decorations, and rifled me of what money I had in my pocket, and every garment on my body, except a thin pair of trousers. So cruel were the merciless savages, that some were forming the barbarous resolutions of taking away my life, lest my escape would lead to a discovery of them; while others less inhuman, opposed the measure, by observing I was too young to injure them, and prevailed on their companions to let me go. I reached the camp with winged feet, and went directly to Mr. Baker, who was much alarmed when he heard of my dangerous situation, but more astonished at my arrival; and when I related by what means my life was spared, and liberty obtained, he admired such humanity in a savage breast.

A few of those ravagers, who loitered behind the rest, were first detected by the guard, pursued, and taken: the track of others was, by this clew, discovered; many of whom were apprehended, and received the punishment due to their crimes, for such wanton depredations. They were flogged through the camp, and their ears and noses cut off, as a shameful example to their lawless confederates. Their rapacity occasioned us to delay longer at Fulwherea, than we intended. We had scarcely suppressed those licentious barbarians, when our quiet was again disturbed by the nocturnal invasion of the jackals that infest this country, ferocious animals not unlike the European fox; they flocked into our camp in the silent midnight hour, carried off a great part of the poultry, and such young children as they could come at. It was in vain to pursue them; we were obliged to endure our losses with patience.

Having dispatched the proper people to supply the markets, we left Fulwherea early on the eighth morning after our arrival, and proceeded in our march towards Chrimnasa, which lay about ninety miles farther off. We reached Turwherea, on the first day's march, where we had a river to cross, which retarded us three days, on account of our numbers. As the weather was very warm, we advanced slowly, and found it exceedingly pleasant to travel along the roads shaded with the spreading branches of fruit-bearing trees, bending under their luscious burthens of bannas, mangoes, and tamarinds. Beneath the trees, were many cool springs and wells of the finest water in the universe, with which the whole country of Indostan abounds: a striking instance of the wisdom of Providence, that tempers "the bleak wind to the shorn lamb," and the scorching heat of the torrid zone to the way-worn traveller.

The former natives of this part of the world, whose purity of manners is still perpetuated by several tribes of their posterity, having foreseen the absolute necessity of such refreshment, and that in the region they inhabited, none could be more seasonable than founts of water for the use of succeeding generations, contrived those inexhaustible sources of relief in situations most frequented; and to prevent any thoughtless vagrant from polluting them, took care to inspire the people with a sacred piety in favour of their wells, and a religious dread of disturbing them. For this reason, they remain pure and undefiled, through every age, and are held in the most profound veneration. Wherever we found them, on the march, our Besties stopped to afford the men some time to recruit themselves, and take in a fresh supply of water, which was carried by bullocks, in leathern hanpacallies or bags made of dried hides, some of which were borne by the Besties on their shoulders.

LETTER VII

Dear Sir,

In about fifteen days after we left Fulwherea, we arrived at Chrimnasa, and encamped on the banks of the Ganges: the Morattoes fled on our arrival. Chrimnasa is an open plain, near which is a small river that flows into the Ganges. We remained here in a state of tranquility, occasionally enjoying all the rural pleasures of the delightful country around us. After a stay of a few months, we received orders from Colonels Morgan and Goddard, to march hence to Monghere [Monghyr]; and Messieurs Baker, Scott, Besnard and the Artillery Quarter Master, set out before the army, between one and two o'clock in the morning, with the baggage and military stores, in the middle of the year 1771. We continued on the march near a month, and when we came within thirty miles of Monghere, a small antique house, built on a rock in the middle of an island, in the Ganges, attracted our notice: we halted towards the close of the evening, at some distance from it: the next day, Mr. Baker, Mr. Besnard, and the other Gentlemen, made a hunting match: I accompanied them: and about noon, after the diversion was over, we turned our horses towards the water side, and taking a nearer view of this solitary little mansion, resolved on crossing the river.

We gave our horses in charge to the sahies or servants, who have always the care of them, and passed over to the island in one of the fishing boats that ply here. When we advanced towards the hermitage, which, as an object of curiosity, is much frequented by travellers, the Faquir or Hermit, who held his residence here for many years, came out to meet us: he wore a long robe of saffron colour muslin down to his ancles, with long loose sleeves, and on his head a small mitre of white muslin, his appearance was venerable from a beard that descended to his breast; and though the hand of time conferred some snowy honours on his head, that negligently flowed down his shoulders a considerable length, yet in his countenance you might read, that health and chearfulness were his companions: he approached us with a look of inconceivable complacency tempered with an apparent serenity of mind, and assured us that whatever his little habitation could afford, he was ready to supply us with. While he was thus speaking, he seemed to turn his thoughts a little higher; for with eyes now and then raised towards Heaven, he continued to count a long bead that was suspended from his wrist; and he had another girt about his waist. We went with him into his dwelling, which was one of the neatest I have ever seen; it was quite square, and measured from one angle to the other, not more than five yards: it rose to a great height, like a steeple, and the top was flat, encompassed with battlements, to which he sometimes ascended by a long ladder. At certain hours in the day, he stretched in a listless manner on the skin of some wild animal, not unlike a lion's, enjoying the pleasure of reading some favourite author. In one corner of the house, he kept a continual fire, made on a small space between three bricks, on which he dressed his food that consisted mostly of rice, and the fruits of his garden; but whatever was intended for his guests, was laid on a larger fire outside the door. When we spent a little time in observing every thing curious inside his residence, he presented us some mangoes and other agreeable fruit, which we accepted; and parted our kind host, having made him some small acknowledgment for his friendly reception, and passed encomiums on the neatness of his abode and the rural beauty of his garden.

We passed over to the continent in a boat, belonging to the Faquir, that conveyed provisions from the island to the people passing up and down the river, who left him in return such commodities as he most wanted; and joined the army, which arrived early the following day at Monghere.

The European brigade marched into a fine spacious barrack: and the Seapoys into the chaumnies inside the fort, which is near two miles in circumference, and built on the Ganges in a square form, with the sides and front rising out of the water, and overlooking all the country seats along the coast.

The Officers' apartments in the front, were laid out with the greatest elegance; the soldiers', quite compact; and nothing could be handsomer than the exterior appearance of the building, which was of glittering hewn stone. The old palace of Cossim Alli Cawn [Mir Kasim Ali Khan], inside the ramparts, still uninjured by the waste of time, was put in order for the residence of Colonel Grant. The entrance into the fort was by four wide gates, constructed in a masterly manner; one at each side, opening into the barrack yard. It was originally built by some of the Nabobs; but since it came into the possession of the Company, it has served as a proper place for our cantonments. There are no other structures of any figure here. About a mile hence is a long row of low, obscure huts (such as the common natives inhabit in several parts of India) occupied by a class of people who prepare raw silk; and, at a little distance from them, reside the manufacturers. The people, in general, here, are remarkably ingenious, at making all kinds of kitchen furniture, which they carry to such an extent, as to be enabled to supply the markets in the most opulent cities around them; and are in such esteem, that they even send for them from Calcutta, and other parts of Bengal. There is a description of inhabitants in this country, who supply the markets, and have continued in this employment through many succeeding generations, always dwelling in one place; and others who follow the army under the denomination of bazars.

LETTER VIII

Dear Sir,

There are some very fine seats and villas round Monghere, built by European Gentlemen in the Company's service, who retire to the country in the warm months of the year: among others, is the house of Mr. Grove, an elegant building finished in the English style, and standing in the centre of every rural improvement; a mile hence is the residence of Mr. Bateman, a very handsome structure, where we spent a few pleasant days in the most polite circles: amid such scenes, the riches and luxury of the East, are displayed with fascinating charms. Our host was that elevated kind of character, in which public and private virtues were happily blended; he united the Statesman with the private Gentleman; the deep Politician with the social Companion; and though of the mildest manners, he was brave in an eminent degree having led the way to victory in many campaigns. Twelve miles from Monghere, is a famous monument erected on a hill called Peepaharea [Pirpahar], which the love of antiquity induced us to visit: it is a square building, with an arch of hewn stone rising over a marble slab, supported by small round pillars of the same, without any inscription: and what is very remarkable, a large tiger, seemingly divested of the ferocity of his nature, comes from his den at the foot of the hill, every Monday and Wednesday, to this very monument, without molesting any person he meets on the way, (even children are not afraid to approach him) and sweeps with his tail, the dust from the lower part of the tomb, in which, it is supposed, are enshrined the remains of some pious character, who had been there interred at a remote period of time. The people have a profound veneration for it, which has not been a little increased by the sudden and untimely fate of a Lieutenant of Artillery, who came hither to indulge an idle curiosity, and ridicule those who paid such respect to the memory of their supposed holy man, who had been deposited here. He imputed their zeal to the force of prejudice and superstition, and turned it into such contempt, that he made water on the very tomb that was by them held sacred: but shortly after, as if he had been arrested by some invisible hand, for his presumption, having rode but a few paces from the tomb, he was thrown from his horse to the ground, where he lay some time speechless; and being conveyed to Monghere on a litter, soon after his arrival expired. Here is an awful lesson to those who, through a narrowness of judgment and confined speculation, are too apt to profane the piety of their fellow-creatures, merely for a difference in their modes of worship. At a little distance from Peepaharea was the bangaloe of Gen. Barker, constructed by him on the most elegant plan. Here he retired to spend some part of the summer, and entertain his friends: it was resorted by the distinguished Officers of his corps, and particularly by Colonels Grant, Morgan, Goddard, Tottingham, and Majors Morrison and Pearce, of the Artillery. At other times, he resided in a stately edifice in the fort, newly built, with exquisite taste and grandeur. Having received orders from Colonel Grant, to proceed to Calcutta, we made the necessary preparations for marching, and set out from Monghere in the beginning of the year 1772. The first day, we reached Sitakund, (where we halted three days) to collect our market people, &c. It is a small village, about twelve miles from Monghere, and in its environs are seven baths or wells, two of which are committed to the care of Bramins, who attend them, and will not suffer any person out of their order, to touch the waters, but such as come with a stedfast faith in their virtues (which they generally possess) to be relieved from various disorders by their application. The other five are common to all who travel this way. The two first are near each other, though very different in their qualities: the water of the one which is of a whitish colour, having an agreeable cool taste, while that of the adjacent well being of a darker hue, is continually boiling up. The people of the country make the most frequent use of them, and the Bramins, who dispatch their orders to all quarters round them in earthen jars filled at their hallowed founts, considerably benefit by their pious credulity. They even send it to the north of the Ganges; and it is held in holy veneration by the Hindoos in Calcutta, and the other districts of Bengal.

As we were advancing on our march, we met a number of Hindoo pilgrims proceeding on their journey to Sitakund, and reached Bohogolpore [Bhagalpur], in about fifteen days after we left Monghere. We encamped outside the town, which is, by no means, inconsiderable for its manufactures. It has a mud fort thrown round it, and contains a regiment of militia, to protect its trade, consisting of a famous manufactory of fine napkins, table cloths, turbans and soucy, a kind of texture composed of silk and cotton, some of which is beautifully variegated with stripes, and some of a nankin colour, used mostly by the Ladies of the country for summer wear. Governor Pelham, who commanded here, entertained our

Officers in a very splendid manner. We halted four or five days to refresh our army, and during the time, the Cooleys were employed to clear and level the rugged narrow road, from Bohogolpore through Skilligurree [Siclygully]. Before we set out, we perceived that Captain Brook [Brooke], a very active Officer, at the head of five companies of Seapoys, stationed in the different parts of the neighbouring country, had been, some time, engaged in the pursuit of the Pahareas, a savage clan that inhabit the mountains between Bohogolpore and Rajamoul [Rajmahal], and annoy the peaceable resident and unwary traveller: numbers, happily! were taken, through the indefatigable zeal of the above Gentlemen, and justly received exemplary punishment; some being severely whipped in a public manner; and others, who were found to be more daring and flagitious, suspended on a kind of gibbets, ignominiously exposed along the mountain's conspicuous brow, in order to strike terror into the hearts of their accomplices.

LETTER IX

Dear Sir,

Hence as we proceeded on our march, we beheld the lifeless bodies of these nefarious wretches elevated along the way for a considerable distance, about half a mile from each other; and having passed through the lofty arches or gateways of Sikilligurree and Tellicgurree [Tiliagarhi] planted with cannon, and erected by former Nabobs, as a kind of battery against the hostile invasions of those Mountaineers, we reached Rajamoul, where we remained a few days.

Our army being very numerous, the market people in the rere were attacked by another party of the Pahareas, who plundered them, and wounded many with their bows and arrows: the picquet guard closely pursued them, killed several, and apprehended thirty or forty, who were brought to the camp. Next morning, as our hotteewallies, grass cutters, and bazar people, went to the mountains about their usual business of procuring provender for the elephants, grass for the horses, and fuel for the camp; a gang of those licentious savages, rushed with violence on them, inhumanly butchered seven or eight of our people, and carried off three elephants, and as many camels, with several horses and bullocks. Such of our hotteewallies, &c. as were fortunate enough to escape with their lives from those unfeeling barbarians, made the best of their way to the camp, and related the story of their sufferings to the Commanding Officer, who kindled into resentment at the recital, instantly resolved to send the three Quarter Masters with two companies of Seapoys, in the pursuit of the lawless aggressors, some of whom, they luckily found ploughing in a field, to which they were directed by two of the men whom Providence rescued from their cruelty; and observed numbers flocking from the hills to their assistance: our men, arranged in military order, fired on them; some of the savages fell on the plain, others were wounded; and the greater part of them, after a feeble resistance with their bows, arrows, and swords, giving way to our superior courage and discipline, fled to the mountains for shelter, and raised a thick cloudy smoke, issuing from smothered fires, in order to intercept our view, and incommode us. Our gallant soldiers, swift as the lightning's flash, pursued, overtook, and made two hundred of them prisoners, who were escorted to Head Quarters, and by order of Colonel Grant, severely punished for their crimes; some having their ears and noses cut off, and others hung in gibbets. Their bows and arrows, and ponderous broad swords that weighed at least, fifteen pounds each, of which they were deprived, were borne in triumph as trophies of the little victory. Two of our hotteewallies, supposed to be massacred by them before this expedition, were found in a miserable state from their unmerciful treatment: they were endeavouring to crawl to the camp, disabled, and almost bleeding afresh from their recent wounds. The elephants, camels, &c. which those useful people took with them, for the purpose of bringing certain supplies to the army, were left behind in the hurry of the sanguinary and rapacious enemy's flight, cruelly mangled and weltering in their blood: our very horses and bullocks had iron spikes driven up in their hoofs, from which they must have suffered extreme torture. They were all, with some difficulty, brought back to the camp, and though taken every possible care of, a few only of the animals were restored, and the rest died in the anguish of exquisite pain.

We continued our march towards Calcutta; and on our way thither, encamped at Gouagochi [Godagarhi], which takes its name from a large black fort built on the banks of the Ganges, three miles from the place of our encampment, where we remained about two months. Our situation was extremely pleasant; the tents being almost covered with the spreading branches of mangoe and tamarind trees, which under the rigours of a torrid sun, afforded a cool shade, and brightened the face of the surrounding country; whilst the Ganges, to heighten the beauty of the varied landscape, rolled its majestic flood behind us. Hence we went to Dumdumma [Dumdum], where we had a general review. Governor Cottier [Cartier] came from Bengal in order to see it, with his Aid-du-Camps, and a numerous train of attendants: his entry into Dumdumma was very magnificent: he was accompanied by our Colonel and some of the principal Officers, who met him on the way: all the army were drawn up, and received him with a general salute. The entire night was spent in preparations for our appearance next day: every individual was employed; and at four o'clock, on the coming morn, we were all on the plain in military array, with twenty field pieces, attended by two companies of Artillery: not a man, through the whole of the business, in which we took up several acres of ground, but displayed uncommon abilities; and was rewarded for his exertions, by the unanimous consent of the Officers, with an extra allowance of pay and refreshment. The natives, who flocked from all quarters, for many miles around, were delighted and astonished at the sight——

> Of martial men in glitt'ring arms display'd,
> And all the shining pomp of war array'd;
> Determin'd soldiers, and a gallant host,
> As e'er Britannia in her pride cou'd boast.

The General received the Governor's compliments on the occasion, who declared that such brave fellows never before adorned the plains of

Asia. The review was over at twelve o'clock, when all the Gentlemen were invited to breakfast with the General. The men, overjoyed with the approbation of their Officers, retired to their tents to talk over their military atchievements, and form, by the creative power of fancy, a second grand review round their copious bowls of *Arrack*, a generous, exhilarating liquor, distilled from the fruit of the tree that bears the same name. The Governor remained a few days here, and was entertained in a style of elegant hospitality, by the military Gentlemen and the most distinguished Personages of the country. The scene of their convivial festivity, was the former habitation of a grand Nabob of this place, constructed on an ancient plan, and containing a number of spacious apartments; but from the change it received from the hand of recent improvement, it had more the appearance of a modern European mansion, than an uncouth pile of building, that reared its gothic head in remoter time.

LETTER X

Dear Sir,

Shortly after the review was over, we marched from Dumdumma to Calcutta, where we arrived in the year 1772. The first brigade that lay in Fort William, and thence proceeded to Denapore, was relieved by a part of our army (which formed the third brigade) consisting of one battalion of Europeans that marched into the fort, and three regiments of Seapoys that occupied the chaumnies at Cheitpore; the other battalion of Europeans, to which Mr. Baker belonged, and three regiments of Seapoys, were ordered to Barahampore [Baharampur], after some short stay here.

Calcutta is a very flourishing city, and the presidency of the English Company in Bengal. It is situate on the most westerly branch of the less Ganges in 87 deg. east lon. and 22, 45 north lat.; 130 miles north east of Balisore, and 40 south of Huegley [Hoogly]. It contains a number of regular and spacious streets, public buildings, gardens, walks, and fish ponds, and from the best accounts, its population has advanced to upwards of six hundred thousand souls. The principal streets are the Chouk, where an endless variety of all sorts of goods are sold; the China Bazar, where every kind of china is exposed to sale; the Lalbazar, Thurumthulla [Dharamtala], Chouringee [Chowringhee], Bightaconna [Baitakkhana], Mochoabazar [Machuabazar], and Chaunpolgot [Chandpal Ghat], where the European Gentlemen, of every description, mostly reside. The greatest concourse of English, French, Dutch, Armenians, Abyssinians, and Jews, assemble here; besides merchants, manufacturers, and tradesmen, from the most remote parts of India.

Near Chaunpolgot is the old fort, which contains the Company's stores garrisoned by the invalids and militia, and inhabited by Collectors, Commissaries, Clerks, and in my time by a Mr. Paxon, the Director or Superintendant of the people employed in the mint, to coin goulmores, rupees, and paissays. Fort William is a mile from the town, and the most extensive in India. The plan of it was an irregular tetragon, built with brick and mortar made of brick dust, lime, molasses, and hemp, a composition that forms a cement as hard and durable as stone. The different batteries surrounding it, are planted with about six hundred cannon: and its inner entrance is by six gates, four of which are generally left open: outside these are fourteen gate-ways leading through different avenues, to the inner gates severally situate in opposite directions to the river, the Hospital, Kidderpore, and Calcutta. Near each gate is a well, from which water is easily raised for the use of the army by engines happily contrived for that purpose. The Commander in Chief resides in an elegant edifice within the fort, where there is also a bazar constantly held to supply the army with every necessary: and the Officers of rank next to him, dwell on the very arches of the gates, in beautifully constructed buildings, that, in such elevated situations, have a very fine effect on the delighted beholder. Inside the fort there are eight barracks, for the other Officers and privates; stores for the ammunition and accoutrements; magazines, armories, and a cannon and ball foundry, almost continually at work, for the general use of the Company's troops throughout India. In short, Fort William is an astonishing piece of human workmanship, and large enough to contain, at least, ten thousand inhabitants.

The other principal public buildings, are the Court-Houses, Prisons, and Churches. There are three Court-Houses; one fronting Loldigee, one near the Governor's mansion, and the other in Chaunpolgot: two prisons; one in Lalbazar, and another in Chouringee: and several Churches, besides the English, Armenian, and Portuguese, which are the most noted places of worship, in point of magnitude, exterior figure, and decoration. On the opposite side of the river are docks for repairing and careening ships; and outside the town is an hospital, encompassed by a sheltering grove; some pleasant villas, the summer retreats of the European Gentlemen, delightful improvements, aromatic flower gardens, winding walks planted with embowering trees on each side, and fish ponds reflecting, like an extended mirror, their blooming verdure on each margin, and Heaven's clear azure in the vaulted canopy above. There is also a very fine canal formed at the expense of Mr. Tolly, which is navigable for boats passing up and down: it was cut through the country, and extended from Kidderpore to Culman [Kalna], a distance of five or six miles, connecting the Ganges with the river Sunderbun [Sunderbans]. Mr. Tolly benefited considerably by this mode of conveyance; as it was deemed more convenient than that of land carriage, and became the principal channel of conveying goods to different parts of Bengal.

LETTER XI

Dear Sir,

Our stay in Calcutta was so short, that I have been only able to give you some account of the town, forts, and environs; and am concerned that I could not contribute more to your entertainment, by a description of the manners of the people, as we received too sudden orders to march to Barahampore, where we arrived in the year 1773, having met with no extraordinary occurrence on the way. The cantonments here are situate on the banks of the river Bohogritee [Bhagirathi], and consist of twenty-two barracks, besides a magazine, stores, and offices. There are two barracks on the south near the river, in which the Colonels and Majors reside: six on the east, and six on the west, occupied by the other Officers: in the northern direction, the privates of the Artillery and Infantry Corps dwell: the Commander in Chief has a superb building, about a mile from the barrack of the privates; and the intermediate space between the different barracks, which form a square, is a spacious plain where the men exercise. Barahampore is very populous, and connects with Muxadabad [Murshidabad] by an irregular chain of building, comprehending Calcapore [Kalkapur] and Casambuzar [Cossimbazar], two famous manufactories of silk and cotton, where merchants can be supplied on better terms than in any other part of India. The city of Muxadabad, to which I had been led by curiosity, is the mart of an extensive trade among the natives, such as the Moguls, Parsees, Mussulmen, and Hindoos; the houses are neat, but not uniform; as every dwelling is constructed according to the peculiar fancy of the proprietor: those of the merchants are, in general, on a good plan, and built of fine brick made in the country; and such as have been erected by the servants of the Company, near the town, are very handsome structures. The city, including the suburbs, is about nine miles in length, reaching as far as Barahampore; and the neighbouring country is interspersed with elegant seats belonging to the Governors, and other Officers; among which, was the Nabob Mamarah Dowlah's [Mubarak al-Daula's] palace, finished in a superior style to the rest, and surrounded with arched pillars of marble, decorated with variegated purdoes—over the arches, native bands of music played on their different instruments, every morning and evening—on one side of the palace flowed the river Bohogritee in winding mazes: on the other, stood the Chouk, where people assembled to sell horses, wild and tame fowl, singing birds, and almost every product and manufacture of India.

Soon after my arrival here, I was dazzled with the glittering appearance of the Nabob, and all his train, amounting to about three thousand attendants, proceeding in solemn state from his palace to the temple. They formed in the splendor and richness of their attire one of the most brilliant processions I ever beheld. The Nabob was carried on a beautiful pavillion, or meanah, by sixteen men, alternately, called by the natives, Baharas, who wore a red uniform: the refulgent canopy covered with tissue, and lined with embroidered scarlet velvet, trimmed with silver fringe, was supported by four pillars of massy silver, and resembled the form of a beautiful elbow chair, constructed in oval elegance; in which he sat cross-legged, leaning his back against a fine cushion, and his elbows on two more covered with scarlet velvet, wrought with flowers of gold. At each side of his magnificent conveyance, two men attended with large whisks in their hands, made of some curious animal's tail, to beat off the flies. The very handles of those whisks were of silver. As to the ornaments of his person—he wore a very small turban of white muslin, containing forty-four yards, which quantity, from its exceeding fineness, would not weigh more than a pound and half; a band of the same encompassed his turban, from which hung silver tassels over his right eye: on the front was a star in diamond of the first water: a thin robe of fine muslin covered his body, over which he wore another of cream-coloured satin, and trousers of the same, trimmed with silver edging, and small silver buttons: a valuable shawl of camel's hair, was thrown negligently about his shoulders; and another wrapped round his waist: inside the latter, he placed his dagger, that was in itself a piece of curious workmanship, the hilt being of pure gold, studded with diamonds, and embellished with small chains of gold.

His shoes were of bright crimson velvet, embroidered with silver, and set round the soals and binding with pearls. Two Aid-du-Camps, one at each side, attended him on horseback; from whom he was *little* more distinguished in splendor of habiliment, than by the diamond star in his turban. Their saddles were ornamented with tassels, fringe, and various kinds of embroidery. Before and behind him, moved in the pomp of ceremony, a great number of pages, and near his person slowly advanced his life guard, mounted on horses: all were clad in a stile of unrivalled elegance: the very earth with expanding bosom, poured out her treasures to deck them; and the artisan essayed his utmost skill to furnish their trappings.

His pipe was of a serpentine form, nine cubits in length, and termed hooka: it reached from his lips, though elevated his situation above the gay throng, to the hands of a person who only walked as an attendant in the train, for the purpose of filling the silver bowl with a nice compound of musk, sugar, rose-water, and a little tobacco finely chopped, and worked up together into a kind of dough, which was dissolved into an odoriferous liquid by the heat of a little fire made of burnt rice, and kept in a silver vessel with a cover of the same, called Chilm, from which was conveyed a fragrant cool smoke, through a small tube connecting with another that ascended to his mouth.

The part which the attendant held in his hand, contained at least a quart of water: it was made of glass, ornamented with a number of little golden chains admirably contrived: the snake which comprehends both tubes was tipped with gold at each end, and the intermediate space was made of wire inside a close quilting of satin, silk, and muslin, wrought in a very ingenious manner: the mouth piece was also of gold, and the part next to his lips set with diamonds.

A band of native music played before him, accompanied with a big drum, conveyed on a camel, the sound of which, could be heard at a great distance: and a halcorah or herald advanced onward in the front of the whole company, to proclaim his arrival, and clear the way before him. Crowds of people from every neighbouring quarter, thronged to see him. I waited for some time, to see him enter into the temple with all his retinue, who left their shoes at the door as a mark of veneration for the sacred fane into which they were entering. The view of this grand procession, gave me infinite pleasure, and induced me to continue a little longer in Muxadabad.

LETTER XII

Dear Sir,

Shortly after the procession, I met with a relation of mine, a Mahometan, who requested my attendance at the circumcision of one of his children. Previous to this ceremony, which I shall describe in the order of succession, it may be necessary to premise, that a child is baptized three times according to the rites of this religion. The first baptism is performed at time of the birth, by a Bramin who, though of different religious principles, is held in the utmost veneration by the Mahometans, for his supposed knowledge in astrology, by which he is said to foretel the future destiny of the child; when he discharges the duties of his sacred function on such an occasion, which consists in nothing more than this prophecy, and calling the child by the most favourable name, the mysteries of his science will permit, he receives some presents from the parents and kindred, and retires.

The second baptism, which takes place when the child is four days old, is performed by the Codgi, or Mulna, the Mahometan Clergyman, in the presence of a number of women, who visit the mother after her delivery; he first reads some prayers in the alcoran, sprinkles the child with consecrated water, and anoints the navel and ears with a kind of oil extracted from mustard seed, which concludes the ceremony. The Priest then quits the womens' apartment, and joins the men in another room. When he has withdrawn, the Hajams' wives enter the chamber, and attend the mother of the child with every apparatus necessary in her situation: one assists to pare her nails, and supplies her with a bason of water to wash her hands in; and others are employed in dressing her in a becoming manner. Several Ladies of distinction come to visit her, presenting her their congratulatory compliments on her happy recovery, and filling her lap, at the same time, with a quantity of fresh fruit, as the emblem of plenty. When this ceremony is over they sit down to an entertainment served up by the Hajams' wives, and prepared by women in more menial offices. Their usual fare is a variety of cates and sweetmeats. The men, who also congratulate the father, wishing every happiness to his offspring, are regaled much in the same manner. Thus is the second baptism celebrated; from which the third, which is solemnized on the twentieth day after the birth, differs only in point of time.

The Mahometans do not perform the circumcision, or fourth baptism until the child is seven years old, and carefully initiated in such principles of their religion as can be well conceived at such a tender age. For some time before it, the poorer kind of people use much oeconomy in their manner of living, to enable them to defray the expenses of a splendid entertainment, as they are very ambitious of displaying the greatest elegance and hospitality on such occasions. When the period of entering on this sacred business is arrived, they dispatch Hajams or Barbers, who from the nature of their occupation are well acquainted with the city, to all the inhabitants of the Mahometan profession, residing within the walls of Muxadabad, to whom they present nutmegs, which imply the same formality as compliment cards in this country. The guests thus invited assembled in a great square, large enough to contain two thousand persons, under a semiana of muslin supported by handsome poles erected at a certain distance from each other; the sides of it were also made of muslin, and none would be suffered to enter but Mahometans. The arrival of the Mulna was announced by the Music, who had a kind of orchestre within the semiana: attended by one of the Hajams, he approached the child who was decked with jewels and arrayed in scarlet muslin, and sat under a beautiful canopy richly ornamented with silk hangings, on an elegant elbow chair with velvet cushions to the back and sides, from which he was taken and mounted on a horse, accompanied by four men, his nearest relations, each holding a drawn sword in his hand, who also wore a dress of scarlet muslin. People of condition, among the Mahometans, contribute largely to the magnificence of this ceremony; and appear on horseback in the midst of the gay assembly, with their finest camels in rich furniture led after them.

But to return—the child was conducted in this manner to a chapel, at the door of which he alit, assisted by his four relations, who entered with him into the sacred building, where he bowed in adoration to one of the Prophets, repeating with his kindred, some prayers he had been before taught by his parents; after this pious duty is over, he is again mounted on his horse, and led to another chapel, where he goes through the same forms, and so on to them all, praying with the rest of the company, and fervently imploring in the attitude of prostrate humility, the great Alla to protect him from every harm in the act of circumcision.

After they had taken their rounds to the different places of worship, they returned to the square in which the semiana was erected, and placed him under the glittering canopy, upon his accustomed chair. The music that played before him suddenly ceased, when the Mulna appeared in his sacredotal robes, holding a silver bason of consecrated water, with which he sprinkled him; while the Hajam slowly advancing in order to circumcise him, instantly performed the operation. In this critical moment, every individual in the numerous crowd, stood on one foot, and joined his father and mother in heartfelt petitions to Heaven for his safety. The Music again struck up, and played some cheerful airs: after which, the child was taken home by his parents and put to bed. The company being served with water and napkins by the Hajams, washed their hands and sat down barefooted on a rich carpet, to partake of a favourite dish called by the natives *pelou*, composed of stewed rice and meat highly seasoned, which they are in general fond of. The entire scene was illuminated with torches, which, by a strong reflexion of artificial lustre, seemed to heighten the splendor of their ornaments.

LETTER XIII

Dear Sir,

I shall now proceed to give you some account of the form of marriage among the Mahometans, which is generally solemnized with all the external show of Oriental pageantry. The parents of the young people, first treat on the subject of uniting them in the bands of wedlock, and if they mutually agree on a connection between them, the happy pair, who were never permitted to see each other, nor even consulted about their union, are joined in marriage at a very youthful time in life, the female seldom exceeding the age of twelve, and the lad little more advanced in years: they must always be of the same cast, and trade; for a weaver will not give his daughter to a man of any other occupation: in the higher scenes of life, each of the parties bring a splendid fortune; but among people of the middle class, the woman has seldom more allotted her than her apparel, furniture, and a few ornaments of some value, as the parents of the man provide for both, by giving him a portion of such property as they can afford; in land, merchandize, or implements of trade, according to their situation. When they conclude all matters to their satisfaction, Hajams are sent with nutmegs, in the usual form, to invite their friends and acquaintance to the wedding, and the houses of each party are adorned with green branches and flowers. Outside the doors they erect galleries for the musicians, under which, are rows of seats or benches for the accommodation of the lower class of people, who are forbid any closer communication. Allured by invitation and the love of pleasure, the welcome guests arrive, and discover the houses by the green branches and flowers with which they are gayly dressed, to distinguish them from others. The entire week is spent in the utmost mirth and convivial enjoyment. The finest scarlet muslin is procured for the young people and their relations, by their parents on both sides: those of the youth supply the dresses of the young woman and her kindred; and her's furnish him and his relatives with suitable apparel.

Thus arrayed, the bridegroom is carried on a palanquin, with lighted torches in his train, attended by a number of people, to the house of the bride, whose friends meet him on the way. At his arrival, the ceremony is performed, if the mansion be large enough to contain the cheerful throng that assemble on this festive occasion; if not, which is generally the case, a semiana is erected in a spacious square, in the centre of which is a canopy about seven feet high, covered on the top with the finest snow-white muslin, and decorated inside with diversified figures representing the sun, moon, and stars. Beneath this temporary dome, the coy maid reclines on a soft cushion, in an easy posture, while the raptured youth, scouring through fancy's lawn, on the wings of expectation, and already anticipating the joys of connubial felicity, leans opposite his sable Dulcinea in a similar attitude. The breathing instruments now wake their trembling strings to announce the coming of the Mulna, who enters the scene with an air of characteristic solemnity: the music gradually ceases, till its expiring voice is lulled into a profound silence; and the Priest opens the alcoran, which is held according to custom by four persons, one at each corner, and reads, in grave accents, the ceremony. The bride and bridegroom interchange rings, which they put on their fingers; and one of the bridemaids, supposed to be her relation, comes behind both, who are veiled, and ties, in a close knot, the ends of their shawls together, to signify their firm union. The Mulna, finally, consecrates a glass of water and sugar, which he presents to them: they alternately taste it, but the man gives it round to a few select friends of the company, who, in turn, put it to their lips, wishing happiness to the married couple. They now sit down to an elegant supper, after which the dancing girls are introduced, who make a splendid appearance, clothed in embroidered silks and muslins, and moving in a variety of loose attitudes that allure admiration and excite the passions.

When the entertainment is over, a silver plate not unlike a salver, is carried about, into which almost every individual drops some pecuniary gratuity to reward the trouble of the Hajams, and the guests retire in company with the newly wedded pair, who are conveyed on separate palanquins to the house of his father, while bands of music in cheerful mood are playing before them, numerous torches flaming round them, that seem with their blaze to disperse the gloom of night, and fire-works, exhibiting in the ambient air, a variety of dazzling figures. When they arrive, the Mulna gives them his benediction, and sprinkles the people about them, with perfumed water coloured with saffron: a second entertainment is then prepared for their friends and acquaintance, which concludes the hymeneal festivity. Among people of rank, merchants, and tradesmen, who have made any acquisitions, in life, the Lady never goes outside the doors after marriage, except when she is carried on a palanquin, which is so well covered that she cannot be seen by any body. A man of any consequence in India, does not stir out for a week after his nuptials, and would deem it dishonourable to suffer his wife to appear in public: the indigence of the poorer kind of people precludes them from the observance of this punctilio. The husband's entire property after his decease, comes into the possession of his wife. It may be here observed, that the Hindoo, as well as the Mahometan, shudders at the idea of exposing women to the public eye: they are held so sacred in India, that even the soldier in the rage of slaughter will not only spare, but even protect them. The Haram is a sanctuary against the horrors of wasting war, and ruffians covered with the blood of a husband, shrink back with confusion at the apartment of his wife.

LETTER XIV

Dear Sir,

The Mahometans are, in general, a very healthful people: refraining from the use of strong liquors, and accustomed to a temperate diet, they have but few diseases, for which their own experience commonly finds some simple yet effectual remedy. When they are visited by sickness, they bear it with much composure of mind, partly through an expectation of removing their disorder, by their own manner of treating it: but when they perceive their malady grows too violent, to submit even to the utmost exertions of their skill, they send for a Mulna, who comes to the bedside of the sick person, and putting his hand over him, feels that part of his body most affected, and repeats, with a degree of fervency, some pious prayers, by the efficacy of which, it is supposed the patient will speedily recover. The Mahometans meet death with uncommon resignation and fortitude, considering it only as the means of enlarging them from a state of mortal captivity, and opening to them a free and glorious passage to the mansions of bliss. Those ideas console them on the bed of sickness; and even amid the pangs of dissolution, the parting soul struggling to leave its earthly prison, and panting for the joys of immortality, changes, at bright intervals, the terrors of the grim Monarch into the smiles of a Cherub, who invites it to a happier region.

When a person dies among them, the neighbours of the same religious principles, bring the family of the deceased to their houses, and use every means to comfort them in their affliction. The corpse is stretched on the death bed, which is covered with white muslin, and adorned with flowers: wax tapers are lit about it, and the room hung round with white cotton. Numbers assemble together to pray for the departed spirit, and twenty-four hours after the decease of the person, on account of the excessive heat of the climate, the body is wrapped up in muslin, and carried towards the grave, near which it is laid down, before it is interred: all the people who attend the funeral kneel in a direct line beside it, imploring the great Alla to give the soul eternal rest: it is then consigned to the silent scene of interment, and the relations throw a little clay on it, after which it is covered. The Mulna consecrates a quantity of thin cakes, which he distributes in broken pieces among the people, who share them with each other, and join in prayer, while the eldest son of the deceased sprinkles the grave with holy water, and spreads a large white sheet over it. Four days after the funeral, the relatives entertain their neighbours and a multitude of poor people with unlimitted hospitality, who, in gratitude for their munificence, offer up their united petitions to Heaven for the kinsman of their benefactors.

People of condition have grand monuments erected to their memory, and lamps lighting at their tombs throughout the year: their houses also, on certain festivals, are magnificently illuminated in remembrance of them. The poorer natives perform this ceremony at the grave and their own habitations, but once in the year, for a short space of time. After the death of a husband, his wife puts on no mourning, and disrobing herself of all the ornaments of dress and jewels, wears only plain white muslin. In the middle walk of life, the widow enjoys the sole property, which, making some reserve for herself, she generally divides in a very equitable manner, among her children: in more elevated situations, the son succeeds his father in rank or employment.

The Mahometans are strict adherents to the tenets of their religion, which does not, by any means, consist in that enthusiastic veneration for Mahomet so generally conceived: it considers much more, as its primary object, the unity of the supreme Being, under the name of Alla: Mahomet is only regarded in a secondary point of view, as the missionary of that unity, merely for destroying the idol worship, to which Arabia had con-

tinued so long under bondage: and so far from addressing him as a deity, that in their oraisons, they do not pray to him, but for him recom-
mending him to the divine mercy: it is a mistaken, though a generally
received opinion, that pilgrimages were made to his tomb, which, in a
religious sense, were only directed to what is called the cahabah or holy-
house at Mecca, an idol temple dedicated by him to the unity of God.
His tomb is at Medina, visited by the Mahometans, purely out of curiosity
and reverence to his memory. Most of his followers carry their veneration for the supreme Being so far, as not only, never to mention the word
Alla or God, on any common occasion, but think it in some degree blas-
phemous to praise or define a Being, whom they consider as so infinitely
transcendant to all praise, definition or comprehension. Thus, they carry
their scrupulosity to such a length, as not even to approve of calling him
good, righteous, or merciful, from their thinking such epithets super-
fluous and impertinent; as if one were emphatically to say of a man that
he had a head, or any other member necessary to the human form: for
they conceive it to be a profanation of the name of God, to accompany
it with human attributes; and that no idea can be so acceptable to that
Being, as the name itself, a substantive infinitely superior and independent of the connexion of any adjective to give it the least degree of additional emphasis.

LETTER XV

Dear Sir,

I shall now change the subject from *grave* to *gay*, and endeavour to entertain you with some account of the dancing girls of this country. At a
very youthful time of life, they are regularly trained in all the arts of pleas-
ing, by a hackneyed matron, worn in the campaigns of Venus, whose past
experience renders her perfectly adequate to the task of instruction, for
which she receives from her pupils a share of the pecuniary favours conferred on them by their gallants, and also procures them every article of
dress that can set them off to advantage. They have different places of

abode, sometimes occupying the handsomest houses in towns or cities; and in the fine season of the year, they retire to the country, where their villas, gardens, bowers, and every other rural improvement, are laid out in such a manner, as to allure the most unconcerned observer. Hither, some of the principal Nabobs and European Gentlemen of the first distinction, are drawn by the love of pleasure, and lavish immense sums on these creatures, who are generally recruited out of the people of all casts and denominations, though not without a peculiar attention to beauty or agreeableness; yet, even the knowledge of their being so common, is with many totally forgotten in the ravishing display of their natural and acquired charms. They dance to the music of cymbals, fifes, and drums, they term tum-tums, and often represent in pantomime such scenes, as a lover courting his mistress; a procuress, endeavouring to seduce a woman from one gallant to another; and a girl, timorous and afraid of being caught in an intrigue. All these love-scenes, they perform, in gestures, air, and steps, with well-adapted expression. In some of their dances, even in public, modesty is not much respected in the motions of their limbs, the quivering of their hips, and other lascivious attitudes, into which they throw themselves, without exposing any nudity. But in private parties, they introduce other dances, in which, though they never offend delicacy, by discovering any part of their bodies, they betray such fascinating looks and postures, as are probably more dangerous. In short, there is no attraction, of which they are not capable, and by these unfailing arts, they frequently arrive at the temple of fortune. In many parts of India, there are several fine Mahometan chapels built by them, and rich factories established, where various artisans and tradesmen find the greatest encouragement.

The dress of these women, which differs according to the custom of the country, is in all, however, the most splendid conceivable. Their persons glitter with jewels from head to toe, since even on their toes they wear rings. Carcanets adorn their necks, bracelets their arms, and chains of gold and silver, enriched with precious stones, their very ankles. They also wear nose-jewels, to which the familiar eye is soon reconciled. Their breasts are covered with thin muslin, embellished with gems, and the swell of the tempting bosom displayed to such advantage, warms even frigid insensibility with a glow of soft sensations. Their necklaces are composed of flowers strung together, which they call mogrees, resembling Spanish double jessamy, but of a more agreeable odor, and preferable to any perfumes, delighting at once the sight and smell. Their dress consists of a long white muslin gown, extremely clear and fine, with a short body and long sleeves, and the skirt which contains near twenty yards, is ornamented in its train, with silver fringe; a long trousers made of fancy silk, exactly fitted to their shapes, and a large shawl, that covers the head and shoulders, embroidered with a deep silver fringe. On the head they wear jewels and flowers; and their long black hair is generally braided. Many of them, especially those in commerce with the Moguls and Moors, follow the old Eastern custom, of forming a black circle round their eye borders, by drawing a bodkin between them, with their eye-lids shut, that both sides may receive the tint of the stibium, or powder of antimony that sticks to the bodkin. The powder is called by them surma; which they imagine refreshes and cools the eye, besides exciting its lustre, by the ambient blackness. They avoid every degree of affectation in their manners, and copy nature, as their grand original, in the imitation and refinement of which, their art chiefly consists. Besides, they have nothing of that gross impudence which characterises the European prostitutes; their style of seduction being all softness and gentleness: their caresses are not only well managed, but well timed in the cloying minutes of satiety. There are some of them, even amidst their vices and depravity, whose minds are finely impressed with generous sentiments. The following authentic account is a striking proof of it:

One of them lived, some years ago, at a pleasant seat a few miles from Cossumbuzar, where she had been visited by some of the principal men of the country, among whom was a rich factor, whose attachments to her diverted his attention from business, in such a manner, that he became a bankrupt. This misfortune preyed so much on his mind, that his melancholy could not well escape the observation of his mistress, from whom he endeavoured to conceal it as much as possible, dreading to be forsaken by her in his poverty. After repeated entreaties on her part, he, at length, made her acquainted with his situation: she suddenly left him, and to his great astonishment, shortly returned with money and effects, to such an amount as enabled him to conduct his business with more spirit and application than ever.

Here is an instance, that even the human heart plunged in crimes and immorality, may sometimes be roused from its torpor by the voice of humanity.

LETTER XVI

Dear Sir,

That part of our army which we left in Calcutta, arrived at Barahampore, before our departure; and shortly after, the entire brigade received orders to march to Denapore, where we arrived in the year 1775. On the Bengal establishment, there are three brigades, who all wear the usual scarlet uniform: that of the first is faced with blue—of the second with black—and the third with yellow. Each brigade contains one regiment of Europeans, six regiments or twelve battalions of Seapoys, three companies of European Artillery, five companies of native Artillery, called Gullendas, and two companies of native Cavalry. A regiment of Seapoys on the present establishment, consists of two battalions, each battalion 500 men or five companies, with a Captain, two Lieutenants, three Ensigns, one Serjeant-Major, Europeans; besides one Comedan, five Subidars, ten Jemidars, thirty Howaldars, thirty Homaldars, five Tombourwallas, five Basleewallas, and five Troohewallas, Natives.

As you may not understand those terms, I shall thus explain them to you.

Comedan signifies	*a Captain*
Subidar	*a Lieutenant*
Jemidar	*an Ensign*
Howaldar	*a Serjeant*

Homaldar	*a Corporal*
Seapoy	*a private Soldier*
Tombourwalla	*a Drummer*
Basleewalla	*a Fife*
Trooheewalla	*a Trumpeter*

The Seapoys are composed of Mahometans and Hindoos, who make no other distinction in their exterior appearance, than that the Hindoos colour each side of the face and forehead with a kind of red paint, produced from the timber of the sandal tree. The dress of both, is a thin muslin shirt, a red coat in uniform, a turban, sash, and short trousers [see figure 2]. The turban, which is of muslin, is mostly blue as well as the sash: it is quite small, fitted very closely to the head, and not unlike a Scotch bonnet in form, except that the front is more flat, to which they affix a cockade of white muslin puffed and trimmed with silver lace, with a star in the middle. It is also ornamented with curious narrow festoons made of thin wire. Round the neck are worn two or three rows of wooden beads, and a shield on the left shoulder. An Officer wears silver or glass beads, a coat of scarlet cloth, in uniform with the brigade to which he belongs, a blue sash and turban, containing twenty yards each, a pair of long trousers, half boots, and a shield on the left shoulder.

The Seapoys, who are in general well disciplined in the use of arms, serve as a strong reinforcement to a much less number of Europeans, and on many occasions, display great firmness and resolution.

As a sequel to this letter, I beg leave to subjoin an alphabetical explanation of Persian and Indian terms, not commonly understood in this country.

EXPLANATION OF PERSIAN AND INDIAN TERMS

Amdanny—*Imports*
Argee—*a Petition*
Assammees—*Dealers in different branches of trade*

Figure 2. A Native Officer (1.); A Seapoy or private Soldier (2.), in the Company's Service, on the Bengal Establishment (Mahomet, *Travels*, Letter XVI).

Bang—*an intoxicating juice of a vegetable*
Bazar—*a Market*
Baudshaw—*a King*
Baudshawjoddi—*a Queen*
Begum—*a Princess*
Betel—*a leaf growing on a vine, and chewed by all ranks of people*
Bramin—*a Priest*
Buckserrias—*Foot Soldiers, with only sword and target*
Buxey—*Treasurer to the Mogul, or Paymaster of troops*
Bundar—*a Custom-house*

Cawn—*a title of dignity*
Codgi—*a Bishop*
Chop—*a small seal, on which is engraved the name of the Mogul*
Choultry—*an open house for all travellers*
Chout—*a fourth part: or a tribute exacted by the Morattoes*
Chowkeys—*Turnpikes; or guards at landing places*
Caffres—*Negroes from Africa, trained up as soldiers by the Europeans*
Cooley—*a Porter, or Labourer of any kind*
Coss—*a distance of two miles and more*
Cossid—*a foot Messenger or Post*
Cowle—*a protection*
Crore of Rupees—*a hundred lack or near 1,250,000 l. sterling*

Dawgahs—*Custom-house Officers, or Collectors*
Decoyt—*a Robber*
Dewan—*King's Treasurer*
Dewanny—*Superintendency over the royal revenues*
Dooley—*a woman's chair, like a sedan*
Dummadah—*a river*
Durbar—*the Court or Council of a Mogul Prince*
Dustuk—*an order*

Firman—*a royal mandate, or grant*
Fouzdar—*a Governor, military Officer, or Renter*

Gentoo—*a native Indian, in a state of idolatry*
Gomastah—*a Broker, Factor, or Agent*
Gunge—*Grain Market*
Gwallers—*Carriers of palanquins*

Hackeries—*Carts or coaches drawn by oxen*
Harkarahs—*Spies*

Jaghire—*a district granted as a mark of honor, or allotted as a pension*
Jaggernaut—*the Gentoo pagoda*
Jemidar—*an Ensign*

Killedar—*the Governor of a Fort*
Kistbundee—*Times of the payment of the country Revenues*

Lack of Rupees—*about 12,500 l. sterling*

Maund—*between 70 and 80 pounds, at Surat only 37 pounds*
Moonshee—*a Persian Secretary*
Mulna—*a Mahometan Priest*
Moories—*Writers*
Muchulcas—*Bonds of obligation*
Musnud—*the throne of an Indian Prince*
Muxadabad—*the capital of Bengal*

Nabob—*a Governor of a Province, appointed by the Soubah*
Naib—*a Deputy to the Governor of a place*

Omrahs—*Privy Counsellors to the Mogul, and men of the first rank in the Empire*

Paddy—*Rice in the husk*
Paddy-grounds—*Rice fields*
Pagoda—*an Indian temple*
Pagoda—*an Indian coin worth 7s. 8d. sterling*

Palinquin—*a kind of canopy bed for travelling*
Parsees—*Worshippers of fire*
Patamar—*a Messenger or Post*
Peons—*Foot soldiers armed with a broad sword*
Pergannahs—*Villages*
Perwannah—*a letter, order, or command*
Pettah—*the town surrounding an Indian fort*
Podor—*a Money Changer*
Polygar—*the Lord of a District*
Ponsways—*Guard-boats*
Pettahs—*Grants*

Raja—*the highest title claimed by the Gentoo Princes*
Royran—*the King's Officer for receiving the revenue*
Rafftanny—*Exports*
Rupee—*a silver coin worth about 2s. 5d. sterl.*

Saneds—*commissions from the Mogul, Soubahs, or Nabobs*
Sardar—*an Officer of Horse*
Seapoys—*Indian foot soldiers, hired and disciplined by Europeans*
Shroff—*a Banker*
Sircar—*a general name for the Government, or those concerned in it*
Sirpah—*a rich dress of the country, worn by way of distinction*
Soubah—*the Viceroy of the Deckan, or of Bengal*

Tank—*a pond, or pool of water*
Tanka—*the Revenue appropriated by the Mogul, for maintaining
    a fleet at Surat*
Tanksal—*a mint for coinage*
Telinga—*the Carnatic country*
Telingas—*Soldiers raised in the Carnatic*
Tum tums—*Drums*
Topasses—*a tawney race of foot soldiers, descended from the Portuguese
    marrying natives, and called Topasses, because they wear hats*

Tunkahs—*Assignments upon lands, or rents assigned to the Company*
Tursaconna—*Wardrobe*

Ginanah—*Seraglio*

Vakeel—*an English Agent, or resident at the Nabob's court*
Vizerut—*the grant for the Viziership*

Zemin—*Ground*
Zemindary—*an Officer who takes care of the rents arising from
    the public lands.*

LETTER XVII

Dear Sir,

On our march from Denapore to Belgram [Bilgram], we halted some days
at Benaras, a rich and populous city on the north side of the Ganges, and
celebrated for its learning in past time. There was once a very fine Ob-
servatory here; and a few years ago, some European Gentlemen, led hither
by the love of science and antiquity, discovered a great many astronom-
ical instruments, of a large size, admirably well contrived, though injured
by the hand of time. It was supposed they might have been constructed
some centuries ago, under the direction of the great Akbar, the fond votary
of science, and the distinguished patron of the Bramins who applied, with
unwearied assiduity, to the study of astronomy.

The country about Benaras, is considered as the Paradise of India,
remarkable for its salubrious air, fascinating landscapes, and innocence
of its inhabitants, whose simple manners had a happy influence on all
who lived near them. While wasteful war spread her horrors over other
parts of India, this blissful country often escaped her ravages, perhaps
secured by its distance from the ocean, or more probably by the sacred
character ascribed to the scene, which had, through many ages, been considered as the repository of the religion and learning of the Bramins,

and the prevailing idea of the simplicity of the native Hindoos, a people unaccustomed to the sanguinary measures of, what they term, civilized nations.

But to return—the city of Benaras is built on the banks of the Ganges, and extends along the river from Rahajgaut, at one end, to Raja Cheyt Sing's [Chait Singh's] palace, at the other, which makes a distance of, at least, four miles. About the centre of the city, stands an ancient and lofty pile of building, called Mawdodasthrohur [Madho Das Dharahara], which strikes the eye, at first view, with a kind of sublime astonishment, and appears like a collection of rising towers that seem to survey in majestic pride the subject town and surrounding country. It is the temporary residence of the Hindoo pilgrims, who occasionally occupy it as they journey through this peaceful region. At some distance from it, is the elegant edifice of Bene, an extensive dealer in diamonds: this mansion is built at a slip, or gaut, called, by being united with the proprietor's name, Benegaut [Beni Madho Rai Ghat]; as if we said, Sullivan's-quay, or French's-slip. There are also other wharfs, or slips, ascending from the river, by many stone steps, termed from the names of the owners, who have built fine houses thereon, Ramgaut [Ram Ghat], Ranagaut [Rana Ghat], Pilleegaut [Pilai Ghat], Chowkgaut [Chawki Ghat], and Marattagaut [Maratha Ghat], &c.

At the east end of the town, there is a large square of building, called Serai, encompassed by walls, and laid out for the reception of travellers of every description; the better sort of people pay for their accommodation: but the poor are entertained free of expence: this laudable institution is supported by the voluntary contributions of the merchants of the city.

There are many other handsome dwellings belonging to the different traders and manufacturers, and several pagodas, or temples, of Hindoo worship.

The streets in Benaras, are rather confined and narrow; and the houses, which are crowded together, are in general very high and flat at the top, where the inhabitants, in the cool hours of the day, enjoy the benefit of the air. In different parts of the town, there are tanks, or wells, for the use of the citizens and the refreshment of passing strangers, who if in indigence, are also humanely supplied with food by persons employed to attend at the tanks for this very purpose. This city is well peopled, and persons of consequence, when they appear abroad, either on horseback or in their palanquins, are attended in great pomp, by numerous retinues. Manufactures of silk are carried on here to a great degree of perfection, and few places in India can surpass this market in such a varied assortment of sattins, keemcaus, and gooldbudthen, an elegant kind of silk, beautifully wrought with flowers of gold, besides muslin shawls, embroidered with gold and silver at each border. It is also remarkable for its fine carpets, saltpetre, sugar, musk, and perfumes; and trades largely with the Morattoes, and other dealers of India, with whom its commodities are bartered for their diamonds, and other articles of value.

About three miles north of the city, stands the Raja's palace, a superb mansion, where he usually spends the summer season, amidst the delightful scenery of groves, lawns, umbrageous walks, ponds, and cascades.

LETTER XVIII

Dear Sir,

You will now expect from me, an account of the Hindoos, the natives of this country; who are classed into four tribes, namely, Bramins, Sittri, Bice, and Sudder. The Bramins, or first class, which are esteemed the most ancient and honourable, are the Priests, the Instructors and Philosophers: the Sittri, or second class, are the military, who are entrusted with the defence and government of the state; in war, the soldiers who fight its battles; in peace, the magistrates and rulers who direct its councils: the Bice, or third class, are the merchants and husbandmen, who provide the necessaries and comforts of life by trade and agriculture, and thereby circulate through various channels the wealth of the nation: the Sudder, or fourth class, are the artisans, labourers, and servants. There is another class, which is the meanest of all, composed of cherwallees or gold-finders, chemars or shoe-makers, and domerah, or basket-makers, who are held in such sovereign detestation, that the very mention of their names conveys to the mind of a Hindoo, every idea of meanness and servility. No person, unless he be excommunicated, can quit his cast, or tribe; nor will he, on any account, be admitted into any other. This distinction of the people into different classes, seems to be an institution of some antiquity, and probably will continue unaltered till the end of time, so steady and persevering is every individual in his attachment to his respective cast.

The Bramins are again divided into five orders: first, into those that eat no flesh: second, into those that eat some kind of flesh; third, those that marry; fourth, those that vow celibacy: and fifth, the Bramins that forbear walking at all, for fear of destroying some living creatures; these wear a piece of silk or muslin before their mouths, lest the smallest fly should be drawn in by their breath. They are so exceedingly scrupulous in this respect, that they will not burn wood, through an apprehension of destroying any insect by it; and they always carry a brush in their hands to sweep the place they design to sit on, lest they should dislodge the soul of some animal. Their scrupulosity arises from a belief in the transmigration of souls, and their followers are so firmly persuaded that departed souls enter the bodies of animals, that they no sooner observe any of them frequent their houses, than they immediately conclude, their deceased friends, under this new disguise, come to visit them. They cannot, without horror, think of depriving any thing of life, and do not less respect it in the smallest insect, than in the huge elephant.

They hold there is but one God infinitely perfect, who has existed from all eternity; but that there are three subordinate Deities, namely, Brama [Brahma], whom he vested with the power of creation; Whistnow [Vishnu], the preserver; and Routeren [Rudra], the enemy and destroyer of mankind. The supreme Divinity is often typified under the form of a Being, with a number of eyes and hands, to impress the minds of the people with a strong idea of his penetration and power, and induce them to be very exact in the performance of moral duties. The Bramins advise their followers to go in pilgrimage to certain places, esteemed holy, and especially to the pagodas near the mouth of the Ganges: washing in that river alone, will, in their opinion, cleanse them from a multitude of sins. Their women rise early in the morning to bathe, carrying pieces of dough on silver salvers, adorned with flowers, to the river side, and lighted lamps in their hands: after bathing, they form the dough into images, which they worship with much adoration, at the same time ringing bells and burning incense, and afterwards commit their images to the bosom of the Ganges, with some formality. However strange their doctrine may appear to Europeans, yet they are much to be commended for the exercise of the moral virtues they inculcate, namely, temperance, justice, and humanity. Amidst a variety of extravagant customs, strange ceremonies, and prejudices, we may discover the traces of sublime morality, deep philosophy, and refined policy; but when we attempt to trace the religious and civil institutions to their source, we find that it is lost in the maze of antiquity. The native Indians, or Hindoos, are men of strong natural genius, and are, by no means, unacquainted with literature and science, as the translation of the Ayeen Akberry [*Ain-i Akbari*] into English, has fully evinced. We may trace the origin of most of the sciences, in their ancient manuscripts. Even before the age of Pythagoras, the Greeks travelled to India for instruction: the trade carried on by them with the oldest commercial nations, in exchange for their cloth, is a proof of their great progress in the arts of industry.

The women in general, except in the higher scenes of life, prepare the food for their husbands and families; as no Hindoo would make use of any but what his wife dresses for him: it consists chiefly of rice, fish, and vegetables, well seasoned with pepper and other spices, to which they add pickles of various sorts. The men, who always eat together, unaccompanied by the women, previously take off their turbans, shoes, and outside garments, and wash before and after meals. They afterwards withdraw to another apartment, where they enjoy themselves with smoking tobacco and chewing betel. They use no spirits or other liquors, but are particularly nice in the taste of different waters, and consider their choice of them a great luxury.

As to the funerals of these people—some bury the bodies of the deceased, which they place in the grave in a sitting posture, with rice and water near them: their dead are generally decked with jewels and other ornaments, of which they are disrobed by their kindred, before the grave is filled up. The usual way, however, is to burn the corpse on a funeral pile erected for that purpose near the water side; the nearest relation in tattered apparel, which is, in their opinion, the expressive garb of sorrow, sets fire to it, and shews every symptom of frantic grief on the occasion: the body being soon consumed, the ashes are collected and thrown into the river. The ashes of the great are placed in an urn, which is carried with some degree of ceremony by a Bramin, and cast into the Ganges, to whose waters they attribute a peculiar sanctity.

LETTER XIX

Dear Sir,

After halting some days at Benaras, in order to refresh the army, we proceeded on our march towards Belgram, delighted, as we passed along, with a continued view of the finest country on earth, diversified with fields of rice, plantations of sugar, and gardens abounding with a variety of fruits and flowers; and encamped at Duci [Joosi], opposite Alahabad [Allahabad], a large fort, about 412 miles to the south of Delhi, 540 from Calcutta, and 850 from the mouth of the Ganges. It is pleasantly situated between that river and Jemina [Jamuna]. Inside the fort is a royal palace, in which are apartments for the Mogul, a Durbar, and Zenanah, with a number of houses occupied by the Officers of the court, and their families. Each house is built like two dwellings joined together, and walled round, for the purpose not only of concealing their women from their neighbours, but even from their own male domestics; and contains very spacious and lofty rooms, opening towards the river, with smaller apartments adjoining them, which are extremely dark, without the least aperture to admit either light or air. To these they retire in the heat of the day, to enjoy the calm refreshment of sleep; for the natives find by experience, that in order to render a situation cool, in this sultry region, they must totally exclude every ray of light, and breath of air, till the fervid sun descends into the lap of Thetis. To the tops of their houses, which are flat, they ascend by narrow, steep, stair-cases, and inhale the evening breeze after Sol's friendly departure.

The palace of Alahabad was entirely built of stone, hewn out of the rocks, at some distance from the banks of the Ganges, and brought hither at a vast expence. It is not unlike the Portland stone, but of a coarser kind, and infinitely more porous. Not only the walls, but the roofs, floors, and pillars of the palace, were formed of it; and even the very squares and passages were paved with it. Neither glass, iron, brick, or other materials for building, were introduced here, until the fort came into the possession of the English. The slightest walls of this great pile are, at least, five feet thick. There are some good houses about it, built in the Indian style, that make a handsome appearance. Nothing can be more striking, nothing can display a more sublime air of grandeur, than the lofty gateways here, which resemble in some manner, the old triumphal arches of the Romans.

The country and climate of Alahabad, are very delightful; when the rains are over, not a cloud is to be seen in the azure Heavens, and the heat of torrid suns is frequently tempered by the breath of fanning gales, which Providence occasionally permits to pant, on the bosom of the sultry air. Vegetation is so rapid, that it seems almost perceptible to the eye; and the naked plains, which appeared, but a week before, to be only a broad surface of sand, are instantly clothed by the benignity of those tears shed from above, with the verdant robes of blooming nature. The face of the country is entirely changed; even the marshy grounds that had been covered with water, produce their golden harvests; and the luxuriant earth, under the genial influence of the clime, pours forth her various plenty. Rice, wheat, peas, and beans, grow here in abundance; and a sort of grain called jow, something like the oats of Europe. The indigo shrub thrives exceedingly in this soil; it is not higher than a rose tree; and its leaves, when stripped off, are steeped in tubs of water, which extracts the blue from them; the sediment, after the water has been drained off, is exposed to the sun, which occasions the moisture to evaporate, and the indigo to remain at the bottom of the vessels. The gardens are painted with a variety of beautiful flowers, that feast the sight, without gratifying the smell: to the rose, and a white flower resembling jessamine, we are only indebted for their fragrance. The fruits are mangoes, guavas, pomegranates, ananas or pine apples, musk and water melons, limes, lemons, and oranges, all which spring up spontaneously, and grow to a great degree of perfection. Ginger, and turmeric, which has much the same qualities of ginger, are produced in this fertile soil, in their highest state of excellence.

LETTER XX

Dear Sir,

Our march from Alahabad was extremely pleasant, until we came to Mendegaut on the river of Ganges, when a violent storm arose, accompanied with hail, lightning, and thunder, which continued for three days, and greatly annoyed both men and cattle. We remained here a week, to repair some damages suffered by the weather, and then crossed over to the plains of Belgram, on the opposite side of the river, where we encamped in the year 1776. These plains take their name from the village of Belgram, situate about two miles farther up the country. In a few months after our arrival, the Nabob Aspa-doulah [Asaf al-Daula], in consequence of a difference with the Fouzdars Maboub and Cossi-bussant [Faujdars Mahbub Ali Khan and Khwaja Basant Ali Khan], arising from their non-compliance to pay the usual annual tribute, due for some time, collected his troops together, in order to march against them, having first dispatched an express to General Stibbert, who commanded our army, acquainting him of his intended expedition, and requesting his immediate assistance. At the instance of Aspah-doulah, two regiments of Seapoys, under the direction of Colonel Parker, were ordered to a place called Coragh [Kora], about eighty miles from Belgram, in order to reinforce the Nabob's troops, which they met on the way, advancing with a few pieces of cannon. Maboub apprized by his scouts, of the route of our detachment, sent Deputies to Col. Parker, to request a personal interview with him. The Colonel wishing to accommodate matters, if possible, without resorting to the horrors of war, agreed on it; and the result of their meeting, was apparently amicable, on both sides. On the next day, our Officers were invited by Maboub, to dine with him: he, in the mean time, prepared his men for a secret attack, and previously poisoned the provisions intended for their entertainment. The Gentlemen, by no means, suspecting his dark design, were actually on the way to their perfidious host, and must have met with an untimely fate at his inhospitable table, had not one of his servants providentially disclosed the secret before their arrival, and informed them that there was a plan concerted to surprise the main body, in their absence. The Colonel, Capt. Gravely, and the rest of the Officers, alarmed at this intelligence, instantly returned to the camp, and perceived at some distance, numbers of Maboub's men, advancing in regular order, to give them battle. Our soldiers, at a moment's notice, were prepared to oppose their force, and made so vigorous a charge on them, at the first onset, when they came up, that their ranks were broken, and the greater part of them discouraged from disappointment, and deserted by the hope of an easy conquest, fled, in the utmost confusion and disorder, after an engagement in which, though soon over, many of the enemy fell. Cossi-bussant escaped with those who made off, at the commencement of hostilities; and Maboub was pursued, taken, and sent prisoner, under a strong guard to Aspah-doulah at Lecknow [Lucknow], where he received that punishment, which his perfidy deserved.

A few of our Seapoys were killed; and the gallant Captain Gravely, no less distinguished for his prowess in the field, than his conduct in private life, received an ill fated wound, of which he died, in a few months after Col. Parker, and the two regiments under his command, returned to Belgram. He was sincerely regretted by his brother Officers; by whom and his weeping Soldiers, his funeral was processionally attended to the grave, and he was interred with due military honours. His afflicted widow erected a very handsome monument to his memory, near the ground where his own regiment usually paraded.

Lecknow, the town, to which Maboub was sent, is a place of considerable trade, and one of the principal factories in the Mogul's dominions. The inhabitants are opulent and industrious; and the Nabob Aspadoulah, with other Noblemen, occasionally reside here, living in all the ease and splendor of eastern luxury, and frequently indulging themselves with their dancing girls. There are some good houses in Lecknow, occupied by merchants and factors; nor is it less remarkable for its cotton manufactories, than for a beautiful kind of porcelain and earthen ware.

The Nabob keeps a kind of a military force here, called Burkendaws, who are not so uniform in dress as the Seapoys. Their arms are match fire-locks, bows and arrows, spears, daggers, swords, and shields.

LETTER XXI

Dear Sir,

At some distance from Lecknow, is the town of Oude [Ayodhya or Faizabad]; and it will ever be a place of constant resort while it holds the remains of Sujah-doulah [Shuja al-Daula], which are deposited here in a magnificent tomb, illumined every night with a number of glittering lamps, and covered with ornamented muslin. It is sheltered by a grand dome supported by pillars, and on each side is placed a large silver jar of water, from an opinion that he may rise in the night to bathe, which the Mahometans look upon as a purification necessary to prepare them for their admission into the regions of happiness. This town is much indebted to him for the great improvements it received during his reign; and the surrounding country also, which appears like one extensive garden. His palace in Oude is an ancient but spacious mansion, and still retains the striking appearance of pristine grandeur.

In the environs of the town, there are lofty groves and wide extending parks, called by the natives, circarga, where he had often passed some of his leisure hours in the pleasures of the chase and riding. His ponds were stored with a variety of curious fishes, both exotic and domestic, with their fins and tails adorned with small golden rings. He frequently made it the amusement of his evenings to feed them with rice, and observe them leap above water to receive it from his hand. He was so extremely fond of curiosities, that he kept a menage constantly supplied with a number of strange animals wild and tame, which he collected from different parts of the world, and confined in iron cages. His great revenues were scarcely sufficient to support his extravagance, and gratify his unbounded love of pleasure.

Some time before Sujah-doulah's death, he repeatedly sent to Mulnahoffis [Maulana Hafiz Rahmat Khan], Nabob of the Rohellas [Rohillas], for the customary tribute, which the latter, on consulting his Officers, not only refused to pay, but even threatened, *vi et armis*, to oppose him. Sujah-doulah, without delay, having acquainted General Champion of his conduct, was reinforced by him, and marched with his brave auxiliaries to the Rohellas, where he met the numerous troops of the enemy on the field of battle, and warmly engaged them, until victory inclining to our side, conferred on us her unfading laurels, as the meed of military virtue. Col. William Ann. Bailie, then Major of artillery, distinguished himself by his intrepid zeal and gallantry in this expedition.

A great part of the enemy's army were killed; the rest fled, and some of them were pursued and taken. General Champion returned with his men to head quarters, at Belgram; and Sujah-doulah directed his course to the very palace of Mulnahoffis, who was also in the number of the slain, and compelled his daughter, a beautiful young woman, whom he found in one of the grand apartments to come along with him to Oude. Having placed this unfortunate Lady in his seraglio, where nine hundred pining beauties, with their attendants, were already immured, he forced her to yield to his licentious desires, but purchased his enjoyment at a dear rate, as his life was the forfeit of it. The violated female, with a soul, the shrine of purity, like that of the divine Lucretia, whose chastity will ever adorn the historic page, fired with indignation at such unmanly treatment, grew frantic with rage, and disdaining life after the loss of honour, stabbed her brutal ravisher with a lancet, which she afterwards plunged into her own bosom, and expired. Notwithstanding the dangerous wound he received, by the appointment of Heaven, from the avenging hand of injured innocence, he might have lingered some time longer in life, had he kept within the bounds of moderation, by restraining the impetuosity of his unruly passions. But his career was pleasure, to which he gave such a loose, that his recent wound opened, and bleeding afresh, reduced him to a state of debility that terminated in his death. On account of his elevated rank in human life, his obsequies were conducted with great pomp and ceremony; and his funeral formed a pageant procession, in which his officers and soldiers walked in solemn pace, to the sounds of pensive music. After his interment, the women who composed his seraglio, laid aside their jewels and ornaments, to denote, at least, in appearance, their sorrow on this mournful occasion.

LETTER XXII

Dear Sir,

I shall now give you some account of the city of Delhi, which is the capital of the province, and situate in the centre of the empire: it lies in 78 degrees, east longitude from London, and 26 degrees north latitude. Its form is something like a crescent standing on the river Jemma, which runs through it. At present it is divided into three spacious towns, about 130 miles to the northward of Agra, in a very pleasant country, and pure, wholesome climate.

The first town of Delhi, is supposed to have contained nine castles and fifty-two gates; and at some distance from it, is a handsome stone bridge. The second town, which had been taken from the Indians, a long time since, by one of the former Mogul's, has a very fine appearance, and fills the mind with ideas of the true sublime, from the ruins of the many grand monuments of their ancient heroes who fell in war, and other magnificent buildings, nearly demolished by Shah Johan [Shah Jahan], the father of Aurengzebe [Aurangzeb]. The third town, which lies close to the second and almost built on its ruins, was called Johan Abad [Shahja-hanabad], but the Moguls have given it the name of Delhi. It is imag-ined, from the frequent wars that desolated a great part of the country of Indostan, at the time of the accession of the Patan Princes, that Shah Johan had laid the foundation of this city in blood, the better (he observed) to cement the stones. This city receives no small embellishment from the delightful gardens that surround it; and forms its principal entrance by a very wide street of a prodigious length, with arches on each side, for the purpose of stores and ware-rooms, to which the merchants and trades-men bring whatever is valuable or curious from all parts of India. This street leads to the royal palace, at the outer gate of which, stand the fig-ures of two huge elephants, with images mounted on them, represent-ing two Rajas, famous in the history of Indostan, for their uncommon valour. They were brothers, who lost their lives in their gallant defence of some possessions, against a powerful army headed by Ekbar [Akbar].

Around the palace, which is two miles in circumference, is a great wall built of hewn stone, and defended with battlements, and a vast number of strong towers, at a little distance from each other. It consists of several courts, and the first of these belongs to the chief nobility, who frequently parade here, on their elephants, in all the pride of Oriental grandeur.

Within this court, is a square adorned with handsome porticos, from which you descend to convenient apartments occupied by the guards: On the east, are the courts of justice; on the west, the apartments of the ladies; and in the middle, an elegant canal formed with vast judgment and art, into basins. From the first court is a grand avenue leading to the second where the Omrahs or Nobles mount guard in person, and deem it a par-ticular honour to wait on the present Mogul, Ahamut Shaw Baudshaw [Ahmad Shah Badshah].

The next object that presents itself to the view, is the Divan, which is held in the third court, where the Emperor gives public audience. It is a superb edifice, open at both sides and covered with a spacious dome, sup-ported by thirty marble pillars of masterly workmanship, ornamented with painted flowers. It contains a grand hall, the ascent to which, is by a flight of marble steps, and in the centre is an alcove magnificently embellished, where the grand Mogul is proudly seated on a brilliant throne, glittering with diamonds, and a profusion of costly jewels.

The history of the revolutions of his court is fraught with so much fiction, that it would be impossible to reconcile it to reason or reflection; yet if we believe the records and traditions of the natives, its sovereigns were the greatest and most arbitrary Monarchs in the world. Their orders, though ever so extravagant, were submissively obeyed; and their mandates observed by the remotest nations. Their very names struck terror into the hearts of their enemies; but so rapid has been the decline of their power, that the race of the great Tamerlane is now little respected since the days of Nizam Almoulud [Nizam al-Mulk]. The royal tenure of the throne, is grown so insecure, that the Mogul has been, of late years, deposed at pleasure, to make way for such of his servants as could gain over the people, that great engine of power! to their cause. His authority, which prevailed, in former ages, over most of the Kings of the earth, now reaches little farther than his seraglio, where he dreams away life, drowned in the enjoyment of dissolute pleasures. His Viziers, who transact the affairs of the state, study rather to promote their own views than advance his interest; and often abridge his power in order to increase their consequence. They make peace or declare war, without his knowledge; and his Viceroys, on the other hand, who were, some years ago, appointed, or dismissed from office by him, have, of late, shaken off their dependence, and even nominated their own successors. They also, like so many independent Sovereigns, grant leases and other privileges to the Europeans, or those whom they wish to serve. His Omrahs are extremely tyrannical, and must, sooner or later by their impolicy, precipitate the ruin of the entire empire. From their oppression its great metropolis has but few manufacturers, who are obliged to work for any price those tyrants please to pay them for their labour, which is always considerably less than the value. This ungenerous treatment has not only compelled the ingenious artisan to seek encouragement elsewhere, and proved the certain means of supplying the English factories with skilful workmen, but reduced the people of Delhi to the necessity of purchasing the goods of other places, at a much dearer rate, than they need pay at home, had they given sufficient support to their own manufacturers.

LETTER XXIII

Dear Sir,

The principal rural sports of the people of Indostan, are hunting and hawking: they purchase hawks and other birds of prey from Persia, which are taught to fly at all manner of game.

The Soubahs and other great characters of the country, find much amusement in the combats of wild beasts. The elephant often encounters the elephant, with a rider mounted on each, to manage them, on a larger space of ground paled in with bamboes to keep off the crowd of spectators: they attack each other with great fury, for several hours, till one of them with its rider, is either killed or disabled. The buffaloe commonly engages with the tyger, and, though ferocious the latter, frequently worsts his quadruped antagonist. It would be endless to enumerate the many diversions of this kind, which consist of various animals attacking each other or combated by men who risque their lives in such dangerous enterprizes.

Among the joyous inhabitants of this country, there are some content to live on what is just sufficient to supply human necessity: which is strictly pursuing the idea of Goldsmith, that elegant writer, who observes in his Edwin and Angelina,

> Man wants but little here below,
> Nor wants that little, long.

They acquire a support, by administering to travellers as they journey along the roads and highways, a chilm, or pipe of tobacco, for which they receive a small gratuity. The rich and poor, sometimes, promiscuously mingle together, and often partake of the same refreshment.

At Muckenpore [Manikpur], a small village sixty miles from Belgram, is the resort of a number of Faquirs, from Delhi, Oude, and the neighbouring provinces. Hither the pious natives flock, to bestow their charity on these holy men, and think it a kind of religious humanity, highly acceptable to their God, to confer their benefactions on his faithful servants.

From the prayers of the Faquirs, great blessings are expected, and many calamities thought to be averted, as they obtain the reputation of sainted martyrs, by torturing their bodies, and suffering a variety of punishments, by way of penance, during this earthly pilgrimage. Some pierce their flesh with spears, and drive daggers through their hands: others carry on their palms, for a length of time, burning vessels full of fire, which they shift from hand to hand: many walk, with bare feet on sharp iron spikes fixed in a kind of sandal: several of their order turn their faces over one shoulder, and keep them in that situation till they fix for ever, their heads looking backward: another sect clinch their fists very hard, till the nails of the fingers grow into the palms, and appear through the back of their hands, and numbers, who never speak, turn their eyes to the point of the nose, losing the power of looking in any other direction. These last pretend to see what they call the sacred fire. Strange as this austerity may seem, if accompanied with purity of intention, it must be considered by the unprejudiced, as less offensive to the Deity, than the indulgence of the passions: though man be not forbid to enjoy the good things of this life, yet an abuse of that enjoyment, which evinces his ingratitude to Heaven, is punished even here below, by wasting the ungenerous being to an untimely grave—but he who foregoes the pleasures of a fleeting period, through an expectation of permanent happiness, and suffers temporary torture in order to obtain endless bliss, with a mind all directed to that great Power who gave him existence, must, notwithstanding the ridicule of the world, meet with a more favourable sentence at his awful tribunal.

Not long before our departure from Belgram, we were honoured with a visit from the Nabob Aspa-doulah, accompanied by General Stibbert, his Aid-du-Camps, and other Officers of distinction, who met him on the way, in his usual style of grandeur, mounted with his Nobles, on an elephant richly caparisoned, and attended by his numerous train of Burkendaws, Chopdars, pages, &c. and a native band of music to enliven the procession, of which the annexed plate will give you a more perfect idea, than this description [see figure 3].

His entry through Belgram was announced by the beating of drums, firing of cannon, and other marks of military honour. After a repast at the General's, he retired to a large decorated tent erected for him, which covered almost an acre of ground; adjacent to his, others were pitched for his attendants.

The day after his arrival, our Commander in Chief issued his orders to prepare for a review. Early next morning, one regiment of Europeans, six of Seapoys, two companies of artillery, and one troop of cavalry, amounting in all to about seven thousand, were in perfect readiness on the wide plain. The Nabob on his elephant, in company with the General, passed the lines. Shortly after, the former descended from the back of the unwieldy animal, and mounted a beautiful Arabian horse, on which he received the salute of the Officers. Colonel Ironside ranged the troops in the following order: the cavalry were placed on the right and left wing; three regiments of Seapoys on each side next to them; and the European infantry in the centre. At first, they were all reviewed in one body, and afterwards formed different corps, observing the most exact discipline and regularity in their various evolutions, which gave much satisfaction to the General, Officers, and numerous spectators. Aspa-doulah, in particular, was exceeding pleased with the beauty and order of our tactics, and expressed his approbation in the terms of that lively kind of gratitude arising from a high sense of received pleasure. After the review, a breakfast was prepared for him, during which, the artillery continued to salute him with their cannon. His fare was served up by his own servants, as he could not touch any thing from the hands of a Christian, consistent with the duties of his religion: however, to shew his politeness, he sat at the same table, with our Officers of rank, and having remained a few days in the camp, returned to his own territories.

Figure 3. View of the Grand Nabob Aspahdoulah of Lechnough and his Retinue (Mahomet, *Travels*, Letter XXIII).

LETTER XXIV

Dear Sir,

Having received orders to march to Calcutta, we quitted Belgram; and finding it unnecessary to keep a force any longer there, on account of the good understanding that prevails, at present, between the Court of Delhi and the East India Company, the chaumnies were entirely demolished, and every vestige of a house or building razed to the ground.

On our way, we passed by some small factories belonging to the Dutch, Danes, French, and others, that were once in the hands of the Portuguese, but being since reduced, have come into the possession of the English. Our brigade, at length, arrived at Fort William in the year 1778, and replaced the other, which marched to Denapore.

About fifteen miles from Fort William, on the opposite side of the river, is a Danish settlement, called Serampour [Serampore]. Its manufactures consist of cotton, baffety, calico, chintz, table cloths, and napkins.

The houses of the inhabitants are very neat, and on the river side is a small battery, with the Governor's castle in the centre, and the Danish flag flying a'top.

In Chinsura, a Dutch settlement, much the same kind of trade is conducted, as at Serampour.

A little farther on, is Chandernagore, or Frasdanga, the scene of many disputes between the French and English; the latter of whom are now the proprietors of it; on the west, it lies exposed to an enemy, though encompassed by a wall, and, in other situations, pretty well fortified. It drives a brisk trade, and carries on, to some extent, the manufacture of handkerchiefs and striped muslins.

Near Frasdanga, and in the same direction, is Gretti, then belonging to the French, under the government of Monsieur Chevalier, but now in possession of the English. The Governor's house, which takes its name from the place about it, was a superb mansion, rising in all the pride of architecture, over the margin of the Ganges, and decorated inside in a style of unrivalled elegance: part of the furniture was covered with a rich embroidered sattin, and the very purdoes of the windows were of scarlet quilted sattin. The avenue to this grand edifice was shaded on both sides, with rows of embowering trees; and the beauty, the fragrance of his gardens, which perfumed the wanton air, ravished the senses: his fish-ponds, cascades, and groves, heightened the imagery of the varied scene; and his expanding lawns were adorned with figures of snow-white marble, that almost started under the artist's hand, from the rude material into life. On the domain was an Opera-house for his amusement. At the outside entrance to the palace, stood the Governor's guard.

Fifty miles from Calcutta lies the town of Hugley, defended by a strong fortress, and surrounded by a deep ditch: it is a place of considerable traffic, particularly in the article of opium, which is brought chiefly from Patna. Notwithstanding the fatal effects of this plant, the irresistible avarice of the Dutch, induces them to raise it wherever they possess a spot of ground in India; but the Chinese, from its destructive qualities, forbid, under the penalty of death, the cultivation of it, and demolish any house, in which it is exposed for sale.

It is used by the people of every class, among the Hindoos and Mahometans: the lower order take it, when they enter on any arduous enterprise, to render them insensible of the danger; and the gentry, who are fond of every thing that tends to a gratification of the passions, consider it as a great luxury. Its effects, however, are various, according to the manner of preparing it. Opium in its original state, is the produce of a species of poppy, the root of which is about the thickness of a man's finger, full of a bitter juice that runs through the whole plant. The flower resembles a rose, and the stem which is commonly pliable, grows to the height of two cubits, and produces a kind of leaves (not unlike those of the lettuce) oblong, indented, curled, and of a sea-green colour. When it is full of sap, a slight incision is made on the outside, from which flow some drops of a milky nature. These drops soon congeal; and when moistened and kneaded with warm water and honey, become more consistent and viscous like pitch; after this process, the glutinous matter is made into small cakes fit for immediate use. The good kind is that, which is soft and yielding to the touch. Patna is allowed to send the best to market: it is there purchased at a cheap rate, though extremely dear in some parts of India. It is nearly opposite qualities, stupifying, at one time, and raising exhilarating ideas at another; it occasions drowsiness, and vigilance; and taken to an excess, brings on a madness that ceases only in death.

LETTER XXV

Dear Sir,

As an instance of the wealth and consequence that aggrandize any situation, where trade is introduced, I shall give you some account of Surat, which lies in twenty-one degrees, thirty minutes, north latitude; and seventy-two degrees east longitude from the meridian of London.

About the middle of last century this place was only the resort of a few merchants, who by extending their commerce, invited numbers to settle among them; and thus, by the introduction of arts, population, and industry, Surat became in a few years, one of the most considerable towns in the world. It is defended by a wall and towers, and has a square castle with a tower at each angle on the S. W. part of it, which commands both the river, and the avenues to the town by land. It is said to contain above two hundred thousand inhabitants: while the Mogul government was in vigour, merchants of all religions and denominations were induced to take shelter under it; and such was the honesty of the traders, that bags of money ticketted and sealed, would circulate for years without being weighed. The Gentoos are very numerous here, particularly the tribe of the Banyans, who are the fairest dealers in the world, and remarkable for plain integrity, and an admirable command of temper, in the course of their transactions. It is impossible to rouse them into passion, and when others are subdued by that temporary frenzy of the mind, they wait with patience till it subsides, and by these means, enjoy a superior advantage over the rest of mankind.

The Governor of Surat keeps his seat of administration at the Durbar or Court, where all actions criminal and civil are brought before him, and summarily dispatched in the Eastern manner. The buildings are in the Gentoo and Morisque style; and the houses of the great are so contrived that their gate-ways are defensible against any sudden irruption of a few armed men. The private apartments are backwards for the greater security of the women, of whom the Moors, especially, are extremely jealous. They have always, at least, one room, in each dwelling, where a fountain is kept playing in the middle of it, by the murmurs of which they are lulled to sleep, and refreshed by the coolness it diffuses through the apartment. Their saloons, which they call diwans, entirely open on one side to their gardens, where fountains, cascades, meandering rills, and variegated flower beds, form the most delightful assemblage of rural beauty and prospect. In summer, they often go in parties, to country recesses, a little way out of town, in order to enjoy themselves in their frescades, by the side of the waters with which they are furnished. The English have a very pleasant garden here, for the use and recreation of the Gentlemen of the factory.

The streets of Surat are irregularly laid out; and the stories of the houses are carried up projecting over one another, in such a manner, that the uppermost apartments on each side, are so close, as to darken the streets below, without excluding a free circulation of air. As to provisions I cannot imagine that there is in the universe a better place. The great plenty of every article, which an unbounded influx throws into the market, renders all kinds of eatables extremely cheap: wild fowl and game can be had at an easy rate; and nothing can exceed their sallads and roots. Among the articles of luxury, which they have in common with other parts of the East, there are public hummums for bathing, cupping, rubbing and sweating, but the practice of champing, which is derived from the Chinese, appears to have been known to the ancients, from the following quotations.

Percurrit agili corpus arte tractatrix
Manumque doctam spargit omnibus membris.

[The female masseuse/shampooer, with her agile art, runs over his
body and spreads her skilled hands over all his limbs.]

MART. Lib. iii. Epig. 82

Seneca, at the end of his sixty-sixth letter, inveighs against it as a point
of luxury introduced among the Romans, thus—*An potius optem ut mala-
cissandos articulos exoletis meis porrigam? ut muliercula, aut aliquis in mulier-
culam ex viro versus digitulos meos ducat?* [Should I desire to be allowed to
stretch out my limbs for my slaves to massage/shampoo: or to have a female masseuse/shampooer pull my finger-joints?] The person who un-
dergoes this operation, lies, at full length, on a couch or sopha, on which
the operator chafes or rubs his limbs, and cracks the joints of the wrist
and fingers. All this, they pretend, not only supples the joints, but procures a brisker circulation to the fluids apt to stagnate, or loiter through
the veins, from the heat of the climate, which is, perhaps, the best recommendation of such a practice.

LETTER XXVI

Dear Sir,

At a small distance from Surat lies Bombay, an island so situate as to form
one of the most commodious bays perhaps in the world; from which distinction it received the denomination of Bombay, by corruption from the
Portuguese Buon bahia. The harbour is spacious enough to contain any
number of ships; has excellent anchoring ground; and by its circular position, can afford them a land-locked shelter against any winds, to which
the mouth of it is exposed. The castle is a regular quadrangle, well built
of strong hard stone; and round the island there are several little out-
forts and redoubts. The English Church at Bombay, is a neat, airy building, standing on the Green, a large space of ground, and pleasantly laid
out in walks planted with trees, round which are mostly the houses of the
English inhabitants. These consist only of ground-floors, after the Ro-

man fashion, with a court-yard before and behind, offices, and out-houses. They are substantially built with stone and lime, and white-washed on the out-side, which has a decent appearance, but very offensive to the eyes from the glare of the sun. Few of them have glass windows to any apartment, the sashes being generally paned with a kind of transparent square-cut oyster-shells, transmitting sufficient light, and excluding, at the same time, the violence of its glare.

At some distance farther on the continent, there are fairs held, that last generally nine or ten days. Hither the Banyans resort, and such dealers as are sometimes disappointed by the Factors or Agents of the Company, (who bespeak their commodities) to expose their goods for sale on banks of earth raised for that purpose, under small sheds. The soil of this country is chiefly employed in cocoa-nut groves, palm-trees, &c.

As to the cocoa-nut tree itself, not all the minute descriptions I have heard of it, seem to me to come up to the reality of its wonderful properties and use. Nothing is so unpromising as the aspect of this tree; nor does any yield a produce more profitable, or more variously beneficial to mankind: it has some resemblance to the palm-tree; perhaps one of its species. The leaves of it serve for thatching; the husk of the fruit for making cordage, and even the largest cables for ships. The kernel of it is dried, and yields an oil much wanted for several uses, and forms a considerable branch of traffic under the name of copra. Arrack, a coarse sort of sugar, called jagree, and vinegar are also extracted from it, besides many other particulars too tedious to enumerate. The cultivation of it is extremely easy, by means of channels conveying water to the roots, and a manure laid round them, consisting of the small fry of fish, known by the name of buckshaw.

There are also here and there interspersed a few brab-trees, or rather wild palm trees; (the word brab being derived from Brabo, which in Portuguese signifies wild) that bear an insipid kind of fruit, about the size of a common pear, and produce from incisions at the top, the toddy or liquor drawn from them, of which the arrack that is made, is esteemed much better than that from the cocoa-nut tree. They are generally cultivated near the sea-side, as they thrive best in a sandy soil. It is on this tree that the toddy birds, so called from their attachment to it, build their exquisitely curious nests, wrought out of the thinnest reeds and filaments of branches, with inimitable mechanism. The birds themselves are about the bigness of a partridge, but of no consideration either for plumage, song, or the table.

The banian tree, which is a species of fig, grows here to an enormous height. Some of its branches shoot forth horizontally from the trunk; and from them proceed a number of less boughs, that fall in a perpendicular direction, downwards, taking root from other bodies, which, like pillars, serve to support the arms they sprung from. Thus, one tree multiplies into twenty or thirty bodies, and spreads over a great space of ground, sufficient to shelter, at least, five hundred persons. Neither is this, nor any other of the Indian trees, without leaves all the year. Under the branches of the banian, the Gentoos frequently place their images, and celebrate their festivals; and the Faquirs inflict on themselves, different kinds of punishment. Milton, in his Paradise Lost, gives a very natural description of it in the following terms:

> The fig-tree, not that kind for fruit renown'd;
> But such as at this day to Indians known
> In Malabar, or Decan, spreads her arms,
> Branching so broad and long, that in the ground
> The bending twigs take root; and daughters grow
> About the mother-tree, a pillar'd shade!
> High over-arch'd, and echoing walks between.

LETTER XXVII

Dear Sir,

As the practice of chewing betel is universal throughout India, the description of it may not prove unentertaining. It is a creeping plant cultivated in the same manner as the vine, with leaves full of large fibres like those of the citron, but longer and narrower at the extremity. It is mixed with the arek and chunam before it is used. The arek-nut is exactly in form and bigness like a nutmeg, only harder: it is marbled in the inside with white and reddish streaks, and wrapped up in the leaf. Chunam is nothing more than burnt lime made of the finest shells. To these three articles is often added for luxury, what they call cachoonda, a japan earth, which from perfumes and other mixtures, receives a high improvement. The taste of it is, at first, little better than that of common chalk, but soon turns to a flavor that dwells agreeably on the palate.

Another addition they use, termed catchoo, is a blackish, granulated, perfumed substance; and a great provocative, when taken alone, which is not a small consideration with the Asiatics in general.

So prevalent is the custom of chewing betel, that it is used by persons of every description; but it is better prepared for people of condition, who consider it a breach of politeness to take leave of their friends, without making presents of it. No one attempts to address his superior, unless his mouth is perfumed with it; and to neglect this ceremony even with an equal, would be deemed an unpardonable rudeness.

The dancing girls are eternally scented with it, as being a powerful incentive to love, and a composition that gives fragrance to the breath and lips. It is taken after meals, during a visit, and on the meeting and parting of friends or acquaintance; and most people here are confirmed in the opinion that it also strengthens the stomach, and preserves the teeth and gums. It is only used in smoking, with a mixture of tobacco and refined sugar, by the Nabobs and other great men, to whom this species of luxury is confined.

In several parts of the country, the soil and climate are very favourable to these latter productions. Tobacco of the finest quality, grows in rich moist grounds, in which it is generally planted, and brought by cultivation to great perfection. The sugar plantations employ thousands of the natives, who alone, inured to the excessive heat of vertical suns, are adequate to the fatigue of this laborious business. The cane commonly shoots up to the height of five or six feet, and is about half an inch in diameter: the stem or stock is divided by knots, above the space of a foot from each other: at the top, it puts forth a number of green leaves, from which springs a white flower. The canes, when ripe, are found quite full of a pithy juice, (of which the sugar is made) and being then carried to the mill in bundles, are cut up into small pieces, and thrown into a large vessel much in the form of a mortar, in which they are ground by wooden rollers plated with steel, and turned either by the help of oxen, or manual labour; during this process, a liquor issues from them, which is conveyed through a pipe in the vessel above described into another in the sugar-house, and thence passes into a copper, that is heated by a slow fire, so as to make it simmer; it is then mixed with ashes and quick lime, in order to separate the unctuous parts, which float upon the surface in a thick scum, that is constantly taken off with the skimmer. After this, it passes through a second, third, fourth, and fifth boiler, which last brings it to the consistence of a thick syrup. In the sixth boiler, it is mixed with a certain quantity of milk, lime-water and allum, and receives its full coction, which reduces it to almost one-third of its first quantity. It is finally put into small baskets, where it remains some time to cool, and, afterwards, becomes fit for immediate use.

This is the manner of preparing the East Indian loaf sugar, so much esteemed in London, and confessedly allowed to be the best made in any part of the world.

LETTER XXVIII

Dear Sir,

The practice of gambling so dangerous in its effects to many of its votaries, is pursued in India with much eagerness, and even sanctioned by the laws of the country. It is, however, regulated under certain restrictions, and permitted only for a limitted time. During the term, which in the Indian dialect, is called dewalli, and continues but a fortnight, the gaming table is frequented by persons of every description. Those who conduct this amusement, are under a heavy license, and give ample security for their observance of peace and good order. On such occasions, they generally keep police guards at their houses, to prevent disputes among the adventurers. Before they enter on this business, every manager, or keeper of a gambling house, is supplied with a large sum of money, for the accommodation of the gamesters, to whom he lends it out, on very advantageous conditions. The winner pays him in proportion to his gain, and the loser secures him in the principal borrowed, with interest. Thus, by a rapid increase of growing profits, he accumulates, in a little time, vast riches.

Notwithstanding the passions of men, and the quick circulation of cash, amid such bustling scenes, it seldom happens that base coin is ever found among the gains of the fortunate. The following is the only instance, within my recollection, of its being passed in the country.

A Seapoy, possessed of fifty rupees, his sole treasure, was going from Calcutta to Patna; on the way, he met a man of genteel appearance, to whom, in the course of a free conversation, he unbosomed himself, and discovered the bulk of his fortune. His fellow traveller, who proved to be a coiner, observed, that as his (the Seapoy's) rupees were the currency of Calcutta, it would be his interest to change them for those of Patna, whither he was going, as he would benefit considerably by the exchange; and that he could oblige him with the coin of that city. The poor soldier, thankfully accepting the offer, counted down his fifty good pieces of silver, for fifty glittering base ones of the sharper, and parting him with a mutual shake of the hands, proceeded on his journey. Not until his arrival at Muxadabad, where he was about purchasing some necessary, did he discover the shining specimens of his friend's ingenuity, and making some very dismal, though pertinent reflections on the occasion, with a countenance, on which you could read in legible characters, A BLANK he exclaims—*I was a stranger, and he humanely took me in.*

After perambulating every street and alley of the large town of Muxadabad, and pervading every corner of its precincts, he, at length, found his quondam companion at a gaming table, and in a paroxysm of gratitude not to be expressed by my unequal pen, seized him by the collar, bestowing on him, at the same time, such violent caresses of rude friendship, as greatly disfigured his person and apparel. When the first transports were over, he requested his money, which after some pressing solicitations, he obtained, and went his way, but not without leaving his worthy acquaintance some visible signs and tokens of lasting remembrance.

Though few the individuals in India, who impose on the unwary by the arts of swindling and fraud, the jugglers, or slight-of-hand men, are numerous, and greatly excel in their tricks and deceptions, any thing of the kind exhibited in Europe.

I have seen one of this astonishing class of men, place in the centre of a bazar, a little shrub or branch of a tree, with only a few leaves on it, over which he has thrown a cloth, and after playing for about half an hour, on a baslee, a sort of instrument consisting of a tube made of the shell of a pumbkin, and connected with two small reeds, through which the sounds pass from the tube applied to the mouth, he has desired some person in the crowd to take off the cloth, and the same branch, to the surprise of every beholder, appeared laden with fruit and blossoms. It would be endless to describe their other deceptions, which are equally unaccountable as wonderful. Their incantation of snakes, in particular, has been attributed by many of your countrymen, to magic and the power of the devil. Their hooded snakes, as they call them, are brought from place to place in close baskets, which are uncovered at the time of exhibition; and these reptiles, when the jugglers begin to play on their instruments, raise up their heads and dance while this strange music continues; but if it should stop, they also cease from dancing, and instantly hiss at each other. The dreadful infection raging in the human blood from the sting of a snake, is effectually cured by a juggler, who, if sent for in time, by playing on his baslee, as usual, calls forth the venomous reptile from its hole, and compels it to bite the person already affected, till its poison is exhausted, after which, it expires, and the patient recovers. Some of these men will sometimes present themselves to public view with two snakes writhing round the neck, without receiving the least injury. There is another species of the serpent, which is very large and long, with a head as big as an infant's, and a beautiful face resembling the human: it has been remarked by several, that this kind is supposed to be the same as that which tempted our first mamma, Eve.

LETTER XXIX

Dear Sir,

Of all the animals in the East or elsewhere, none can equal the elephant in magnitude. To excite your wonder, and, at the same time, afford you some entertainment, I shall here give you a particular description of this quadruped, which is (nem. con.) the largest in the universe. It is from twelve to fifteen feet high, and seven broad: its skin about the belly is so tough, that a sword cannot penetrate it: the eyes of it are exceeding small, the ears large, the body round and full, and the back rises to an arch: it is of a darkish colour and very much seamed: on each side of its jaws, within the mouth are four teeth or grinders; and two teeth which project outwards: in the male, they are stronger and thicker; in the female, they are sharper and smaller: both male and female use one, which is sharp as a defensive weapon, and the other, which is blunted to grub up trees and plants for food. The teeth of the male sometimes grow to the length of ten feet, and have been known to weigh three hundred pounds each; the teeth of the female, though less, are the most valuable ivory. They naturally shed their teeth once in ten years, and bury them carefully in the earth, to prevent, as it is imagined, their being found by man. The elephant's tongue is small, but broad; the feet round and ample, and the legs have joints, which are flexible: the forehead is large and rising; the tail resembles that of a hog; and the blood of this creature is colder than that of any other; but the organ which most peculiarly distinguishes it, is the trunk. This singular member is crooked, grisly, and plaint, about seven feet in length, three in circumference, and gradually diminishing to the extremity. At the root, near the nose, are two passages, the one into the head, the other to the mouth; through the first, it breathes; and by the latter, it receives its provisions, the trunk serving the purposes of a hand to feed it, and a weapon to defend it. So strong is this powerful animal, that it can lift a prodigious weight; and so delicate in the sensation of feeling, that it can take the smallest piece of coin from the ground. It delights much in water, and will swim a great way.

They are taken by stratagem in different parts of India, as they descend from the mountains, where they feed, to the lakes or rivers, to water. The hotteewallies, or people employed to take them, dig deep trenches in their direction, which they conceal with reeds covered over with earth and grass; the elephants, on their way to the watering places, unacquainted with the danger before them, fall into the pit contrived by these artful men who often risque their lives in the execution of such hazardous projects. The old animals, by some means, extricate themselves, and escape to the woods, but the young ones, who thus become an easy prey to their pursuers, are suffered to remain in this situation, for some days without food, till they are almost spent, and unable to make any resistance: an easy descent is then opened into the pits or trenches, and collars thrown round their necks, after which they are mounted, and following a tame elephant as their leader, conducted with great facility to the next town or village. When a considerable number of them, is collected in this manner, they are regularly trained by the hotteewallies, for the use of the Nabobs and other great men; and when rendered by age unfit for their amusements, they serve to carry the equipage of camps and other burdens. Under the management of their tutors, they are taught to do any thing, and, in a short time, become as tractable as the horses of the most famous riders in Europe.

It is related of one of them, that when the child of its keeper, lay some time in a cradle, crying for want of nourishment, in the absence of the parents, this huge but generous animal took it up gently, gave it suck, and afterwards laid it down in the cradle with the utmost solicitude. This tenderness, which is not unlike gratitude in our species, proceeded from the kind treatment of its keeper.

An elephant is commonly sold by measurement; and some of those animals, which are young and well trained, are purchased at the rate of 150 rupees per cubit: they are measured from the head to the tail, which is about seven cubits long, and at this calculation will amount to above one hundred pounds sterling each.

Next to the elephant in bulk and figure, is the rhinoceros, called by the modern Indians, abadu; it is not unlike the wild boar, but much larger, having thicker feet, and a more unwieldy body. It is covered with large hard scales of a blackish colour, which are divided into small squares, raised a little above the skin, and nearly resembling those of the crocodile. Its head, which is large, is wrapped up behind in a kind of capuchin; its mouth is little; but its snout extends to a great length, and is armed with a long thick horn, which makes him terrible to other animals, its tongue is as rough as a file, and a sort of wings like those of the bat, cover the belly.

In the Eastern territories, there is no beast more useful than the camel, either for burden or dispatch: some of them will carry a thousand weight, and travel, at least, seven or eight miles an hour: they have no teeth, except in the lower jaw, and one bunch on the back: none of the brute creation, of such a bulk, less voracious than this creature. They lie down on their bellies to receive their loads, and are always governed by the voice of the driver, who could never mend their pace, by beating them. They are naturally fearful, and extremely patient under fatigue.

LETTER XXX

Dear Sir,

In the year of 1779, we marched from Fort William to Barahampore, and in some time after our arrival, the strong fortress of Ganlin [Gwalior] was taken by our troops; the particular account of which, is as follows:

The Morattoes, whose depredations in every quarter, had given a general alarm, were making constant sallies from the different posts they fortified in many parts of the country. Their strongest hold, however, was the fort of Ganlin, in which they centred all their hopes of security, as it was always considered to be impregnable. It stands on a rock about two coss in length, and in many places above four hundred feet high, in some three hundred, but in no situation less than one hundred and fifty feet in height. The table is entirely surrounded by a rampart of stone, rising immediately from the edge of the rock, which in most parts, is rendered perpendicular. Within the rampart are many fine buildings, large tanks, innumerable wells, and cultivated land.

The only access to the fort, is by a flight of steps, defended by the rock on the one side, and a large stone wall on the other, flanked with bastions; and on the summit, is a passage through seven gate-ways. The craggy rock frightfully lofty, into which are hewn many caves, at whose entrances are gigantic figures of men and animals; the rampart seeming almost a continuation of this awful precipice; and the rising edifices, whose solemn domes, battlements, and balconies, are suspended, as it were, over the dreadful steep, forming all together, the most sublime view I ever beheld, strike the imagination with a kind of horrible astonishment far beyond simple admiration. A tribe of Morattoes, who lived by robbery, about this place, informed the Rana, that they ascended the fort in the night, and found the Chokeedars asleep; and offered, if encouraged by a sufficiently pecuniary recompense, to lead his troops to the very spot from whence they climbed up, promising also their assistance, by fixing ladders to help them to mount; but the Rana, through want of confidence in his troops, declined the enterprise.

Captain Popham, one of the English Officers, having procured some intelligence of the proposal made to the Rana, requested of him to send those men to him: they accordingly came, through the hope of reward, and went to the appointed place, with some of his own spies, who were particularly directed to watch their actions. The accounts brought back were so satisfactory, that he made instant preparations for a surprise, which he conducted with secrecy and dispatch.

In a month's time, during which he obtained some knowledge of this important situation, he was in perfect readiness for the intended attack, and on the third of August, about eleven o'clock, at night, Captain William Bruce, at the head of his British grenadiers, was ordered to march in front, attended by Lieut. Cameron, engineer, with his apparatus for scaling; Captain Popham, with two battalions, followed soon after, to support the assailants, and direct the entire expedition. Captain McClary was ordered with his battalion to march round towards the town, and intercept Ambassee [Ambaji Inglia], a Morattoe Chief, who had cantoned in it with four hundred horse; and Captain Clode was left in charge of the camp, at Raypore [Raipur], near four coss from Ganlin. In this disposition, the party advanced by private roads, and arrived at the foot of the rock, an hour before day-break. Captain Bruce's people were provided with sacks of coarse cloth, stuffed with cotton, to prevent the noise of their feet in mounting, and just as they arrived, the guards of the fort were going their rounds, (as is the custom with the Chokeedars,) their lights were seen, and the men distinctly heard. This seemed to portend the ruin of the plan, but firmness and resolution conquered every apprehension of danger. The spies observing the utmost silence, mounted the rock, and ascended the wall, from whence they brought intelligence that was all quiet: Lieut. Cameron then fixed the wooden ladders by which he mounted, and gave those of rope to the spies, who fastened them by a noose round the battlements of the wall.

Every thing in readiness, Capt. Bruce ascended with twelve men, and when he had got within the fort, he ordered them to sit down as closely as possible under the wall, till the others would come up. Near the place where they concealed themselves, three Chokeedars lay asleep, and three Seapoys rashly fired, which had almost defeated the success of the enterprize, and sacrificed the lives of the little party, which was soon surrounded by alarmed numbers of the garrison. Before they had recovered from their astonishment, of seeing our gallant soldiers within their walls, thirty Seapoys had ascended, and the rest followed very fast: a few shot and rockets were exchanged, and their principal Officer being wounded, the enemy dismayed and confounded at the boldness of the undertaking, took shelter in the inner buildings of the fort, from which they escaped in the utmost confusion.

Their Officers collected within one house, with their women, and hung out a white flag: a detachment of the English was sent to receive their arms, and give them quarters.

Thus fell, in less than two hours, the great and, as it was deemed, impregnable fortress of Ganlin, without the loss of a man; and twenty only were wounded. The place where the assault was made, from the foot of the rock to the wall is above two hundred feet high; to behold it even, must astonish you, beyond description, and you would have considered the execution of such a project all together impracticable, and not within the compass of human courage or abilities.

The enemy hitherto regarding any intention of disturbing them, as the greatest presumption, attributed our success to the divine interposition: such an attempt was indeed above common conception, and it had never succeeded, but for the terror, with which the boldness of the enterprise, had struck the unwary dupes of heedless security. The greatness of the undertaking, reflects the highest honour on the Officers and men employed in it; and proves the general opinion that there is no difficulty so arduous which may not be subdued, by the resolution and perseverance of a British soldier.

The Morattoe parties in this country, having heard with astonishment of the surrender of Ganlin, began to dread, and venerate the very names of the conquerors; and shortly after it was surprised, they evacuated eight forts, which they had formerly taken from the Raja of Ghoad [Gohad]. From one of the apartments of the Imperial palace, built by Akbar, within the fort, I looked down, and beheld, as it were from the clouds, the town, four hundred feet below me: such an awful scene forms a subject for the pencil of the most sublime artist.

About this time, Col. William A. Baillie, who was marching with a detachment of two hundred Europeans, and a battalion and half of Seapoys, from one of the provinces to join the main army, which was going to the relief of Arcot, was attacked by Hyder's son, with a large force, and repulsed him with slaughter. The Colonel as usual, distinguished himself on this occasion with great firmness and intrepidity.

LETTER XXXI

Dear Sir,

In the year of 1781, Captain Baker, after his appointment to the command of the Seapoys' battalion, in the second brigade, with Lieutenants Simpson and Williamson, two companies of Europeans, and two companies of Seapoys, marched from Barahampore, in order to join the second brigade in Caunpore [Cawnpur]: on his promotion, he appointed me market-master to supply the bazar. We halted at Denapore to refresh the party, and draw their pay; and as they proceeded on their march, I was dispatched, with an escort of two Seapoys to Gooldengunge [Golding's Ganj], which was considered the cheapest market, to purchase corn for the army, and had in my possession for that purpose, four hundred goolmores, with bills on the Commissary there, amounting in all to fifteen hundred pounds sterl. As we journeyed onwards, one of the Seapoys happened to trample some melons in passing through a plantation near the river side, and on being observed by the proprietor, who desired him to be more cautious in his career, he returned him some impertinent answer, which roused the peasant's resentment, and discord expanding her gloomy wings, a battle ensued; the neighbouring cottagers thus alarmed, flocked to their friend's assistance, and cruelly stabbed his adversary, who fell a breathless corpse beneath their murderous weapons. The other Seapoy made off through the country, but I was dismounted from my horse, which I was obliged to leave behind, and having plunged into the Ganges, on whose verge I stood trembling for my fate, with the utmost difficulty I gained the opposite shore, fainting under the fatigue of my exertions in crossing the wide river, with my clothes on, and such a weight of gold about me. A few of the peasantry, who beheld me thus struggling for life, ran to my assistance, and after supporting me to the next cottage, kindly ministered what relief was in their power. As the night approached, I sunk to rest, and forgot the dangers of my late journey in the sweet oblivion of sleep. Next morning, finding myself tolerably restored, I made my acknowledgements to these humane people, whose foot-steps, an all-ruling

Providence must, in that crisis, have directed, to save me from impending dissolution; and having gone forthwith to the Fouzdar of Gooldengunge, and given him up my money and bills, I related the story of my adventures: he seemed much affected at the recital, and detained me till the supplies for the use of the troops were purchased; a part was sent by water to Caunpore; and the rest by land, consisting of several loads of corn drawn by bullocks, with which I travelled, and joined the army at Buxar. From the early intelligence of the Seapoy, who escaped before me, the greatest surprize, and even doubt of the reality of my existence at my arrival, was almost graven on every countenance, as the prevailing opinion unanimously agreed on by all parties, was, that I had fallen a sacrifice with the other Seapoy to the rage and resentment of the country people.

From Buxar we marched for Caunpore, where we arrived in the latter end of February. On the first of March, Capt. Baker took the command of the battalion of Seapoys in Major Roberts' regiment, to which he had been recently promoted, and by his recommendation, I was appointed Jemidar in the same battalion.

Having received an account of the insurrections of the Morattoes in the vicinage of Caulpee [Kalpi], on the banks of the river Jemina, the entire brigade, by order of Colonel Morgan, proceeded to that town, and a part of the main army in different detachments, scoured the neighbouring country, in order to disperse those disturbers of the public tranquility, who, after some slight skirmishes, entirely fled, overawed by the terror of our arms.

We remained a few weeks in Caulpee, and then returned to Caunpore, where our stay was of no long continuance.

About this time Governor Hastings having required of Cheyt-sing his stipulated subsidies, towards defraying the expences of the late war with Hyder Ally; and finding him either unwilling or unable to pay them, sent a guard consisting of two companies of Seapoys to arrest him: the alarming news of his being made a prisoner, soon spread through the country, and roused the indignation of his troops, who were seen in a large body, crossing the river from Ramnagur to the palace, in which he was confined. The two companies of our Seapoys, who formed the guard in an inclosed square outside the palace, were mostly massacred by this powerful force which rushed onward, like an irresistible torrent, that sweeps all away before it.

Ramjaum [Ramjiwan], one of the Raja's Generals, after killing a serjeant of the Seapoys, who opposed his entrance, broke into the royal mansion, and made way for the soldiery, who escorted their Prince through a garden which led to the river. As the banks were high above the surface, they let him down by turbans tied together, into a boat that conveyed him to the other side, whence he escaped under the friendly shade of night, to Lutteefgur [Latifgarh], one of his strongest fortresses, with a chosen band of men to protect him.

LETTER XXXII

Dear Sir,

The day following, a large party of the Raja's, with Ramjaum at their head, went in pursuit of Governor Hastings, who proceeded to Chunargar; and having fought him in vain, they returned to Ramnagur, where they attacked a strong body of the English under the command of Capt. Mayaffre, of the artillery, who was hemmed in on every side by the narrow streets and winding alleys of the town, with which he was unacquainted. Being thus exposed to the fire of the enemy from all quarters, and particularly to that of a covered party that greatly annoyed him, he fell in the scene of battle, with upwards of one hundred and fifty of his men, among whom were Captain Doxat, and Lieutenants Stalker, Symes, and Scott, besides eighty wounded. After many brave struggles, Captain Blair, at last, effected a regular and steady retreat, which gained him much honour. He prevented the eager pursuit of the enemy, who followed him till he came within a few miles of Chunar, from having any bad effect.

This success gave fresh ardour to the Raja's friends, and plunged Governor Hastings into new difficulties.

Ramjaum having put Ramnagur into a state of defence, conducted his principal troops to a fort called Pateetah [Patita], to which a detachment under the command of Major Popham was directed, composed of what men could be spared from the garrison of Chunar. In mean time Captain Blair was dispatched with his battalion and two companies of grenadiers to surprise the fort; and Lieutenant Polhill, who just arrived from Allahabad, with six companies of Seapoys from the Nabob Aspah-doulah's life guards, was ordered to encamp on the opposite shore, in order to keep the communication at that side open. In two days after his arrival, this spirited Officer defeated a considerable body of the enemy at a small fort called Seekur [Sacrut], where he found a vast quantity of grain, which proved an acceptable prize, as it was much wanted.

Major Popham and Captain Blair having arrived within about a mile of Pateetah, nearly at the same time found a party of the enemy in seeming readiness to oppose them. They fought on both sides, with great ardor and intrepidity, till victory perplexed with doubt, waited the arrival of Lieutenants Fallow [Fallon] and Berrille [Birrell], whose gallant conduct with the united bravery of their countrymen, preponderating in the scale of her unbiassed judgment, induced the Goddess to bestow on them, her unfading laurels, as the reward of their exertions. After a dreadful carnage of killed and wounded on each part, the conquered fled for refuge to their fort, and the victors advanced to Chunar to recruit their losses. At the commencement of these commotions, Governor Hastings dispatched a courier to Colonel Morgan, at Caunpore, with instructions directing him to send an immediate reinforcement to Chunar: three regiments were accordingly sent with the utmost expedition; two of which were under the command of Majors Crabb and Crawford [Crawfurd] with one company of artillery, and two of European infantry; and the other under Major Roberts, which marched by the route of Lecknow. Early on the tenth of September, Majors Crabb and Crawford, at the head of their respective corps, appeared within view of Chunar on the opposite shore: the following day, the Nabob Aspa-doulah arrived, and encamped at the same side of the river; and shortly after Major Roberts came from Lecknow, with his troops. The English crossed the river, and joined Major Popham, who had now the command of four complete regiments, one battalion of Colonel Blair, another of the Nabob's life guards, two companies of Europeans, one of artillery, and one of French rangers. From this main body, Major Crabb, with one detachment, proceeded against Lutteefgur, Major Crawford with another, crossed the mountains to Seckroot and Lora; and two companies under the direction of Captain Baker, and Lieutenant Simpson, advanced towards Pateetah with a twelve pounder, which they played on the north side of the fort, for, at least, an hour, with good effect, till an halcarah, who just arrived, informed them that there was large tank on the eastern situation with a great heap of earth thrown up about it, which might answer the purpose of a temporary battery. When the tank was discovered, and found adequate to the description given of it, an additional supply of cannon and ammunition was directly sent for. We now began the siege with the most lively ardor, and continued it for three days without intermission: on the fourth morning, at three o'clock, Captain Baker and Gardner kept up a brisk cannonading, and threw the enemy into the utmost confusion, amidst which, Captain Lane, Lieutenants Simpson and Williams, with whom I adventured and three companies of determined Seapoy grenadiers, stormed the fort and rushed on the disordered enemy with manly resolution. After some opposition, they evacuated their strong hold, with Ramjaum at their head, and made off towards Lutteefgur, leaving their military equipage, elephants, camels, bullocks, &c. behind them.

Captain Baker distinguished himself in this action, as in many others, by the greatest exertions, and displayed the courage of the active soldier united with the experience of the hoary veteran.

Whilst memory dwells on virtues only thine,
Fame o'er thy relics breathes a strain divine.

Major Crabb having met Ramjaum on his way to Lutteefgur, gave him battle, and obliged him with his vanquished forces to fly for shelter to Lora, and from thence to Bidgegur [Bijigarh], whither Cheyt-sing had escaped. The Raja, however, not finding himself safe in Bidgegur, fled for refuge to the mountains among the Morattoes, taking with him what diamonds and other valuable effects he could possibly convey on his camels.

LETTER XXXIII

Dear Sir,

Captain Baker with the detachment under his command, marched to Ramnagur, where he remained till further orders; and Major Popham advanced with his troops, in pursuit of the enemy, to Bidgegur, which lies about fifty miles to the south east of Chunar: the fort is erected on the summit of a lofty rock, and rises to the great height of seven hundred feet above the surface of the country. It was considered next to Ganlin, among the strongest in India, being deemed, like that fortress, impregnable. The Raja, however, not judging the strength of Bidgegur a sufficient security against the conqueror of Ganlin, abandoned it, leaving behind him a part of those treasures, which were the cause of his misfortunes; and resigning that honour in the persons of his women, which he had so highly estimated, himself a wretched fugitive flying for protection to the uncertain asylum of those who were only in a state of precarious security.

The Ranee, his mother, besides his women, and such of the descendants of Bulevant-sing [Balwant Singh], as still adhered to him, continued in the fort, with a certain military force, as guardians of the remainder of his treasure, which, in diamonds and specie amounted to a very considerable value.

Major Popham, who behaved with great spirit and firmness, spent an entire month in subduing the utmost difficulties, and, at length, as he was on the point of springing a mine, the Ranee, who seemed to have the sole direction of affairs after the departure of her son, surrendered the fort by capitulation, in the terms of which, she was to be allowed fifteen per cent. on all the effects given up by her, and to have her choice of residing unmolested, either with her son, or elsewhere in the country. In the one case, she was to be escorted by a proper guard to the frontiers; in the other to meet with the greatest protection.

A principal part of the property taken at Bidgegur, became a prize to the captors, as a reward for their services. A letter written by the Governor to Major Popham, during the siege, was understood as giving a sanction to such a distribution of the spoil. The Officers acted with so much expedition in the business, that their dividend, with that of the privates, was apportioned in two days after the place was taken, and the residue went to the Company. Scenes of joy and conviviality now succeeded the toils of war; and the private soldier, as well as the Officer, forgot his dangers in the indulgence of his pleasures.

Such was the issue of the war with the unhappy Raja Cheyt-sing, whose humility and sufferings cannot be better described than in his own words; thus, expressing himself in a letter to the Governor, when he was arrested by his order, he says,

> Pity me, I pray you, in remembrance of the services done by my
> father, and in consideration of my youth and inexperience: whatever
> may be your pleasure, do it with your own hands—and as I am your
> slave, what occasion can there be for a guard?—It depends on you
> alone to deprive me, or not, of the country of my ancestors—what
> necessity is there to deal in this way with me, who am ready to
> devote my life and property to your service.

—Many other letters followed this, and all were equally pathetic.

His manifesto, addressed to the native Princes, abounds with many sublime sentiments, free from that sounding phraseology too frequently used in India; and expressive of the most lively sensibility for the fate of a country, which he thus finely contrasts with the other territories surrounding it.

In vindication of his government, he says,

> Look to my country; look to others—Do not the different pictures
> they present to you, mark the limits of them more, than the bound-
> aries which nature itself has drawn out. My fields are cultivated; my

villages full of inhabitants; my territory a garden; and my subjects happy. From the security I have given to property, my capital is the resort of the first traders of India; and the treasures of the Morattoes, the Jairs [Jains], and the Saiks [Sikhs], are deposited here, as well as those brought hither from the remotest borders of the eastern world. Hither the widow and the orphan convey their property, without dread from the violence of rapacity, or the gripe of avarice. The way-worn traveller, within the bourne of my country, lays down his burden unmolested, and sleeps in security.

Look to other provinces, there famine and misery stalk hand in hand, through neglected plains and deserted villages: there you meet with aged men drooping under the weight of years, and unable to transport themselves from the grasp of the prowling ruffian, watching to waylay their helplessness.

Here every passing stranger has been used with kindness, his hardships alleviated, and even his weary Cooleys have had their loads taken off their shoulders, and carried for them, through the humanity of my peasantry, from village to village.

To men of condition, who have travelled here, I have sent my Officers to enquire their wants, and supplied them with provisions and carriages at my own expence: their interior testimony will evince the truth of these assertions, and enable them to form a discriminative comparison between mine and the neighbouring districts.

Such was the happy situation of the Prince, and the philanthropy of the man, who shortly after became the sport of fortune, amidst the vicissitudes of life, and the trials of adversity.

LETTER XXXIV

Dear Sir,

This commotion had scarcely subsided, when a fresh disturbance arose at Gochipour [Ghazipur], a place famous for distilling rose water, between the natives and the Fouzdar of that quarter, who enjoyed the same post which he held under Raja Cheyt-sing. As he availed himself of a general pardon granted by the Governor, he was permitted to continue in his employment. The people dissatisfied with the fate of their late Raja, could, by no means, be reconciled to the sovereignty of the English; and when the Fouzdar, consistent with his duty, attempted to collect the customary revenues, he was every where opposed, and with the greatest difficulty escaped the fury of the natives.

On the first rise of the male-contents, he wrote to the Governor for a reinforcement of troops to assist his own, which were quite insufficient to quell the insurrection. Captain Baker was therefore sent to his relief from Ramnagur, with his battalion. The day after our arrival at Gochipour, we marched onward to a little village called Bellua, where the motley crew were assembled within a small mud fort, seemingly determined to maintain an obstinate defence.

After withstanding the fire of our musquetry with a degree of courage not to be expected in an undisciplined rabble, on the approach of our cannon, some fled, were pursued and taken, and the rest, who were still very numerous, sent Deputies to the Captain, requesting a cessation of hostilities, which he granted on receiving the most solemn assurances, that they would peaceably return to their respective employments, and disturb, no more, the public tranquility.

One of the captives, before he obtained his liberty, having informed us that there were some cattle belonging to Ramjaum in a neighbouring plain, to which he offered to direct us, I was ordered to accompany him with an escort of Seapoys to the very place he described, where I found two elephants, two camels, and twelve Arabian horses, under the care of a few peasants, who made off on the appearance of our arms. I seized the cattle as the property of an enemy, and drove them to Gochipour, where the party waited my return.

Captain Baker reserving only one horse for his own use, generously divided the spoil among the soldiers as the well earned meed of their military labours.

After a month's stay here, we were relieved by Captain Lane, and marched hence to Jouanpour [Jaunpur], which has little to recommend it but a good fort and a few tolerable buildings: it is however equally remarkable, as our last cantonments, for its rose water and rose oil, which are peculiarly esteemed throughout Asia for their odoriferous excellence.

We were again involved in new broils, and obliged to penetrate farther into the country, in order to disperse the unruly natives who assembled in a hostile manner within a fort, which they put into some state of defence. They were armed with bows and arrows, and long barreled guns of their own construction, generally known by the name of matchlocks. They held out so obstinately, that they kept possession of the fort for nine or ten days, and then escaped under the favouring gloom of night, leaving a number of their dead behind them.

After this commotion, the country became quiet, and no future disturbances were heard of, at least, in this quarter.

The refractory were awed into submission by the terror of our arms; yet humanity must lament the loss of those whom wasting war had suddenly swept away.

> Alas! destructive war, with ruthless hand,
> Unbinds each fond connection, tender tie,
> And tears from friendship's bosom all that's dear,
> Spreading dire carnage thro' the peopled globe;
> Whilst fearless innocence, and trembling guilt,
> In one wide waste, are suddenly involv'd.
> War wake's the lover's, friend's and orphan's sigh,
> And on empurpled wings bears death along,
> With haggard terror, and with wild dismay,
> And desolation in the savage train:
> From slow-consuming time, his lazy scythe,
> With ruffian violence is torn away,
> To sweep, at once, whole Empires to the grave.

Near Jouanpour is a spacious chapel much frequented by the Mahometans, under which is a subterraneous cavern extending a considerable length of way. It is a fort or arsenal, and serves as an asylum for the natives in time of war, as the entrance to it, is only known to themselves. When peace was restored to this distracted country, we returned to Chunargur.

LETTER XXXV

Dear Sir,

A few months after our arrival at Chunargur, Captain Baker disclosed his intentions of going to Europe: having a desire of seeing that part of the world, and convinced that I should suffer much uneasiness of mind, in the absence of my best friend, I resigned my commission of Subidar, in order to accompany him. We took boat at Chunargur, and proceeded to Calcutta, by the way of Dacca, sailing along the Ganges a distance of three hundred miles. Our passage was very agreeable, as the season was fine, and the farmers were just returning from the fields with the fruits of the harvest. It was not uncommon to see two thousand bullocks carrying corn, the property of one yeoman, to the granaries. There are many fine seats on each side of the river, with a continued variety of beautiful improvements, striking landscapes, and sublime scenes of rural imagery, which, at once astonish and delight the enraptured view.

Having completed the most pleasant voyage imaginable, we, at length, arrived at Dacca, one of the most extensive cities in the province of Bengal, which lies in twenty-four degrees north latitude, on an eastern branch of the Ganges. It is near five miles in length, but very narrow, and winding with the river.

Dacca is considered the first manufactory in India, and produces the richest embroideries in gold, silver, and silk. It also receives considerable advantages from its cottons, of which the finest striped and worked muslins, callicoes, and dimities, are made, much superior to those finished in other parts of the country. The best kind manufactured for the immediate use of the Great Mogul, and his Zannanahs, are of exquisite workmanship, and greater value than any permitted to be sold either to the natives or foreigners.

The filligrane, in particular, is admirable, the workmanship being more costly than the metal itself. It is not perforated, as with us, but cut in shreds, and joined with such inimitable art, that the nicest eye cannot perceive the juncture. The embroidery and needle-work, for elegance, surpass all description, and greatly exceed any thing of the kind done in Europe: but it is remarkable that there are no female embroiderers or sempstresses here; the men do all the work in these branches, and their patience is astonishing, as their slowness is singular. Provisions of all sorts are exceeding cheap and plentiful in Dacca: the fertility of its soil, and the advantages of its situation have, long since, made it the centre of an extensive commerce; it has still the remains of a very strong fortress, in which, a few years back, was planted a cannon of such extraordinary weight and dimensions, that it fell into the river, with the entire bank on which it rested; the length of the tube was fourteen feet, ten and a half inches, and the diameter of the bore one foot, three and one eighth inches: it contained two hundred and thirty-four thousand four hundred and thirteen cubic inches of wrought iron, weighed sixty-four thousand four hundred and eighteen pounds avoirdupoise, and carried a shot of four hundred and sixty-five pounds weight.

Here is also the residence of a grand Nabob, who, at his accession to the throne, conformable to an old custom, something similar to that of the Doge of Venice on the Adriatic, enjoys a day's pleasure on the river, in one of the most curious barges in the world, called a samsundar. It is sheathed with silver, and in the centre is a grand eminence of the same, on which his crown is placed on the day of coronation: nearer the stern is a brilliant seat encompassed with silver rails, and covered with a rich canopy embroidered with gold, under which he reclines in easy majesty. This boat and another of considerable value, that conveys his attendants, are estimated at a lack of rupees. He is accompanied by a number of the most distinguished personages, and there are no bounds to the lavish waste of money expended on this occasion, in order to aggrandize the pomp of this ancient ceremony. Travellers of every description, who pass this way, are led by a prevailing curiosity to see these elegant boats.

LETTER XXXVI

Dear Sir,

Before we left Dacca, the celebration of the festival of two supposed saints, whom the Mahometans call Hassan, Hussen, was commenced on the first day of the new moon, and continued, with great solemnity, for ten days. The first day, several parties forming in different quarters of the town, assembled together in one spacious square appointed for the general meeting, where they raised an extensive canopy on eight poles, in the centre of which were three others composed of finer materials of various colours, and under the smallest canopy was a silver salver filled with clay, to represent the remains of these saints. The Mahometans, during this ceremony, cease from the pursuits of business, and spend the time in repeating their prayers, singing canticles, and other pious exercises, to which they add many exterior marks of devotion, emphatically expressed by thwacking the bosom, extending the arms, upturning the eyes, muttering ejaculations, fetching deep sighs, and emitting hollow groans on a tremendous key. The Gentoos and other dissenters are excluded from their society, by a railing of bamboes, which in the night time is hung with glittering branches that illuminate the entire scene, while a number of colours are flying from the poles. There are four other colours of a particular kind, trimmed with a beautiful gold fringe, within the small canopy: under this the salver is placed, to which the entire Mahometan assembly kneel in adoration, whilst bands of music swell the strain of religious enthusiasm.

On the ninth day, they exhibit a kind of edifice made of stained paper, which is perhaps one of the most curious specimens of filligrane work ever attempted by human ingenuity. It consists of many spires, rising above each other, and gradually diminishing towards the top; the variety of ornaments about it is admirable, and the taste with which it is executed, inconceivable: you can form but an imperfect idea of such a masterly piece of workmanship, and I am therefore unhappy that my abilities will not permit me to pursue such a combination of inimitable art and elegance, through all the complicated minutiae of an adequate description.—It is carried in grand procession through the town, during the night, with the salver and two turbans placed on the battlements of the fourth spire: before which, were thousands in the attitude of prostrate humility, paying their adoration and distributing alms to their indigent fellow creatures around them, whilst numbers followed, with flams and torches lighting, colours flying, and various instruments of music, on which they played the most solemn airs. The tenth day this paper structure, which in the Indian dialect, is termed Gouwarrah, is carried to the burial ground of their supposed saints or holy men, and thrown into a large tank, which concludes the ceremony.

The Mahometans keep a strict lent once in the year, in the month Ramzaun, for a space of thirty two days: during this time, they never sleep on a bed, nor cohabit with their wives, and live only on rice and vegetables: they also abstain from off their usual enjoyments of chewing betel, and smoking tobacco, avoiding every kind of amusement, and spending the time in prayer, and the performance of charitable offices. They are so extremely tenacious of their principles that even under the painful longing of excessive thirst, they will not taste a drop of water, each day, till seven in the evening. As an instance of their severity in the observance of their religious tenets, I shall introduce the following real anecdote. A considerable Banyan merchant was on his passage from Bombay to Surat, in an English ship, and having made such a provision of water in vessels under his own seal, as might serve for that short voyage, which was commonly completed in two or three days; it happened however that, through retardment by calms and contrary winds, his liquid store was expended, and he reduced to a condition of perishing with thirst, though there was plenty of water on board: but, no entreaties could prevail on him to use it, as his religion forbade it, which to him was more dear than life itself. He felt all the torments occasioned by the fever of thirst, and would have actually sunk under them, had not a favourable breeze springing up, brought him to Gundavee [Gandevi], near Surat; but he was so faint on his arrival, that his soul was almost panting between his lips.

LETTER XXXVII

Dear Sir,

Having remained some time in Dacca, we proceeded on our voyage to Calcutta, and, in about two days reached the river Sunderbun, which is extremely narrow, and winds into many branches, that feast the delighted eye with a variety of new scenery: the land on each side is low, and covered with great trees, close to the water's edge: the water was smooth and transparent when we passed through, and appeared like an extended mirror reflecting the tall trees that grew upon each border. Creation seemed to be at rest, and no noise disturbed the silence which reigned around; save, now and then, the roaring of wild beasts in the adjacent woods: the scene was truly great, and raised into unaffected grandeur, without the assistance of art.

The most remarkable trees that grow on each margin of the river, are the sandal, aumnooze, and ceesoe. The woods are infested with ferocious animals of different kinds, which frequently destroy the unwary traveller; and the tygers in particular are daring enough to approach the river side, and dart on the very passengers in the boats going up and down, of whom they make an instant prey. Along the banks are many villages, at about ten or twelve miles distance from each other, where we sometimes laid in a fresh supply of provisions. There is no display of art in the construction of the cottages, which are only composed of broad green flags fastened together, and supported by frames of bamboes. When the floods begin to overflow the country, the natives, with much ease, remove their dwellings from one place to another, first taking them asunder, then rolling up the partitions and roofs, and finally carry them in bundles, wherever convenience of situation, out of the reach of danger, might allure them to fix their moveable abodes. The inhabitants live in a state of nature, sequestered from the tumult of bustling crowds: their wants, which are few, are easily satisfied; and their manners are rendered simple, from the unvarying tenor of their lives, and their remote distance from great towns and cities, where vice finds an asylum amidst luxury and dissipation, and guilty greatness lords it over the trembling wretch who crouches at her feet. Between the villages, we observed a few scattered huts, built by some European adventurers, as a temporary residence, while they are employed in cutting down timber which they sent to different parts of Bengal for ship-building, and other uses.

In January 1783, we arrived at Calcutta, that great emporium of wealth and commerce, where people of rank appear in a style of grandeur far superior to the fashionable eclat displayed in the brilliant circles of Europe. Every private gentleman is attended by twenty servants, at least, eight of whom called bahareas, are alternately employed in carrying his palanquin: and two footmen termed halcarahs, walk before this travelling vehicle: he also keeps three or four domestic servants, namely, a consumma or butler, a bowberchee or cook, and a kizmutgaur or valet: to these may be added seven or eight others under the following appellations, viz. a hookeburdar or person whose chief business is to prepare his master's tobacco pipe, and attend him when smoking, an offdaur to cool the water for his drinking, two or three sahees who have the care of the horses, a gusseara or grass cutter, and three or four mussalchees or torch bearers.

Great characters still increase the number of attendants, by adding to the train already described, nakeeves or criers, to clear the way before them, chowkdars or pages, who carry large silver rods in their hands, sotiburdars the bearers of small silver rods, and piadas or letter carriers.

Those elevated personages, who bask in the sun-shine of exalted life, look down, as from a lofty eminence, on your second-rate people of quality, with as much supercilious disdain, as the second-rates survey all, without distinction, in the humbler walks of life, in which are some sentimental souls whose wounded sensibility gives rapture to enjoyment, when they behold *them* held in such sovereign detestation and sneering contempt by their distant superiors.

I have frequently seen a circar or writing clerk, attended in the day time, by a servant holding an umbrella over his head to shade him from the sun, and one or two torch bearers illuming the way before him by night.

Every man of rank has a derawan or door-keeper at his gate, to announce the arrival of a visitant, whose name he cries out in a vociferous tone, which is heard in the gentleman's mansion, and repeated by a servant at the foot of the grand stair-case leading to his apartment: pages posted in different situations on the stairs, usher the sound to each other, till, at last, it reaches the jemidar or principal page, at the drawing-room door, who conveys it, with great formality, to his master, in order to prepare him for the reception of the visitant.

In passing through some parts of the town, I have observed several men employed in repairing the streets, who had logs chained to their feet, as a punishment, which the law inflicts for the commission of small crimes. Women guilty of petty offences, appear abroad quite bald, their heads being close shaved, in order to expose them to public scorn. Persons in the matrimonial state, detected in criminal conversation, are mounted on a large jackass, with two spears or bayonets fastened round the brows of each, to denote their shame, and render them more conspicuous to the populace. These examples are indeed like black swans, and very seldom seen in Asia, where a breach of conjugal fidelity is considered an odium that must doom the parties to eternal solitude, for ever precluding them from the benefit of society.

LETTER XXXVIII

Dear Sir,

Having passed through a variety of scenes in India, we left Calcutta in January 1784, and went by water to Belcoor, a little village about twelve miles down the river, where a Danish East-Indiaman, commanded by a Captain Duck [Doack], bound for Copenhagen, lay at anchor waiting for the passengers, who embarked with us, and proceeded on our voyage for Europe. The weather being fine, and the wind favourable, we reached Madapallam in seven days, and came to an anchor. The Captain and passengers went ashore, some remaining here, and others, whom I accompanied, being led by curiosity to visit Madras about eight miles hence, while the ship, which was to continue here a fortnight, was taking in some bales of chintz and callico.

Madras or Fort St. George is a regular square about a hundred yards at each side, with four bastions, built with what they call iron stone, being of the colour of unwrought iron, and very rough, on the outside like honey-comb. There is no ditch about the fort, and the walls are arched and hollow within, and are therefore not cannon proof. It has two gates, one to the east, and the other to the west.

The western gate which looks towards the land, is pretty large, and here the main guard is kept, the soldiers of the guard lying on the right and left of it, under the wall, which being hollow, serves them instead of a guard house. The east gate towards the sea, is but small, and protected only by a file of musqueteers. In the middle of the fort stands the Governor's house, in which are apartments for the Company's servants: it is a handsome, lofty, square, stone building; the first rooms are ascended by ten or twelve steps, and from thence another pair of stairs leads to the council chamber and the Governor's lodgings.

The fort stands near the centre of the white town where the Europeans inhabit. This is an oblong square, about a quarter of a mile in length, but not half so much in breadth. To the northward of the fort are three handsome streets, and as many to the south: the buildings are of brick; and several of the houses have one floor above the ground floor. Their roofs are flat, and covered with a plaister made of seashells, which no rain can penetrate. Opposite the west gate of the fort is a long room where the soldiers lodge when they are off the guard, and adjoining to it, on the north, is a commodious hospital; at the other end is a mint, where the Company coin gold and silver. On the north side of the fort is the Portuguese church, and to the southward the English church, which is a neat elegant building, and moderately large: it is floored with black and white marble, the seats regular and convenient, and all together, the most airy lightsome temple any where to be found, for the windows are large and unglazed to admit the cooling breezes in the warm season.

Here is also a free school, where children are educated in reading and writing; besides which there is a library. On the west part of the town a river runs close to the buildings, which are protected by a large battery of guns commanding the plain beyond them. On the east there is a slight stone wall, built on an eminence, that appears something grand to the shipping in the road; but here is very little occasion for any fortification, the sea coming up close to the town, and no large vessels can ride within two miles of the place, the sea is so very shallow; nor is there any landing but in the country boats, the surf runs so high, and breaks so far from the shore. The north and south ends of the town, are each of them defended by a stone wall, which is hollow within, like the fort walls, and would hardly hold out one day's battery. To the southward is a little suburb, inhabited only by black fishermen; it consists of low thatched cottages, which hardly deserve the name of buildings. Beyond this is an outguard of Blacks, who serve to give intelligence to the fort; but there is no other fortification on this side.

The black town, situate to the northward, adjoins the white town, and is considerably larger. Here Portuguese, Indians, Armenians, and others dwell. It is built in the form of a square, and more than a mile and a half in circumference; being surrounded with a brick wall seventeen feet thick, with bastions at proper distances, after the modern way of fortification: it has also a river on the west, and the sea on the east; and to the northward a canal is cut from the river to the sea, which serves for a moat on that side. The streets of the black town are wide, and trees planted in some of them; and having the sea on one side and a river on the other, there are few towns so pleasantly situated or better supplied; but except some few brick houses, the rest are cottages built with clay and thatched. The houses of the better sort of Indians, are of the same materials, and built usually in one form, with a little square in the middle from whence they receive all their light. A stranger seldom comes farther than the door, before which is erected a little shed supported by pillars, where they sit cross-legged morning and evening, to receive their friends or transact their business. The great streets and the bazar, or market place, are thronged with people, for notwithstanding the houses are low and small, they are well filled; and the people from the highest to the lowest are exceedingly cleanly, washing themselves several times a day. In this black town, there is an Armenian church and several little pagodas or Indian temples, to which belong great numbers of female choristers, who spend half the time in singing to the idols, and the rest in intriguing or chanting in companies before the great men as they pass along the streets. The Governor of Madras makes a splendid appearance, and his usual guard is upwards of an hundred black men: when he goes abroad on any public occasion, he is attended by trumpets, fifes, and drums, with streamers flying, and accompanied by his principal Officers on horse-back, and their ladies in palanquins.

Having returned to Madapallam at the appointed time, we continued our voyage till we came within view of the Cape of Good Hope, and met with no extraordinary occurrence on the passage. We saw several kinds of the finny inhabitants of the liquid element, a description of which I must here omit, as uninteresting to a gentleman of your information. A speck now observed in the mariner's horizon, was to him an evident sign of the impending storm, which collected with rapid increase, and bursting with resistless impetuosity over our heads, incessantly raged for three days. The howling of the tempest, the roaring of the sea, the dismal gloom of night, the lightning's forked flash, and thunder's awful roll, conspired to make this the most terrifying scene I ever experienced.

Fair weather providentially succeeding this violent tornado, we reached St. Helena in a week, and met with the Fox English Indiaman, which received some damage by touching on a rock at some distance from the shore. There were also lying here at anchor, three more Indiamen, in one of which was Governor Hastings' Lady on her return to Europe, and in another the remains of that great and gallant Officer, Sir Eyre Coote. Having laid in a supply of fresh provisions and water, and proceeded on our voyage, we arrived at Darmouth [Dartmouth] in England in September 1784.

THREE

Dean Mahomet in Ireland
and England (1784–1851)

DEAN MAHOMET ENTERS CORK

Arriving at Cork late in 1784, twenty-five-year-old Dean Mahomet created a new life for himself. Through his patron, Godfrey Evan Baker, he gained access to the Anglo-Irish Protestant elite but he stood separate from them in origin, color, and culture. Nor did he fit among the colonized Catholic Irish peasantry. A few other Indians passed through or lived in Cork: Indian sailors, servants, wives, and mistresses, their Anglo-Indian children, and even the occasional Indian dignitary. Whatever relationships Dean Mahomet may have had with these other Indians, his situation remained quite different from any of theirs. Yet he quickly made a distinctive place for himself in Cork. He soon married a woman from a Protestant Irish gentry family. His literary achievement, *Travels*, received the endorsement of hundreds of Ireland's leading citizens, proof that they regarded him as a man of culture. Yet he remained someone quite apart from Irish society at the time.

When Dean Mahomet and his patron Baker reached Cork, Baker immediately assumed a prominent place in elite society. The Bakers stood as an established landholding clan, one of the pillars of the Protestant Ascendancy in southeast Ireland. His father, Godfrey Baker, had made himself a wealthy merchant in Cork. The city fathers had already elected the senior Baker to most of the important offices in Cork including Burgess, Mayor, Sheriff, and Water Bailiff.[1] Godfrey Evan Baker, within a year of his return, married the Honorable Margaret, second daughter of the Commander-in-Chief of Munster, Lieutenant General Lord Baron Massey (1700–88).[2] Godfrey Evan Baker's wealthy marriage added to whatever fortune he brought back from India. Dean Mahomet undoubtedly benefited from the Baker and Massey connections.

Soon after his arrival in Cork, Dean Mahomet began to study (under the Bakers' sponsorship) to advance his education. He particularly cultivated his knowledge of English language and literature. As clearly illustrated by the rhetoric and content of *Travels*, he mastered the classically polished literary forms of the day, complete with poetic interjections, erudite allusions, and classical quotations in Latin. Occasional poetry remained very much a part of the cultured life of some of the elite of Cork, reflected in the "Poet's Corner" found in nearly every newspaper. Much of this poetry was published anonymously; some liberally imitative of more established poets. We can never know if Dean Mahomet himself contributed his own verse to the "Poet's Corner," but the unattributed poetry he included in his *Travels* is typical in style, content, and quality of such work.

In 1786, the same year Godfrey Evan Baker died, Dean Mahomet eloped with a teenage woman student, Jane Daly.[3] Suggestion of the haste or desire for privacy of this marriage comes from their decision to post a bond with the church where they were married rather than have the banns read for weeks previously from the pulpit, as was customary. This substantial bond would then indemnify the church should the marriage prove illegal. Any wedding between a Protestant and a Catholic was unlawful at this time in Ireland, with the officiating clergyman held responsible. Although Dean Mahomet must have already become a member of the established Protestant Church, we can imagine a lingering doubt in the mind of the clergyman who performed the wedding of this unusual couple, particularly since they had eloped. The substantial wedding bond also testifies to Dean Mahomet's own comfortable financial position: he either owned considerable capital or he had sufficient credit to borrow it for such a personal undertaking as his elopement. The newly married couple seem to have been accepted by Cork society, suggesting that Dean Mahomet's marriage to Jane may have enhanced his social status. Nonetheless, he remained too distinctive to assimilate fully into the Protestant Irish elite around him.

PUBLICATION OF *TRAVELS*

Dean Mahomet's most lasting representation of himself as an Indian living in Cork remains his book *Travels*. In March 1793 (at age thirty-four), he took out a series of newspaper advertisements proposing to publish *Travels* by subscription, as was usual at the time.[4] He apparently supplemented his public advertisements with personal visits to many of the leading families in southern Ireland. Testifying to his acceptance as a literary figure, a total of 320 people entrusted him with a deposit of 2 shillings 6 pence each long in advance of the book's delivery.

Dean Mahomet clearly appealed to the social elite of Ireland, both men and women. Of the 238 males who subscribed, over 85 percent were gentlemen distinguished by a title, rank, or the epithet "esquire" (the rest bore the label "Mr."). Included among the male subscribers were 17 members of the nobility, 10 military officers (up to Colonel), 17 clergymen (including 3 Bishops), and 3 medical men. The 82 women, over a quarter of the subscribers, included a Viscountess, 5 Ladies, and several Honorables (i.e., daughters of titled families). In addition, the Catholic Ursuline Convent purchased a set (which still remains in their library over two centuries later).[5] A number of Protestant Irishmen who had served in India and held estates in southern Ireland also appeared prominently among Dean Mahomet's patrons; he dedicated his book to one of them, Colonel William Annesley Bailie (1740/41–1821).[6] Having drawn great wealth from India, such officers continued their bonds to it, sponsoring Dean Mahomet and, sometimes, naming their estates after places in India: for example, William Popham's "Patna."

Dean Mahomet chose to use for *Travels* the epistolary form then fashionable in Britain for fiction and travel literature. The epistolary style enabled an author to write more intimately and confidently—notionally to address a friend, rather than a faceless world of unknown readers. England had produced some eight hundred epistolary novels by 1790; this form was especially strong in the 1750–1800 period, when approximately every sixth work of fiction used it.[7] Like most contemporary authors of epistolary works, Dean Mahomet used the fiction of pretending to have written his letters contemporaneously with the events they described. Unlike many other authors of his day, however, he did not backdate these letters or devise a fictional dialogue with an imaginary correspondent.

Although Dean Mahomet began each of the thirty-eight letters in *Travels* with "Dear Sir," he did not seem to have any single real or imagined person as his intended audience. Rather, internal evidence suggests he was addressing two types of readers. First, he was presenting India, and himself, to the elite society around him. Authorship proved him an educated man. Second, he intended, at least in part, *Travels* to be a functional guide for European travelers: young men or women considering a career in, or tour of, India. To this end, Dean Mahomet delineated Indian cities, industries, geography, flora, and fauna, he included a glossary of Persian and Indian terms and factual descriptions of major cities which he did not himself visit, and he designed the book in duodecimo format as two small volumes for easy portability.

When Dean Mahomet determined to write a travel narrative about India, he studied earlier travel narratives and copied parts of them, including Jemima Kindersley's *Letters from the Island of Teneriffe . . . and the East Indies* (1777) and, more extensively, John Henry Grose's *Voyage to the East Indies* (1766).[8] Kindersley and Grose present unsympathetic pictures of India and Indians. Nonetheless, Dean Mahomet found aspects of their work worthy of emulation, since he paraphrased or directly lifted material from them without attribution—a practice today termed plagiarism. To illustrate how Dean Mahomet used Grose's words without accepting his perspective or interpretation, I include a sample of both texts, underlining the words which he took from Grose. These passages describe eating betel leaf, something Dean Mahomet knew well without having to rely on Grose, and yet he clearly did so:

Grose (vol. 1, p. 238)

Another addition too *they use* of what they call *Catchoo,* being *a blackish granulated perfumed* composition, of the size of a small shot, which they carry in little boxes on purpose. They are pleasingly tasted, and are reckoned *provocatives, when taken alone, which is not a small consideration with the Asiatics in general.*

They pretend that this use of Betel sweetens the breath, fortifies *the stomach*, though the juice is rarely swallowed, *and preserves the teeth*, though it reddens them; but, I am apt to believe, that there is more of a vitious habit than any medicinal virtue in it, and that it is like *tobacco*, chiefly a matter of pleasure.

Dean Mahomet (XXVII)

Another addition they use, termed *catchoo,* is *a blackish, granulated, perfumed* substance; and a great *provocative, when taken alone, which is not a small consideration with the Asiatics in general.*

It is taken after meals, during a visit, and on the meeting and parting of friends or acquaintance; and most people here are confirmed in the opinion that it also strengthens *the stomach, and preserves the teeth* and gums. It is only used in smoking, with a mixture of *tobacco* and refined sugar, by the Nabobs and other great men, to whom this species of luxury is confined.

Where Grose used this passage to indicate his condemnation of such "vicious" habits indulged in by natives, Dean Mahomet used some of the same words to describe a healthful and luxurious practice, conducive to polite social intercourse. Overall, Dean Mahomet took 7 percent of the words in *Travels* from Grose, yet reconstructed them into his own voice.

Although Dean Mahomet wrote *Travels* twenty-five years after the first events it narrated, and ten years after its last events, the specific details of names and places which he presented have proven quite precise when checked against English Company and other records. It is highly unlikely that Dean Mahomet himself took notes about all his adventures at the time, especially since they began when he was only eleven. He may have supplemented his recollection—and perhaps later notes—with the memories, diaries, or other papers of the Anglo-Irish officers then living in Cork who served with him in India. Nevertheless, the text stands clearly as his own. He orchestrated his various sources into his own narrative, as he understood and wished to present it to his patrons. The writing of such an elevated and refined work of literature, and its acceptance by elite society, buttressed his respectability, yet his self-presentation as Indian stressed his difference.

CORK SOCIETY

During the quarter century that Dean Mahomet lived in Cork, its citizens encountered a variety of images of India, quite apart from those he presented. Many had personal experience of Asia: as soldiers, officials, merchants, or travelers. Some had Indian mistresses and Anglo-Indian children. Cork newspapers periodically published lists of "Nabobs": Britons who had returned from India with vast fortunes and exotic tastes.[9] Much of the literature and theater available in Cork held attitudes toward India or Islam that clashed with those espoused by Dean Mahomet.

One image of India prevalent in Cork remained that of the exotic. Traveling carnivals and circuses, books, plays, and newspaper articles all presented India and Muslims as alien curiosities.[10] For example, during Dean Mahomet's years in Cork, two plays proved particularly popular, staged repeatedly with a professional lead but with townspeople in the other roles. In 1788 and 1796, Cork produced the Reverend Mr. Miller's translation of Voltaire's *Mahomet, The Impostor: A Tragedy* which presented the Prophet Muhammad as a religious tyrant, using the faith of his followers to advance his corrupt personal agenda.[11] In 1791, 1804, and 1807, Cork performed *The Sultan; or, a Peep into the Seraglio* by Isaac Bickerstaff, which presented a plucky English slavewoman resisting the sexually and physically subordinated role specified for her by Islam, thereby winning over the Sultan, becoming Queen, and freeing the rest of the harem from bondage.[12] This theme of an English Christian woman converting a Muslim to her "higher" principles and then marrying him may have seemed to the people of Cork to be relevant to the marriage of Jane and Dean Mahomet.[13]

Some images, in contrast, emphasized the virtues of Indians. Cork newspapers included anecdotes illustrating the extreme pride and sense of honor of Indians: a high-caste Rajput servant who, hit unjustly by his master, committed suicide rather than accept the shame of either being struck or betraying his employer; grenadier sepoys who claimed the right to be executed first among "mutineers," since grenadiers always had the honor of entering battle first.[14] Indeed, Dean Mahomet or one of his fellow veterans may have been the source of such newspaper stories designed to illustrate the exceptional virtue of Indians. Despite his representation of India and Indians in his own terms, the images that prevailed in Britain were those by European authors; the message of his book received little lasting attention from the British public.

Dean Mahomet and Jane seem to have lived fairly comfortably during their years in Cork. He may have brought some capital with him from India to Ireland. Godfrey Evan Baker may have helped establish Dean Mahomet in Cork, using money Baker had acquired in India, the Baker family's extensive properties, or money brought by Baker's wealthy marriage. The Baker clan's wide range of commercial enterprises would have had room for Dean Mahomet. Jane Daly may also have brought property with her into their marriage. Most plausibly, Dean Mahomet worked as manager of the Baker household, probably not a servant in livery, but not an independent gentleman either. He later claimed much experience in marketing and running a kitchen.[15] As manager, he would have had some status in society but would also have been dependent on his patrons, the Bakers.

In 1796, Captain William Massey Baker (well known by Dean Mahomet as Godfrey Evan Baker's younger brother who had served with them in the Bengal Army, once in the same battalion), returned to Cork on leave from the Company's army. William Massey Baker had done extremely well financially in India, as a Quartermaster and as an entrepreneur in a variety of private commercial activities, rather than depending on his modest army salary.[16] It is not clear if he brought his Indian mistress and their teenage Anglo-Indian daughter, Eleanor, with him to Cork.[17] Soon after his arrival in Cork, William Massey Baker purchased —for a reported £2,500—a large estate a few miles from Cork and built a fine Georgian house, with all the latest conveniences, on the site.[18] His mansion, Fortwilliam, still stands today (figure 4). When the Bakers shifted their household from downtown Cork to Fortwilliam, Dean Mahomet may have set up his own household on the estate.[19] There, in 1799, through a chain of remarkable coincidences, he met an Indian traveler who recorded their meeting.

Abu Talib Khan came from much the same Muslim service elite as Dean Mahomet, albeit from a slightly higher class. By 1799, however, Abu Talib found himself unemployed, and accepted an invitation from Captain David Richardson to visit London. Adverse winds kept Abu Talib's ship from reaching London directly, instead it sought shelter in Cork's harbor. Tired of the sea and shipboard fare, Abu Talib went ashore. He spontaneously decided to travel by land to Dublin, where he hoped to renew the acquaintance of his old patron, Marquis Cornwallis, formerly Governor-General of India (1786–93), currently Viceroy of Ireland (1798–1801), and later Governor-General of India again (1805). While dining in Cork, Abu Talib fortuitously encountered William Massey Baker, whom he and Captain Richardson had known in India. Baker impulsively invited Abu Talib to Fortwilliam, to show off its modern conveniences. While there, on December 7, 1799, Abu Talib met and

Figure 4. Fortwilliam, Cork (courtesy Fitzpatrick Silver Springs Hotel, Tivoli, Cork).

chatted with Dean Mahomet. Abu Talib went on to a triumphant season in London's high society as a self-proclaimed "Persian Prince," before returning to India. Thirteen years later, he wrote up a Persian-language account of his travels in Europe based on his notes of the trip. My translation of Abu Talib's account of Dean Mahomet suggests much about the latter's status:

> Mention of a Muslim named Dean Mahomet: Another person in the house of the aforementioned Captain [William Massey Baker] is named Dean Mahomet. He is from Murshidabad. A brother of Captain [William Massey] Baker raised him from childhood as a member of the family. He brought him to Cork and sent him to a school where he learned to read and write English well. Dean Mahomet, after studying, ran off to another city with the daughter, known to be fair and beautiful, of a family of rank of Cork who was studying in the school. He then married her and returned to Cork. He now has several beautiful children with her. He has a separate house and wealth and he wrote a book containing some account of himself and some about the customs of India.[20]

Abu Talib's tone suggests that he considered himself socially superior to

Dean Mahomet. Nevertheless, he states that Dean Mahomet had an independent income and living arrangements, clearly not the status of a servant. Further, Abu Talib considered Dean Mahomet still a Muslim, at least by culture. In Abu Talib's writings and self-reported behavior, he showed a particular interest in sexual relationships between Indian men and European women, so he appears to have probed the Bakers about Dean Mahomet's marriage and Jane's status.

Around 1807, Dean Mahomet decided to leave Ireland and move to London. The most probable cause of his departure was a change in his relationship to the Bakers. After a second stay in India (1800–1806), William Massey Baker returned again to Ireland. He soon made a distinguished marriage (February 19, 1807) to Mary Towgood Davies, the daughter of a prominent Protestant minister. We can speculate that her assumption of authority over the Fortwilliam household may have made Dean Mahomet's place there uncongenial, leading to his emigration. Whatever factors pushed him from Ireland or attracted him to London, he was at this time nearly fifty, unusually late in life in that era to undertake such a radical change.

In future, Dean Mahomet would expunge the quarter century he had lived in Ireland from his life story. He never later mentioned it in print or in reported conversation; indeed, he explicitly stated that he had come directly from India to England in 1784. Thus, he evidently never fully identified himself with society in Ireland and started a new life in the British capital.

IMMIGRATION TO LONDON

When Dean Mahomet and his family (including a ten-year-old son William, and perhaps other children born in Cork) moved to London, they entered a cosmopolitan city quickly becoming an imperial capital. London surpassed Calcutta and Cork in scale and power. England was growing wealthy from its industrializing economy and from exploitation of its colonies—particularly India and Ireland. Its capital became the dwelling place for a variety of peoples drawn by the imperial process, including Irish and Indian workers (among the proletariat) and British officials, officers, and merchants who had grown rich in the East (among the elite).

As England developed its national identity, it largely did so over and against the people of its colonies.[21] Irish people, attracted by the growing English economy, often found themselves in the bottom social and economic strata in London. Some two thousand Asian sailors made London's docklands their abode—either temporarily between voyages or terminally marooned there. Many hundreds of Indian servants or slaves had accompanied their masters or mistresses back to England, only to be abandoned with no means of return to India.[22] By law, the East India Company had the financial obligation to repatriate destitute Indians, but it was reluctant to discharge this responsibility.[23] Further, a number of Indian wives, mistresses, and children of British men lived on the margins of whatever social class that man occupied.[24] Finally, a few Indian noblemen visited England during Dean Mahomet's lifetime.[25] Thus, Dean Mahomet and his family, combining as they did both Indian and Irish identities, would have had a particularly difficult time establishing their place in London.

Significantly, Dean Mahomet and his family did not settle among either merchants doing business with India or Indian sailors. Rather, they lived near one of the most fashionable new centers of London high society: Portman Square. A few blocks north, in St. Marylebone Church, Dean Mahomet and Jane baptized Amelia (born August 8, 1808) and Henry Edwin (born December 15, 1810).[26]

DEAN MAHOMET WORKS FOR A NABOB

After his arrival in London, Dean Mahomet began to work for a rich and controversial Scottish nobleman, the Honorable Basil Cochrane (1753–1826), sixth son of the eighth Earl of Dundonald. Cochrane had himself returned from India in 1805 as one of the wealthiest of the Nabobs and took the largest house in Portman Square.[27] Here, too, the Ottoman Turkish Ambassador established an imposing residence and a mosque.[28]

Much of Cochrane's vast fortune came from his contracts (which totaled £1,418,236) to provision the Royal Navy in India. Cochrane spent much of the rest of his life successfully disputing Navy charges of embezzlement against him. Meanwhile, Cochrane claimed to have developed a form of vapor cure while in India; he determined to improve the health of London's lower classes, and his own reputation, by establishing a vapor bath for their therapy at his plush home in Portman Square early in 1808. Dean Mahomet served in this vapor bath but Cochrane never acknowledged any Indian contribution to his invention.

Although Cochrane claimed that he hit upon the original idea of a vapor bath while he was in India, he attributed his inspiration not to Indian tradition but rather to a British innovation which he encountered there: "an accident about this time threw in my way '*Mudge's Inhaler*,' and I made use of it . . . this naturally produced reflection on the superior advantages that might be obtained from vapour, upon an extensive scale, and with a more general application."[29] In a work published later, Dean Mahomet's son, Horatio, acknowledged that the impetus for the establishment of the vapor bath in London had been Cochrane's, but then asserted that the "bath was fitted for" Cochrane by Dean Mahomet.[30] Diagrams supplied and captioned by Cochrane in 1809, showed the design he and his staff developed using flannel, whalebone, and metal pipe fittings and boilers (see figures 5 and 6).[31] Over the years, Cochrane's wealth and social standing enabled him to enlist large numbers of the most prominent members of the medical establishment to authenticate his innovation.[32] Cochrane publicized his contribution to public health repeatedly and widely. His most famous work, *An Improvement on the Mode of Administering the Vapour Bath* (1809), in many ways epitomized the self-promotional, quasi-medical literature of that era.

Despite Cochrane's assertions, the practice of vapor bathing in London was not original to him. Institutions using a range of forms of such baths had existed for centuries. Hamams, or Turkish steam baths, had

Figure 5. Vaporizer (Cochrane, *Improvement* [1809], fig. 4).

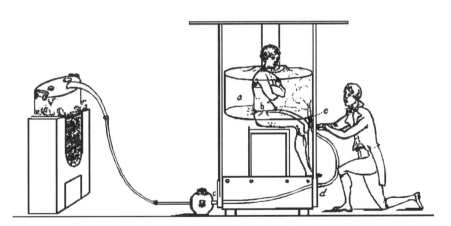

Figure 6. Patient and attendant in vapor bath (Cochrane, *Improvement* [1809], fig. 1).

been established in London as early as 1631 and have continued in various guises up to the present.[33]

The British conquest of India and Napoleon's invasion of Egypt (1798–1801) had brought ever larger numbers of Europeans into contact with—and power over—the "East." In terms of medicine and health treatments, the perception of the Orient as exotic led to conflicting valuations. On one hand, Asia represented to many Europeans a largely unknown storehouse of wealth, including a wealth of medical knowledge, drugs, and treatments. On the other hand, the growing European conception of Asians as essentially different from themselves suggested that such medical knowledge and medicine might be specific to Asians and inapplicable or even dangerous for Europeans, particularly to Europeans who had not been subjected to the environment of Asia.[34] While Cochrane's innovation had no particular Indian associations, Dean Mahomet apparently added to Cochrane's bath a practice that he would make famous in England as "shampooing" (therapeutic massage).

Dean Mahomet later claimed to have been practicing shampooing in England from 1784.[35] Nevertheless, in *Travels* (Letter XXV) Dean Mahomet gave an unflattering account of this art, reproducing Latin citations giving derogatory descriptions by Seneca and Martial of such massage in imperial Rome as immoral and emasculating.[36] In the original context, Martial was castigating Zoilus, a sybarite who feasted surrounded by his catamite, concubine, slave boy, and female shampooer. Furthermore, in *Travels*, Dean Mahomet attributed this practice of shampooing ("champing") to the Chinese. Yet by the time he made himself a practitioner of shampooing in England, he had clearly changed his attitude toward it.

Shampooing (*champi*) and the related art, *malish*, were widely practiced in India. As in Rome, however, many professional practitioners were servants or people of low status, both male and female. One of Dean Mahomet's contemporaries in Patna described a noble's attendants: "one of his . . . favourite women . . . presented herself at the foot of his bed . . . whose office was to chuppy [*champi*, shampoo] his limbs. . . . Within the seraglio, these . . . offices must be performed by women; and . . . they must be pretty, elegantly dressed, witty, and ready at repartees."[37] European commentators about India also described practitioners of this art: " . . . of lulling to sleep in India . . . by the chuppy, a method of handling, from the feet upwards, all the members successively, opening the palm of the hand as if going to grip hard a handful of flesh, and yet grasping it so gently, as hardly to make any impression. The person that operates, is always a young one, and with long fingers, and a satined skin."[38] Further, within a household, a wife or servant might regularly shampoo the elders of the family or a child to induce relaxation and sleep.

After Dean Mahomet began to shampoo in Cochrane's celebrated vapor bath, the idea of shampooing for health quickly entered the popular medical jargon of London; many commercial bathhouses included shampooing among their advertised therapies.[39] Dean Mahomet, however, gained little credit from Cochrane or the London public for his shampooing at this time. Instead, he began a new career: representing Indian culture and cuisine to the British elite.

THE HINDOSTANEE COFFEE HOUSE
(1809–12)

Late in 1809, Dean Mahomet opened a public eating house. He distinguished it from the thousands of other public houses then scattered across London by calling it the "Hindostanee Coffee House," thus marketing his Indian identity.[40] In the location, furnishing, and advertising of this public eating house, he clearly sought to appeal and cater to the same type of men who had been his patrons in the past: Europeans who had worked or lived in India, men they called "Indian gentlemen." He located his establishment near Portman Square: on the corner of George and Charles Streets, two short blocks directly behind Cochrane's mansion.[41] In selecting "coffee house" as the genre of his enterprise, he summoned up the Oriental origins which Londoners continued to attribute to coffee.[42] Like many other nominal coffeehouses of the day, however, he did not feature coffee at all. Rather, he created a restaurant, but one with a difference.

Unique among coffeehouses and other public houses then found in London, the Hindostanee Coffee House provided what Dean Mahomet and Jane intended their European patrons to recognize as exotic Indian cuisine and ambience. He prepared a range of meat and vegetable dishes with Indian spices and served with seasoned rice. He constructed bamboo-cane sofas and chairs on which his patrons would recline. He adorned the walls with a range of paintings including Indian landscapes, Indians engaged in various social activities, and sporting scenes set in India. One observer reported "Chinese pictures" as well, so he may have drawn upon Asia generally rather than India alone. In a separate *en suite* smoking room, he offered ornate hookas (water pipes), with especially prepared tobacco blended with Indian herbs.[43]

Soon after he inaugurated his coffeehouse, he presented his creation to the British public through a newspaper advertisement:

> HINDOSTANEE COFFEE-HOUSE, No. 34 George-street, Portman square—MAHOMED, East-Indian, informs the Nobility and Gentry, he has fitted up the above house, neatly and elegantly, for the entertainment of Indian gentlemen, where they may enjoy the Hoakha, with real Chilm tobacco, and Indian dishes, in the highest perfection, and allowed by the greatest epicures to be unequalled to any curries ever made in England with choice wines, and every accommodation, and now looks up to them for their future patronage and support, and gratefully acknowledges himself indebted for their former favours, and trusts it will merit the highest satisfaction when made known to the public.[44]

This advertisement indicated his continuing public orientation toward Europeans who had traded or ruled in India, but also his effort to attract patronage from other segments of the British elite as well.

The Hindostanee Coffee House received a favorable reception in some quarters. During their first year, he expanded his enterprise into the adjacent building.[45] One connoisseur of fine dining later listed Dean Mahomet among the "Artists who administer to the Wants and Enjoyment of the Table."[46] To be profitable, however, public houses either had to generate a loyal and substantial clientele or to have a prime location, drawing many occasional visitors. Particularly successful London coffeehouses had already established themselves as hosts for specialized constituencies. Lloyds Coffee House over the previous half century had become central for ship insurers.[47] By the time Dean Mahomet began his enterprise, the Jerusalem Coffee House (in Cornhill, far closer to the City of London financial center) already held the patronage of European merchants and veterans of the East Indies.[48] The elite of the Portman Square neighborhood, including wealthy Nabobs, had their own private kitchens where their personal tastes would be satisfied; they could easily hire Indian servants, or Europeans with experience in India, if they sought to eat or smoke in an Indian style regularly.[49] Therefore, the relatively exclusive location of the Hindostanee Coffee House and its novel and specialized cuisine and ambience meant that its start-up costs exceeded Dean Mahomet's limited capital. After less than a year running the Hindostanee Coffee House on his own, he took in a partner, John Spencer, perhaps to infuse more cash into the business.[50] Spencer's partnership, however, proved either an inadequate recapitalization or simply a mistake, bringing with it even more financial difficulties. Less than a year after that (March 1812), Dean Mahomet (but not Spencer) had to petition for bankruptcy.[51] As a regretful aficionado of the former house suggested: "Mohammed's purse was not strong enough to stand the slow test of public encouragement."[52] While the Hindostanee Coffee House apparently did eventually generate a loyal clientele and may have continued on the same site until as late as 1833, neither Dean Mahomet nor Jane held any further financial interest in it.[53]

Dean Mahomet's bankruptcy stripped him of his financial assets and kept him and his family enmeshed in complex legal processes until July

27, 1813—when his assets were publicly divided among his creditors in front of London's Guildhall. While this bankruptcy left the fifty-four-year-old Dean Mahomet free to begin yet another career, it must have been an extremely difficult period for him and his family. We can only imagine their frustration, particularly since they were recent immigrants trying to establish themselves in a distinctly English society which relegated most Indians and Irish to the lower classes. Not surprisingly, Dean Mahomet soon excised all reference to his life in London from his subsequent autobiographical writings.

Bankrupt, Dean Mahomet had to find a new way to support himself and his family. Late in 1812, he moved his family out of the Hindostanee Coffee House to a boardinghouse on Paddington Street, in a less attractive neighborhood a few blocks north. Their son William, in his mid-teens, may already have started working as a postman, an occupation he followed in London until his death.[54] The salary of a beginning postman, however, could hardly have supported the entire family. Further about this time, Dean Mahomet and Jane had another son, whom they named Deen, junior.

Dean Mahomet, lacking any other satisfactory employment, offered himself as an upper servant, hoping to revert to his earlier life running a wealthy household. His newspaper advertisement read: "MAHOMED, late of HINDOSTANEE Coffee House, WANTS a SITUATION, as BUTLER, in a Gentleman's Family, or as Valet to a Single Gentleman; he is perfectly acquainted with marketing, and is capable of conducting the business of a kitchen; has no objections to town or country."[55] Virtually unique for such "Situations Wanted" advertisements in this period, he gave his name and his previous situation. Thus, he must have still identified himself with his failed business and have thought that he would be known to potential employers for his accomplished cuisine. Although he sought a position as the majordomo in a respectable household, based on his experience with the Bakers in India and Cork, he found employment in a vapor bathhouse, apparently based on his experience working for Cochrane.

THE WORLD OF BRIGHTON

Brighton, during the half century prior to the arrival of Dean Mahomet and his family, had been growing into a fashionable seaside spa. A series of popular medical texts drew public attention to sea bathing and the reputedly healthful marine environment of Brighton.[56] Sea bathing increased in popularity despite the fact that relatively few Englishmen or women actually knew how to swim. A growing number of English families could afford, and felt they deserved, a holiday by the seashore. Nevertheless, these same families were also developing a bourgeois mentality about revealing the body in public. To accommodate their interests and concerns, horse-drawn bathing machines, segregated by sex, sprang up along the Brighton shore to convey the bather into the water. Professional "dippers" stood at the foot of these machines to encourage the occasionally terrified bathers, via the dipper's arms, into the shallow seawater.

In addition to outdoor sea bathing, Brighton emerged as distinctive for its indoor activities as well. A series of medical promoters popularized their particular water treatments: indoor bathing in, or drinking, various types of waters as highly therapeutic for a broad range of maladies. In 1769, Dr. Awsiter established a hot and cold bathing institution at the foot of the Steine (the open area that ran down the middle of Brighton).[57] Other indoor bathing establishments followed, each with its own special method.[58] Thus, long before Dean Mahomet and Jane's arrival in Brighton, a range of bathhouses flourished there.

The flamboyant George IV—as Prince of Wales and then King— added a significant element of social prestige, and much income, to the expanding town. From his first visit in 1782 or 1783 onward, George's almost unbridled expenditures and increasing notoriety focused attention on the resort. For example, in 1784 he dramatically demonstrated his own prowess and the accessibility of Brighton by riding on horseback from Brighton to London and back in ten hours on one day.[59] Brighton offered George release from the social and moral restrictions of London and his father's court. Over the years, George remodeled a rented house into the striking Brighton Marine Pavilion.[60]

The Pavilion's major theme became eclectic Oriental exotica. A gift to George of Chinese-style wallpaper (c. 1802) led to extensive decoration and redecoration of the Pavilion in what George and his architects believed was "Eastern luxury." While chinoiserie had been fashionable long before, a new amalgamation of putatively "Indian" themes made the Pavilion a striking expression of England's rapidly expanding eastern Empire, with India as its crown jewel (see figures 7 and 8). The Pavilion's final reconstruction into its current "Indian" form took place between 1815 and 1823, during Dean Mahomet's rise to fame in Brighton. He contributed a further fillip of the exotic to Brighton, which proved more receptive to his Indian offerings than London.

DEAN MAHOMET AND JANE MOVE TO BRIGHTON

Burgeoning Brighton offered Dean Mahomet and Jane the opportunity to create new lives for themselves. By September 1814, they were established as bathhouse keepers at 11 Devonshire Place, on the eastern edge of town.[61] Here, Dean Mahomet advertised a range of exotic luxuries: "INDIAN TOOTH POWDER, which possesses extraordinary excellence. It is the first ever offered to the public in this country . . . also just introduced from India, the celebrated CULEFF [*kalaf*, Persian for red-black hair dye], for changing the Hair, of whatever colour it might be, to a beautiful glossy permanent BLACKNESS, which will ever remain unaffected by the attacks of time."[62] Soon, however, they dropped the marketing of these substances to concentrate on a more promising line.

Dean Mahomet and Jane began to treat invalids using their own distinctive form of the therapeutic bath, Brighton's mainstay. They distinguished their form of the vapor bath from others by adding medical herbs and other substances to the vapor and calling it "the Indian Medicated Vapour Bath." Dean Mahomet apparently simply modified Cochrane's

Figure 7. Front of the Brighton Marine Pavilion (etching by John Nash, 1826).

Figure 8. Rear of the Brighton Marine Pavilion (Horsfield, *History* [1835], vol. 1, p. 148).

apparatus (figures 5–6) with the addition of purportedly Indian elements. He used the same type of white flannel cloth and chair with footstool but, in place of Cochrane's whalebone framework, Dean Mahomet used wood, painted to resemble bamboo, suggesting the Orient. Into the vaporizing chamber, Dean Mahomet placed various "herbs and essential oils, . . . brought expressly from India, and . . . known only to myself."[63]

Dean Mahomet also featured "Shampooing with Indian oils." His son—and a successor as shampooer—explained:

[Shampooing] . . . consists of friction and extention of the ligaments, tendons, &c., of the body, the operation commencing by briskly administering gentle friction gradually increasing the pressure, along the whole course of the muscles; imperceptibly squeezing the flesh at the same moment: the operator then grasps the muscles with both hands whilst he kneads it with his fingers; this is succeeded by a light friction of the whole surface of the body . . . anointed with a medicated oil, . . . the muscles are then gently pounded with the thick muscle of the hand below the thumb. . . . [64]

This description seems to indicate a conventional massage, although the exact nature of his proprietary "Indian oils" may never be known.

For Dean Mahomet and Jane to succeed, they had to make clear both that their Indian methods were unique to their bathhouse and that those methods cured a broad range of complaints. To expand his clientele, Dean Mahomet took out a long series of ambitious newspaper advertisements, from early 1815 onward, to tout his treatments as a virtual panacea:

Mahomed's Steam and Vapour Sea Water Medicated BATHS . . . are far superior to the common Baths, as they promote copious perspiration, and never fail in giving relief when every thing else has been tried in vain, to cure many Diseases, particularly Rheumatic and Paralytic Affections of the extremities, stiff joints, old sprains, lameness, eruptions, and scurf on the skin, which it renders quite smooth; also diseases arising from the abuse of mercury, consumption, white swellings, aches and pains in the joints; in short, in all cases where the circulation is languid, or the nervous energy debilitated, as is well known to many professional gentlemen and others in this country.—Mr. M. has attended several of the Nobility with the happiest results, can give most satisfactory references.

N.B. Board and Lodgings in his House, if required.

→Mr. and Mrs. MAHOMED Possess the Art of SHAMPOOING.[65]

In format and broad claims, these early advertisements differed little from other aspiring practitioners of other cure-alls; in featuring "Indian" vapor and shampooing, however, they were distinctive, although later imitated.

Their success and their family grew. Dean Mahomet claimed by 1815 to have treated "a thousand Cases."[66] Jane gave birth to their daughter, Rosanna, early in 1815.[67] After only a year or so, they moved from the Devonshire Place baths to a more distinguished establishment.

THE BATTERY HOUSE BATHS (1815–20)

By December 1815, they had shifted to the Battery House, a more prominent location overlooking the sea, just down the Steine from the Royal Pavilion. The British Board of Ordinance still owned the Battery House, but vibrations from cannon fire and the erosion from the sea had combined to weaken this building's foundations and the cliff beneath.[68] As a result, the Board of Ordinance removed the cannon and rented out the building. There Dean Mahomet established his baths and lived with his growing family through 1819. This was their home when they baptized their sons Horatio (1816), Frederick (1818), and Arthur Ackber (1819) and buried their two-year-old daughter, Rosanna (1818).[69]

Increasingly, publicists who touted Brighton and its growing health care industry featured the Battery House Baths in their guidebooks. One stated that, with Dean Mahomet's treatment "the universal remedy . . . has at length been discovered."[70] In addition to a growing body of loyal and distinguished clients, he also developed a personal history that presented him to his clients in a suitable manner.

From about 1818, Dean Mahomet began to publicize the title he apparently invented for himself: "Shampooing Surgeon" (see figure 9). In 1820, Dean Mahomet extended his publicity campaign by publishing a book containing both descriptions of many of the cases he had treated and glowing testimonials from his grateful patients. Such tracts, while expensive to produce, were a frequent vehicle for bathhouse advertising.[71] He entitled the work *Cases Cured by Sake [Shaikh] Deen Mahomed, Shampooing Surgeon, And Inventor of the Indian Medicated Vapour and Sea-Water Baths . . .* (1820). He modestly attributed the impulse to publish this book to his distinguished patients: "By the pressing desires of many of

Figure 9.   S. D. Mahomed, Shampooing Surgeon, Brighton (Mahomed, *Shampooing*, frontispiece).

the Nobility, and others of the first consideration, Sake Deen Mahomed has caused the few cases, herein presented to the public, to be printed." In his brief opening "Address," he implied that he had been doing shampooing since 1780. In later works, he would gradually make this claim more specific. By 1822, he had begun to assert that he had started shampooing in England in 1784 (see figure 10).[72]

During Dean Mahomet's years in the Battery House Baths, the entire medical bath industry continued to expand dramatically. Numbers of therapeutic baths sprang up across Britain, using a variety of types of vapor, chemicals, electricity, and other fluids as their healing medium. Like Dean Mahomet, the promoters of these other baths published numerous tracts, pamphlets, and books advertising their baths as universal remedies.[73] So, in order to prosper, he created a special niche for himself in the industry and in Brighton.

Since the Battery House building proved limiting, Dean Mahomet designed a magnificent, purpose-built bathhouse on the cliff top nearby. At the same time, the Brighton Town Council was developing the shorefront by building the Kings Road past that site. During the period when construction of this road disrupted traffic and commerce and/or while his new baths were under construction, Dean Mahomet shifted temporarily (1820–21) crosstown to a West Cliff location.[74]

The arrangements in his West Cliff establishment may not have been fully satisfactory. Two distressing incidents occurred there which could have ruined Dean Mahomet's budding career. John Claudius Loudon, a promising landscape gardener, took treatment at Mahomet's bath for a badly rheumatic right arm. The shampooers working under Dean Mahomet misjudged the brittleness of Loudon's humerus and snapped that bone close to the shoulder. This bone never healed properly; ultimately Loudon was compelled to have it amputated.[75] In the second incident, an elderly gentleman of means, Mr. Spode, died while undergoing a shower at Dean Mahomet's West Cliff baths. According to a newspaper report, Spode "ordered a shower bath, when he was ready, the water was, in the usual manner, discharged upon him, when, shocking to relate, he

SAKE DEEN MAHOMED,

Shampooing Surgeon,

INVENTOR OF THE

Indian   Medicated   Vapour   and   Shampooing

BATHS;

No. 39, EAST-CLIFF, BRIGHTON.

THE soothing efficacy of the application of steam to the human body, has been long known in the eastern parts of the world. Medicated with fragrant herbs of peculiar virtue, the vapour is rendered more beneficial, whilst the addition of Shampooing the various parts of the body envoloped in steam, augments its sanative energies throughout the whole animal system. In Rheumatism, Parylitic, Gouty Affections, Asthma, Roughness and Diseases of the Skin, Stiff Joints, and Old Sprains, it is a safe and certain remedy ; and in all cases of corporeal weakness, or where the circulation is languid, or the nervous energy debilitated, its effects have excited astonishment. Scarcely any disease, to which the human frame is liable, but may be relieved by the use of these Baths. They have been sanctioned by the first medical men in the united kingdom ; and have been patronized by many of the nobility, both of England, France, and other places on the Continent, who have received relief from them in many hopeless cases, and whose written testimony of approval may be seen at the Baths.

The art of Shampooing first introduced into England, by S. D. Mahomed, in 1784.

☞ *Cupping performed by* **D. MAHOMED,** *Jun. late pupil of Mr. Mapleson Cupper to his Majesty.*

Figure 10.   Advertisement for Mahomed's Baths (Pigot's *National Directory* [1826]).

fell instantly dead. He death is supposed to have been produced by the shock being too severe for a frame already much debilitated, or from apoplexy. The coroner's verdict was—*Died by the visitation of God.*"[76] Despite these untoward incidents, the town of Brighton stood behind Dean Mahomet and his career continued to flourish. Kings Road officially opened on New Year's Day 1822 and Mahomet's new baths reopened for business about the same time.

MAHOMED'S BATHS (1821–43)

Mahomed's Baths stood as the most concrete expression of Dean Mahomet's professional success. He and a wealthy London backer, Thomas Brown, constructed the splendid baths at a particularly striking location, just down the Steine from the Brighton Pavilion, and perched on a prominent vantage point overhanging the shore on the new main seaside road (see figure 11).[77] This building first opened when Dean Mahomet had already turned sixty-two. Its location, imposing form, and elaborate internal decoration stood as testimony to the prominence he had reached in the community and in the bathhouse profession. A composite of several descriptions of his bathhouse from the time of its glory enable us to describe its design and ornamentation.[78] These descriptions convey the elements which Dean Mahomet evoked in his patients: Oriental and classical Grecian exotica, an almost religious faith in his method, his scientific medical professionalism, and the patronage of the elite. This combination made his bathhouse the epitome of fashion in Brighton for nearly two decades.

Visitors entered his bathhouse through a splendid vestibule off the fashionable Kings Road. Dean Mahomet covered the walls of this entrance room with a mural of "Moguls and Janissaries . . . represented in rich dresses, and the Muses . . . in plain Grecian attire." Over the years, he further festooned the walls of this entry with relics, what a visitor called his "trophies in the shape of crutches, spine-stretchers, leg-irons, head-strainers, bump-dressers, and club-foot reformers . . . [bestowed by] for-

Figure 11. Mahomed's Baths (Mahomed, *Shampooing*).

mer martyrs to rheumatism, sciatica, and lumbago. Mahomed's vigorous and scientific shampooing having restored them to health." In this entryway as well, he kept his "visitor's books," open for testimonials from his distinguished patients. He divided his patients by sex and class reserving one book, for example, for "Ladies of the Nobility." He later mined these visitor's books, selecting particularly important patients or glowing tributes for his extensive and colorful publicity.

From this entry, ladies mounted the stairs to the floor above, while gentlemen proceeded directly ahead down a corridor. A naturalist described the walls of this corridor:

> [a] profusion of trees laden with their fruits and rich foliage, meet the eye on every side, and description of the Duranta Plumina, the Chinese Limodoron, the large flowing sensitiloe plant or mimosa grandiflora, the rencalmina nutens or nodding grandiflora, the bouvardia versicolor, the bright rencalmis, is given with a correctness that is delightful. Birds of the gayest colours are represented also winging their rapid flight through sylvan groves, and Hebe is seen reclining on the ambent air, and strewing the earth with flowers, symbolical of the efficacy of the Medicated Baths, which are prepared in a peculiar manner from herbs, etc. the growth of India.

Awaiting their baths on separate floors, ladies and gentlemen amused themselves in reading rooms furnished with a variety of local and metropolitan newspapers and journals selected for the expected interests of their respective genders. These rooms faced south, overlooking the sea and, to the east and west, the Brighton seashore and open-air sea bathing machines. The walls of these rooms

> were beautifully painted in the most glowing colours, with Indian landscapes, from designs of Mr. Mahomed himself. On one side is seen a superb pagoda, surrounded by a variety of figures in the costume of the country, making their profound salams. On another is a gorgeous temple, beneath which is represented an enormous idol, the object of idolatrous worship. Here is the celebrated car of

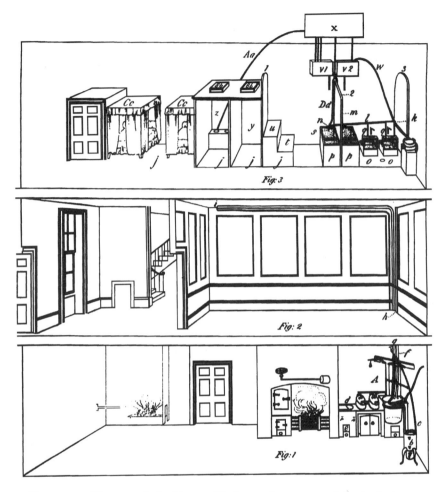

Figure 12. Diagram of a bathhouse (Cochrane, *Improvement* [1809], pl. 5).

Jaggernaut, and here a messenger just dispatched on a distant journey, on his camel, and armed as they are seen in India. On one side is a Rajah's mausoleum, and on another a group of Brahmins, and on a third a group of native musicians sitting beneath the umbrageous trees of that prolific soil. Here is a lake whose liquid surface is lost beneath the rising bosom of those distant mountains whilst the swan, swelling with pride, gently breaks the monotonous stillness of the scene and the rich plumage of the Balearic and Numidian cranes.

In addition, ladies had a "boudoir" and gentlemen a "private parlour" in which to await their turn in the baths. Elevated balconies surrounded the building, including "an elegant sun screen" room.

Arranged symmetrically off each of the central corridors stood the bathing rooms themselves, four per floor. All of the bathing rooms "[are] fitted with a marble bath, and have the means of giving in the same room hot water, cold water, shower, and douche baths. Four of them are also fitted with the Indian vapour or shampooing baths, two of which are appropriated for ladies and two for gentlemen." Above, five bedrooms awaited any patient who desired to remain for more extended treatment. Dean Mahomet located water closets discretely at various places within the building.

Unseen by the patients, but essential to the functioning of the Baths, were a basement with "a large coal and store cellars, breakfast room, a manservant's room, kitchens, scullery, and other offices. A spacious area, in which is the steam engine room, surrounds the west and south sides of the house, enclosed with an iron fence, which is a most important benefit to the comfort and security of the building." This steam engine pumped the large volume of sea and fresh water used by the establishment. Figure 12 shows the structure and apparatus of such baths.[79]

Two men and three women lived as servants and bath attendants on the premises. No one on the staff, except Dean Mahomet, was Indian. Adjacent to the Baths stood a comfortable house where Dean Mahomet, Jane, and their growing family lived (figure 13 shows the only known portrait of Mrs. Jane Mahomet).[80] To accompany this majestic new bathhouse, Dean Mahomet developed a new public persona for himself.

SHIFTING SELF-PRESENTATIONS

Following the opening of his grand bathhouse, Dean Mahomet's fame and popularity grew dramatically. He enhanced this growth through frequent

Figure 13.   Mrs. Mahomed, Wife of Mr. Mahomed, Shampooing Surgeon, Brighton (courtesy of East Sussex County Library).

self-promotional publicity, projecting himself and his method as the latest in medical science and exotic fashion. In addition to his continuing newspaper advertisements, he expanded his book *Cases Cured* into a full medical casebook. Dean Mahomet followed the popular medical casebook genre by organizing his book around a quasi-scientific analysis of diseases, symptoms, methods, cures, and testimonials: *Shampooing, or, Benefits Resulting From the use of The Indian Medicated Vapour Bath, As introduced into this country by S. D. Mahomed (A Native of India)*. In all, he published three editions of this book: 1822, 1826, 1838. Each edition expanded the previous one, adding another layer to the identity he had constructed in order to reflect the self-image that he wished to project at that time (see figure 9). This work received serious attention in at least one leading literary journal.[81]

In an age when each medical faculty (Physicians, Surgeons, and Apothecaries) was gradually organizing itself into a Royal College, with specified requirements for admission, Dean Mahomet came to feel the need for formal medical credentials.[82] In the first edition of *Shampooing* (1822), he claimed medical training in India, prior to his entry into the Company's army. To accommodate these years of medical training, he modified his life-story, increasing his putative age by a decade:

> The humble author of these sheets, is a native of India; and was born in the year 1749, at Patna, the capital of Bihar, in Hindoostan. . . . I was educated to the profession of, and served in the Company's Service as, a Surgeon, which capacity I afterwards relinquished, and acted in a military character, exclusively for nearly fifteen years. In the year 1780, I was appointed to a company under General, then Major, Popham; and at the commencement of the year 1784, left the service and came to Europe, where I have resided ever since.[83]

In the entrepreneurial environment of the early nineteenth century, a range of self-proclaimed experts made fortunes selling medicine and medical treatments to the public.[84] Dean Mahomet remained well within the bounds of medical and advertising ethics of the day.

Later family traditions among Dean Mahomet's descendants attributed to him professional training as "a medical student at the Hospital in Calcutta . . . [His commission as] Soubadar of the 27th Regiment . . . was offered by the Colonel . . . in grateful recognition of his skillful treatment of cholera among the soldiers."[85] This family tradition is not supported either by East India Company records or Dean Mahomet's own *Travels.* A descendant rationalized the decadewide discrepancy in the dates Dean Mahomet gave for his birth in *Travels* and in *Shampooing* as due to the "difficulty" of conversion from the lunar Muslim calendar to the solar Christian calendar.[86] While Dean Mahomet may have given this implausible explanation to the curious and his descendants, the 1759 date of birth he stated in *Travels* accords perfectly with existing records and the chronology of the events of his life, while the 1749 date he claimed in *Shampooing* does not.

In the next edition of *Shampooing* (1826), Dean Mahomet further enhanced the amount of scientific testing that had gone into his "invention." He explained how he developed his hypothesis about the properties of his vapor and shampooing, echoing the format of a scientific paper. He portrayed himself as an inventive, but disparaged, medical practitioner whose empirically derived method eventually triumphed over prejudice. This prejudice, however, rested not on racial grounds, but rather on his challenge as a newcomer to more established and conventional medical practitioners:

> It is not in the power of any individual to . . . attempt to establish
> a new opinion without the risk of incurring the ridicule, as well as
> censure, of some portion of mankind. So it was with me: in the face
> of indisputable evidence, I had to struggle with doubts and objections
> raised and circulated against my Bath. . . . Fortunately, however, I
> have lived to see my Bath survive the vituperations of the weak
> and the aspersions of the [in]credulous. . . . Upwards of a hundred
> medical gentlemen . . . of the first professional reputation . . . have
> since tried the experiment on themselves; most of them were

invalids, but many were merely prompted by an honourable desire to ascertain truth.[87]

Thus, by this time, Dean Mahomet had located his medical methods within the European scientific discourse.

In addition to "modern" medicine, Dean Mahomet also drew upon the European classical tradition to support his treatment: "Homer mentions the use of private baths, which baths possessed medicinal properties. . . . [T]he Romans directed their attention in particular to the actual cure of disease by impregnated waters."[88] This passage contrasts strikingly with the scathing classical references to shampooing by Martial and Seneca cited in *Travels* (Letter XXV).

Dean Mahomet further took authority for his method from ancient Hindu practice: "To the Hindoos, who are the cleanest and finest people in the East, we are principally indebted for the Medicated Bath. . . . "[89] Many among the British public never understood the distinction between Hindu and Muslim, or Dean Mahomet's relationship to either religious community, even after he had lived in Britain for over half a century.[90]

Nowhere, indeed, did Dean Mahomet specify his own training in shampooing or vapor bathing that would have prepared him for this career. He implied that his self-identification as a "native" of India had qualified him as a master of "Eastern" knowledge generally. Familiar as we are now with his earlier years, we can understand why, although he came to this career in his mid-fifties, he sought to indicate to his patients and potential patients a far longer commitment to the medical profession.

THE INDIAN METHOD

Through his medical career, Dean Mahomet argued that, as an Indian, he was uniquely able to provide his patrons with access to Indian (and in a larger sense, "Oriental") medical knowledge. He thus sought to preempt his rival European bathhouse keepers who sought themselves to represent the Orient. Nevertheless, as his fame grew, various competitors sought to appropriate the terms and methods "Indian Medicated Bath" and "Shampooing" for themselves.

One of his most competitive rivals, John Molineux, opened a bath-house similar to Mahomed's Baths, but somewhat smaller and less elegant, two doors down on East Cliff in 1821.[91] In clear imitation of Dean Mahomet's shampooing and Indian medicated vapor baths, Molineux offered first "affriction" and then, in an effort to shift the origin of this method away from Dean Mahomet's area of expertise: "TURKISH MEDICATED SEA-WATER, VAPOUR, AND SHAMPOOING BATHS."[92] Much to Dean Mahomet's disgust, many patrons and guidebooks confused the two baths, so similar were they in advertisements and location.[93]

In response to this situation, from June 1821 onward Dean Mahomet ran a series of front-page newspaper advertisements warning the public not to be fooled by

> . . . the many IMITATIONS of and the repeated attempts to rival his celebrated Indian Bath. . . . [T]he art of SHAMPOOING, as practiced in India, is exclusively confined to himself in Brighton. . . . [T]hough the outward appearance may be copied, the EFFICACY of it defies competition.
>
> To avoid mistake the public are particularly requested to enquire for MAHOMED'S BATHS, NO. 39, EAST CLIFF.[94]

Molineux replied directly in his own advertisements, impugning Dean Mahomet's motives and medical training:

> J. MOLINEUX thinks it his duty in answer to an advertizement that appeared in last week's Gazette [containing] unhandsome and unmanly allusions. . . .
>
> J. M. does not, in the vulgar term, wish to *gull* the public by saying, that he was the first person that introduced Shampooing into this country, but, with the greatest confidence, he can say he understands it equal to any one who practices it, having, for the last eighteen years, been constantly employed therein, under the directions of the FIRST MEDICAL MEN IN THE WORLD, and

thereby obtained a necessary knowledge of the human frame. . . .
"Let man live without envy."[95]

Even as these rivals battled over the provenance of shampooing (India or Turkey) and similarly the legitimacy of Dean Mahomet's claim as an Indian or Molineux's claim as a professional medical man, other bath proprietors also sought to capitalize on Dean Mahomet's reputation. In 1823, the oldest bathhouse in Brighton, the "Royal Original Hot, Cold and Improved Shower Baths" (founded in 1769), revised the treatment it featured to "Improved Indian Medicated Vapour and Shampooing." The initial advertisement for this "new" method featured the term "improved" six times and "Indian" four times.[96] Eventually, however, these rivals gave up their direct imitation of Dean Mahomet's methods.

On his part, Dean Mahomet broadened his range of treatments. He provided courses of "vegetable pills," "Paste or Wooptong baths," "electuaries," "dry cupping," and "electrification"—some of which were not particularly Indian.[97] Thus, to attract broad-based attention and patronage, he did not restrict his publicity or methods to "Indian" traditions alone. Nevertheless, he rose out of the welter of claims and counterclaims among bathhouse keepers in a large measure because his undeniable identity as an Indian distinguished him from his rivals in the eyes of his patrons: the British public and royalty.

SHAMPOOING SURGEON TO ROYALTY

During Dean Mahomet's career, Brighton's most celebrated attractions, and sources of income, remained the courts of Kings George IV (r. 1820–30) and William IV (r. 1830–37). Dean Mahomet provided both Kings with shampooing and vapor bath treatments and received Warrants of Appointment as royal "Shampooing Surgeon" to their Majesties.[98] For attendance on such noble patients, he charged a royal rate of 1 guinea each for a shampoo and vapor bath. Further, his official court costume, modeled on Mughal imperial court dress, added another

Figure 14.   Sake Dean Mahomet in court robes (Erredge, *History of Brighthelmston* [1862], vol. 4).

exotic touch to their royal assemblies and the Brighton horse races (see figure 14).

Over the years Dean Mahomet did much business with the royal household. He sold it baths and shampoos, an Indian Vapour Bath apparatus, bathing gowns of twilled calico and swanskin flannel, and other bathing gear.[99] In addition to Kings George and William, continental royalty, British aristocrats, and members of their entourages also took treatments from him.[100] A course of treatment from him became de rigueur for a fashionable visit to Brighton, even for Indian dignitaries.[101]

Even more valuable to Dean Mahomet than his fees from such royal patronage was the attention among the general public that it brought to him and his baths. His visits to the Royal Pavilion to supervise his vapor bath apparatus excited the fascinated gossip of Brighton society, in part because he received advanced word of the King's arrival in town.[102] Dean Mahomet capitalized on these royal connections by inserting the royal coat of arms in his newspaper advertisements (March 1822 onward). He also publicized his fervent expressions of loyalty to the royal family. He dedicated his book *Shampooing* to King George. He adopted a small, but for him unusual, public role in Brighton politics, placing himself among the inhabitants calling publicly for a Town Meeting to organize a reception for the newly crowned King William IV.[103] Further, he celebrated royal arrivals and anniversaries through elaborate gas-lamp signs and transparencies on the walls of his bathhouse. Such expressions were duly noted in the Brighton newspapers:

> [Mahomed's baths displayed] portraits of the King and Queen [with the] motto "Welcome to Your People." Under the portrait of the King was written "King William, Neptune's Favourite Son," and under that of Her Majesty "Queen Adelaide, Patroness of Every Virtue" . . . [also] a transparency, representing Fame crowning William IV, Britannia supporting the portrait.[104]

When the newly crowned Victoria (r. 1837–1901) first visited Brighton, Dean Mahomet displayed "a transparency of large dimensions, representing Her Majesty walking into Brighton, preceded by a number of damsels strewing flowers before her. . . ."[105] His public expressions of loyalty to the royal family were not unusual among entrepreneurs in Brighton, where royal patronage bestowed the greatest cachet and attracted the attention of a less elevated but more broad-based market. Nevertheless, his arrays were repeatedly among the grandest.

By the late 1830s, however, his connection to the British royal family faded. King William's favor changed to other baths, making them more fashionable. Queen Victoria, despite Dean Mahomet's effusive expressions of loyalty, never graced his Baths or submitted herself to a bath or shampoo at his or Jane's hands. Ultimately, she found Brighton uncongenial, closed the Pavilion, stripped its furnishings, and sold it the year Dean Mahomet died (1851). Nevertheless, Dean Mahomet's transient entry into the circle of attendants on the royal family did much to draw the attention of society at large to him and his mode of treatment.

SOCIAL POSITION IN BRIGHTON

Dean Mahomet's rise and then decline in royal favor paralleled his reputation in Brighton society generally. His very identity as an Indian that made him stand out in society also marginalized him. Through the 1820s and early 1830s, he placed his name prominently before the public as a patron of worthy causes.[106] He further offered his medical treatment gratis to the deserving poor, as his advertisements and the press noted.[107] Although he had a reputation as a poor judge of horses, he contributed handsomely to the Brighton Race Fund through the 1820s, thus locating himself among the patrons of this sport of kings.[108] Such public acts of benevolence, however, were expensive; each one of his £5 donations represented the gross income from sixteen Indian vapor baths with shampooing.

Dean Mahomet and Jane's lives had been uneven financially prior to arriving in Brighton, and this continued during their years there. On a good day, Mahomet's bathhouse could provide twelve Indian Medicated

Vapor baths and thirty hot water baths. In theory, this worked out to be nearly £8 per day. Such an income, however, would rarely be sustained. In contrast, his fixed expenses remained high: rental to the building's owner, salaries to the attendants, expenses including coal and laundry, subscriptions to many newspapers, advertising costs, and taxes. Given the seasonal nature of resort life in Brighton, long periods of little or no business would have to be expected. Nevertheless, in flush times, there would be a handsome income, no doubt enhanced with tips. However, Dean Mahomet never controlled sufficient capital to free himself from financial dependence on his British backers.

Brighton's ambitious rebuilding of its seashore periodically disrupted his business. From the 1820s, the town built broad seawalls in front of the cliff and filled in the intervening space eventually to create a wide "Grand Junction Road" and esplanade. Beyond any financial losses incurred by this disruption in his usual custom, Dean Mahomet had to pay for part of the construction.[109] While the ultimate result was a more secure foundation for his bathhouse, during the construction, anyone seeking to visit his baths would have encountered noise and debris. Complaints by Dean Mahomet to the Town Commissioners about inadequate lighting and disruption met with little satisfaction.[110] Perhaps to compensate for obstructed access to his bathhouse, in 1838 he advertised a mobile bath service which carried attendants and a portable vapor bath apparatus to the patron's own rooms.[111] Further, all this construction isolated his bathhouse from the seashore. Instead of a prominent—if perhaps insecure—location on the cliff top, his bathhouse by about 1830 had become landlocked. Figure 15 shows that strollers now looked in at eye level to both the ground floor gentlemen's bathrooms and to the lowest level of the balcony, one of the building's most attractive architectural features.

Most British pen portraits of Dean Mahomet tended to paint him in sympathetic but eccentric terms, as an established Brighton "character," identified with exotic India and Islam.[112] Some of his supporters identified him as in the forefront of modern medical innovation.[113] Among his detractors, the most consistent theme remained that his self-promotional

Figure 15. Mahomed's Baths (computer-altered version of Berthou and Georges, *Album de Brighton* [Brighton: The Authors, 1838], pl. 5).

advertising and his fashionable reputation were out of proportion to the medical benefits of his method.[114] Nevertheless, at the height of his career, Dean Mahomet had inserted "shampooing," and, to an extent himself, into English popular culture as exotically attractive.

By the end of the 1830s, Dean Mahomet's leadership in Brighton's bathhouse industry had begun to falter. Already into his eighties, he may have found life as an inventive entrepreneur exhausting. Reviewers of bathhouses began to criticize his establishment as having become something of a "museum," lacking "the air of freshness and sweet atmosphere" found in rival bathhouses. While his baths appeared passé, he personally remained "[o]ne of the greatest curiosities at Brighton."[115]

Over the years, Dean Mahomet and Jane proved very interested in preparing three of their sons for careers as medical men. They apprenticed one son, Deen junior, to the King's own "Cupper"; "dry cupping" (applying vacuum cups to a patient's skin) and "wet cupping" (therapeutic bleeding of a patient) were highly fashionable at the time. Deen junior first worked at his father's bathhouse in Brighton. Dean Mahomet then established a branch bathhouse for Deen in a fashionable district of London, at 11 St. James Place, quite near both St. James Palace and numerous gentlemen's clubs.[116] Unfortunately, it seems Deen died some-time in 1836 and the bathhouse went to a competitor, George Fry.[117]

In response to Fry's unauthorized use of the name "Mahomed's Baths" for his establishment, Dean Mahomet opened another London bathhouse a few blocks away, at 7 Little Ryder Street, early in 1838. Dean Mahomet was nearly eighty years old and admitted a reluctance to take on this new operation. Nevertheless, he vowed to defeat Fry's rival business "carried on in [Dean Mahomet's] name, [but] with which he has not, nor ever had the slightest connection."[118] Having beaten off his imitator, Dean Mahomet gradually withdrew from active involvement with the Ryder Street Baths, leaving them to his son, Horatio, to manage.[119]

Back in Brighton, an unfortunate financial blow hit Dean Mahomet. After his silent partner, Thomas Brown, died, his executors determined in 1841 to sell Mahomed's Baths by public auction. Despite twenty years of flourishing practice, Dean Mahomet himself did not have enough cap-ital to purchase it.

In the auction notice, Dean Mahomet's personal reputation featured as the establishment's greatest asset. However embarrassing this open ad-vertisement of his dependence may have been, he offered in the auction announcement to lease the bathhouse from whomever made the highest bid. To add to this public embarrassment, the first auction (October 16, 1841) failed, since no one was willing to meet the reserve price. His bath-house was not worth in a public market what the owners expected. Thus, even as the railway opened between London and Brighton in 1841 (soon carrying up to seventy-four thousand visitors in a single month), Dean Mahomet and Jane were already moving toward a somewhat inglorious retirement.[120]

On August 12, 1843, Brown's executors once again offered the bath-house at public auction, this time with no bottom price. The purchaser, William Furner, leased the bathhouse not to Dean Mahomet but rather to a rival, William Knight. Dean Mahomet, Jane, and their youngest son Arthur moved to a far more modest rented establishment at 2 Black Lion

Street.[121] While Dean Mahomet and Jane sought to revive their fortunes in this smaller and more obscure house, Knight capitalized on Dean Mahomet's lingering reputation. Knight hired the same bath attendants and servants who had worked for Dean Mahomet. Further, he advertised the Baths almost exactly as had Dean Mahomet:

> Original Indian Medicated Vapour and Shampooing Baths . . .
> known as MAHOMED'S BATHS, the CELEBRATED INDIAN MEDICATED
> VAPOUR AND SHAMPOOING BATHS, (first introduced into England at
> this Establishment) . . . are still to be had in precisely the same way,
> *and with every attention* to comfort as originally. The same attendants
> who have for many years lived in the house and given such universal
> satisfaction, being retained by W. K.[122]

In response to this marketing of his name and claim to primacy, Dean Mahomet and Jane took out counteradvertisements announcing that they had no connection with their former establishment and now practiced the profession in their home on Black Lion Street.[123]

Interestingly, in these later years (1844–45), Jane's name resurfaced in their announcements, from whence it had faded since the initial advertisements of 1815: "The Ladies Bath is under the entire personal administration of Mrs. Mahomed."[124] Indeed, Dean Mahomet and Jane continued to advertise in newspapers for clients at least until late in 1845, and local directories listed him as active until just before his death, although their youngest son Arthur may have been doing much of the actual shampooing.[125]

By the time Jane and Dean Mahomet died (December 26, 1850 and February 24, 1851 respectively), they had largely fallen from public attention. Newspaper obituaries uniformly took the tone that Dean Mahomet, once so important to the town's development, had largely been forgotten. They presented him as too innocent to be a successful entrepreneur.[126] Thus, as prominent as he had made himself through entrepreneurial and medical innovation, Dean Mahomet could not sustain his honored place in Brighton.

DEAN MAHOMET'S LEGACIES

Dean Mahomet's life and works illustrate the complex movement of peoples and ideas inherent in the British empire. Over his lifetime, he passed through many worlds: India as it came under British control, Ireland as an English colony, and England as it became an imperial power. In each of these worlds, Dean Mahomet crossed cultural boundaries.

During his youth, India contained a diversity of polities and cultures, with little national unity. As the Mughal imperial state and regional powers —including both indigenous rulers and nominally Mughal appointees— declined, he and his family, as well as hundreds of thousands of other Indians, entered into the service of the English East India Company during its formative years. He remained with the English Company's Bengal Army for fifteen years as it expanded British control over additional Indian territories, suppressed insurrection by enemies and subordinate Indian allies alike, and crushed resistance to this new order among the Indian rural population. Yet, *Travels* reveals the inherent contradictions of his intermediate position and his conflicted attitudes toward the colonial process. He served the British but also saw the costs of such service.

In 1794, Dean Mahomet published the first account of this imperial process from an Indian's perspective that was intended directly for an anglophone audience in Britain. His very act of asserting his own narrative challenged European assertions of monopoly over representations of the "Orient." Yet he selected a fashionable English genre and addressed the British elite as his "friend."[127] His book's anomalous nature meant that it had limited influence on British colonial attitudes as a whole, however much it added to his personal prestige among the elite of Cork.

Living, writing, marrying, and raising a family in colonial Ireland, Dean Mahomet felt how "hybrid historical and cultural experiences are, . . . how they . . . cross national boundaries."[128] Over his quarter century in Cork, diverse groups bitterly contended about Irish national identity and its relationship to the developing British empire. He carved out a place for himself distinct from both the Catholic Irish colonized and the Protestant Anglo-Irish colonizers. Besides his own narrative, our most extensive image of him in Ireland comes from an Indian traveler and self-styled "Persian Prince" on a triumphant tour of the British capitals. Unfortunately unavailable to us today are Dean Mahomet's interactions with the Indian sailors, servants, mistresses, and families of the British elite who also passed through Cork. We also know little about his growing Anglo-Irish-Indian family.

For forty-five years in England, Dean Mahomet tried, eventually with some success, to market his version of Indian cuisine and medical practices to the British public. London and Brighton both already contained a variety of "foreign" elements, as the British elite likewise sought to represent the exotic "Orient." Dean Mahomet's "Hindustanee Coffee House," his "shampooing," and his "Indian medicated vapour bath" all founded their appeal on, and sought to profit from, this British attraction for his Indian identity. He merchandised nothing purely Indian yet his services proved particularly attractive precisely because he presented them as exotic. Ultimately, however, Dean Mahomet lacked the capital to sustain his career or establish his independence.

Over the nineteenth century, a growing British sense of imperial supremacy over Asia meant that Britons sought control over such representations of the "Orient." After his death, his "shampooing" became a name for hair-wash and the Turkish Bath—under British management—displaced his Indian Vapour Bath.[129] Thus, British society appropriated Dean Mahomet's creations with little recognition of his role.

Dean Mahomet's descendants became British, yet were always marked with a difference. Despite the accomplishments of his progeny, particularly in the medical field, many English contemporaries continued to remark upon their "Oriental" features: "dark and typically Eastern."[130] Most of them retained the name Mahomed—although Britain's changing racial prejudices led one branch to change its surname to Dean.[131] Their stories, and those of other Asian immigrants and their descendants, also deserve to be told in the context of the conflicted development of multicultural British society.

During the late twentieth century, a few scholars and activists have been drawing attention to the achievements of early Indian immigrants. Some have pointed to Dean Mahomet as one of the first Asian professionals in England, making him a symbol of early Indian contributions to British society.[132] In recognizing Dean Mahomet's achievements, we should ensure that his image is not divorced from his own deeds and writings.[133]

Overall, Dean Mahomet and his *Travels* illustrate the circulation of people and ideas brought about by European imperialism. His writings and other accomplishments allow us access to these formative years in the development of the British empire in India, Ireland, and England. As Said asserts: "[T]o ignore or otherwise discount the overlapping experience of Westerners and Orientals, the interdependence of cultural terrains in which colonizer and colonized co-existed and battled each other through projections as well as rival geographies, narratives, and histories, is to miss what is essential about the world . . ."[134]

NOTES

PREFACE

1. Throughout this book, except in direct quotations, I spell Dean Mahomet as he did in *Travels*. His name was not uncommon for Indian Muslims; indeed, "Din Muhammad" was a war cry within his community. For a more extensive study of Dean Mahomet's life, see Michael H. Fisher and Dean Mahomed, *The First Indian Author in English* (1996).

2. Prabhu Guptara, *Black British Literature* (1986).

3. For Ranajit Guha and other members of the Subaltern Studies Collective, Dean Mahomet's class origins and role in the English Company's army would have placed him in the "indigenous elite," oppressive of the Indian "subaltern" classes. See Ranajit Guha et al., eds., *Subaltern Studies*, volumes 1–8 (1982–94).

4. This figure is compiled for covenanted officials from East India Company, *List* (1771). Much scholarship on colonial India (and European imperialism generally) has focused on Dean Mahomet's class of intermediaries or "compradores" who served as the interface between Europeans and the subordinated peoples. E.g., C. A. Bayly, *Indian Society* (1988); Ronald Robinson, "Non-European Foundations of European Imperialism" (1976); Shubhra Chakrabarti, "Collaboration and Resistance" (1994).

5. See Thomas R. Metcalf, *Ideologies* (1995).

6. Edward W. Said, *Orientalism* (1979), pp. xiii, 283.

7. Mary Louise Pratt, *Imperial Eyes* (1992).

8. E.g., Homi Bhabha, "Signs Taken for Wonders" (1985); Homi K. Bhabha, *The Location of Culture* (1994); Henry Louis Gates, Jr., "James Gronniosaw and the Trope of the Talking Book" (1988); Edward W. Said, *Culture and Imperialism* (1993).

9. While there are parallels between Dean Mahomet's *Travels* and Equiano's and other former slaves' narratives, it is important to emphasize the fundamental differences as well. For example, Dean Mahomet never experienced slavery nor mentioned his conversion to Christianity, two vital elements in their works. See Henry Louis Gates, Jr., ed., *The Classic Slave Narratives* (1987).

10. Said, *Culture and Imperialism*, pp. xxiv–xxv; Metcalf, *Ideologies*.

11. Consider, for example, that Equiano, in addition to his antislavery activities, once purchased slaves for his employer. He explained that he selected his "own [Igbo] countrymen" to buy as slaves, in preference to other African peoples. Equiano, *Interesting Narrative*, Chapter 11.

12. Pratt, *Imperial Eyes*, p. 6.

13. E.g., Sudhir Kakar, ed., *Identity and Adulthood* (1992); and Sudhir Kakar, *The Inner World* (1981).

14. For various positions on this problematic, see Karl Weintraub, "Autobiography" (1975); Stephen F. Dale, "Steppe Humanism" (1990); and Gustav E. von Grunebaum, *Medieval Islam* (1953).

15. These three engravings are signed by J. Finlay, an obscure artist. He may have been a military officer, with technical training as a surveyor, who passed through Cork at this time. The frontispiece portrait of Dean Mahomet appears to be based on an oval ivory painting but the original artist's name has been garbled as H. Ghaylbamdy. Significantly, Figures 2–3 both foreground a hooka, which Dean Mahomet would feature in his London coffeehouse; see Chapter Three.

16. Scholars who have studied Muslim and/or Asian visitors to Europe include Susan Gilson Miller, *Disorienting Encounters* (1992); Jonathan D. Spence, *The Question of Hu* (1988); Simon Digby, "An Eighteenth Century Narrative" (1989); and Ibrahim Abu-Lughod, *The Arab Rediscovery of Europe* (1963).

17. Studies of early Asian immigrants to Britain include Rozina Visram, *Ayahs, Lascars and Princes* (1986); and Peter Fryer, *Staying Power* (1992).

18. For examples from England: Meer Hasan Ali married an English gentlewoman sometime between 1810 and 1816; David Octerlony Dyce Sombre (a man of mixed Indian and European ancestry) married an English Viscount's

daughter in 1840; Abu Talib Khan and Mirza Abul Hassan Khan, among other travelers, wrote about their free social intercourse with elite Englishwomen. Mrs. Meer Hassan Ali, *Observations on the Mussulmauns of India* (1832); Abu Taleb Khan, *Travels of Mirza Abu Taleb Khan* (1810; 1814); Mirza Abul Hassan Khan, *A Persian at the Court of King George, 1809–10* (1988). "Interracial" marriages within the lower classes in Britain also appear to have been relatively common. For example, of the sixty-one families that left Britain to settle the British colony of Sierra Leone in 1786, forty-four were interracial: mostly British women and men of African descent. Douglas A. Lorimer, *Colour, Class and the Victorians* (1978).

19. Pratt, *Imperial Eyes*, p. 4.

20. E.g., G. Willis, *Willis' Current Notes* (March 1851), pp. 22–23; Review of John Henry Grose, *Voyage* (1757) in *Monthly Review* (1757).

ONE: THE WORLD OF EIGHTEENTH-CENTURY INDIA

1. Abul Fazl Allami, *Ain-i Akbari* (1988), 2:141–368. Dirk H. A. Kolff compiled these figures; see *Naukar* (1990), p. 3. Not all of these men were, however, prepared to serve as professional soldiers in the Mughal imperial armies.

2. See Irfan Habib, *Agrarian System of Mughal India* (1963).

3. From CoD July 12, 1782, FTWM 9:61.

4. To CoD April 5, 1783, FTWM 9:378.

5. See Henry Dodwell, *Sepoy Recruitment* (1922), pp. 1–12.

6. P. J. Marshall, *East Indian Fortunes* (1976), p. 15.

7. Arthur Broome, *History* (1850), 1:92–93; John Williams, *Historical Account* (1970 reprint), p. 4

8. E.g., Sayid Ghulam Husain Khan, *Seir Mutaqherin* (1902).

9. Marshall, *East Indian Fortunes*, pp. 163–66, 179.

10. See Henry Yule and A. C. Burnell, *Hobson-Jobson* (1903), s.v. "Sepoy."

11. See Letter to Court September 3, 1766 in J. Long, *Selections* (1869), 1:427; Bruce P. Lenman, "Weapons" (1968); Gayl D. Ness and William Stahl, "Western Imperialist" (1977).

12. Mir ʿAbdul-Latif Khan Shustari, *Tuhfat al-ʿalam va zayl al-tuhfah* (1992), p. 10.

13. See BSMC May 1, 1770; Great Britain, Parliament, "Account" (1773); Lenman, "Weapons," p. 119; Raymond Callahan, *East India Company* (1972), p. 6.

14. See Bayly, *Indian Society*; and Douglas M. Peers, "War and Public Finance" (1989).

15. See Michael H. Fisher, *Politics of the British Annexation* (1993), pp. 1–49.

16. Broome, *History*, 1:455–58; Charles Caraccioli, *Life of Clive* (1775–77), 2:46–47.

17. Despite the English Company's policies against military labor contractors, it continued occasionally to recruit bodies of soldiers from them. Dodwell, *Sepoy*, p. 19; Madras Military Consultation March 15, 1781, ff. 668–69; Military Consultation February 19, 1799, ff. 1018–19; Provincial CinC June 10, 1782, BPbC July 9, 1782.

18. From CoD April 11, 1781, FTWM 8:295; BSMC August 6, 1781.

19. For differing interpretations of the sepoy in the English Company's armies, see Philip Mason, *Matter of Honour* (1974); Douglas M. Peers, *Between Mars and Mammon* (1995); Seema Alavi, *The Sepoys and the Company* (1995); and Dodwell, *Sepoy*, pp. 29–30.

20. See Thomas Williamson, *East Indian* (1810), 1:426.

21. Minutes of Council May 7, 1781, BMCG May 11, 1781.

22. Broome, *History*, Appendices; Williams, *Historical*, p. 3.

23. GRT July 31, 1770. See also Statement of the Army, BPbC December 16, 1769; and From CoD March 16, 1768, FTWM 5:99–100.

24. Broome, *History*, Appendices P-W; Callahan, *East*, p. 6.

25. See From CoD May 27, 1779, FTWM 8:242; HMS 24, p. 113; Committee on Shipping Report December 3, 1776, in Arthur N. Gilbert, "Recruitment and Reform" (1975); Callahan, *East*, p. 5.

26. Minutes of CoD, September 16, 1785.

27. E.g., From CoD April 16–17, 1777, FTWM 8:85–86, 103–4.

28. Smith Letter, November 2, 1768, in BSMC November 17, 1768.

29. I calculated these figures from "Infantry Native Officers and Sepoys Examined . . . " BMC 1778–84. The Madras Army had similar proportions, Dodwell, *Sepoy*, pp. 11, 40–49.

30. Minutes of Council April 22, 1782, BMCG April 29, 1782; GOCC May 11, 1782.

31. "Circumstances of the People . . . in Confinement . . . ," in Alexander Letter March 16, 1770, BSMC March 29, 1770. The specific names which Dean Mahomet used—Adams, Boudmal, and Corexin—do not appear in surviving Company records. Nevertheless, he recounted a typical scenario.

32. Broome, *History*, 1:552–54; Innes Munro, *Narrative* (1789), p. 186.

33. To CoD March 18, 1770, FTWM 6:197.

34. H. Palmer, June 15, 1771, Patna Factory Records January 1, 1771 to July 30, 1771, pp. 228–30.

35. The Brigade spent nine months in Monghyr cantonment, resuming its journey to Calcutta in February 1772. To CoD March 26, 1772, FTWM 6:390.

36. The Brigade left Baharampur in February 1775 and paused at Denapur until November 1775 when it transferred west to Bilgram in Awadh, remaining there through October 1777.

37. Dean Mahomet visited Allahabad in December 1775 but parts of his description of that city (Letter XIX) paraphrase an earlier account in Jemima Kindersley's *Letters* (1777), pp. 251–53. We cannot tell if he went to Delhi (some 225 miles from Bilgram) but since he anachronistically referred to Emperor Ahmed Shah (r. 1748–54) instead of the incumbent, Emperor Shah Alam II (r. 1759–1806), he may also have taken his account of Delhi from an earlier visitor. Dean Mahomet never saw Surat or Bombay; his descriptions of these cities come from Grose, *Voyage* (1766), pp. 29–52, 98–99, 107–14. I analyze Dean Mahomet's use of these European sources in Chapter Three.

38. BSC January 20, 1776.

39. For details of this march, see Stibbert Letters October 28, 1777, November 18, 1777, BMC November 21, 1777, December 5, 1777. The Third Brigade reached Calcutta on January 22, 1778.

40. After some ten months in possession, the Company restored this fortress to its ally, the ruler of Gohad. Two years later, the Marathas recovered it by strategem. Warren Hastings, *Memoirs* (1841), 2:378–81. Dean Mahomet either quoted or paraphrased a first-hand account by an unnamed participant in the capture of this fortress.

41. This Regiment was raised in 1778 as the Thirty-Seventh sepoys, renumbered as the Thirtieth Regiment in 1781, again renumbered as the Thirty-Third Regiment in 1784, and disbanded in 1785.

42. Baker had induced the Commander-in-Chief of the Bengal Army to supersede the Colonel of the Third Brigade so as to transfer Baker's profitable appointment as Quartermaster to his younger brother, Lieutenant William Massey Baker. BPbC November 23, 1780.

43. Foreign Secret Original Consultations March 19, 1781 No. 8; April 14, 1781 No. 6; April 27, 1781 Nos. 16–18; May 7, 1781 Nos. 8–9.

44. Since these events occurred prior to Dean Mahomet's arrival, his dating the death of Stalker, Symes, and Scott one day prematurely is understandable.

45. Warren Hastings, *Narrative* (1782), pp. 180–84.

46. William Popham Letter October 9, 1781, BSMC October 29, 1781.

47. Hastings, *Memoirs*, 2:415–16, 428–29, and *Narrative*, p. 190n.

48. Baker and Simpson Letter November 9, 1781, BPbC December 17, 1781.

49. From CoD August 28, 1782, To CoD February 14, 1782, July 15, 1782, April 5, 1783, January 17, 1785, FTWM 9:70, 318–19, 381, 526.

50. The Company's Resident, William Markham, oversaw the Regent, Drigbijai Singh, father of the infant Raja.

51. Dean Mahomet's promotion to *subadar* must have come through Baker's influence. Ordinarily, promotion to *subadar* came only after many years' service, going by regulation to the battalion's most senior *jemadar*.

52. Hastings Letter July 15, 1782 in Hastings, *Memoirs*, 2:584–87. Hastings to Doorbijey Sing July 15, 1782, Persian Correspondence, Translations of Issues, 1781–85, No. 26, pp. 1–18, No. 38, NAI.

53. Minute of Council June 16, 1786 in Henry Grace, *Code* (1791), p. 11.

54. Baker Letter November 27, 1783, BPbC December 18, 1783; Minutes of CoD September 10, 1784, IOL.

55. Of the 107 writers of the years 1768–70, 43 percent had died and about 8 percent returned to Britain. HMS 79, p. 3.

56. From CoD March 17, 1769, FTWM 5:186; To CoD February 12, 1771, From CoD July 12, 1782, FTWM 9:58–59.

57. To CoD April 5, 1783, FTWM 9:374; see also CoD to Madras July 8, 1782, HMS 163, pp. 175–86.

58. To Fredricksnagore March 6, 1783, BPbC March 6, 1783; From Bie March 18, 1783, BPbC March 24, 1783.

59. To CoD July 15, 1782, FTWM 9:314.

60. Ole Feldbaek, *India Trade* (1969), appendix.

61. Foreign Letter from Bengal March 16, 1784, To CoD March 16, 1784, FTWM 15:242–43; To CoD January 14, 1785, FTWM 15:328–31; HMS 57, pp. 53–86, 227; Foreign Department Consultation, December 16, 1783, Nos. 28, 31.

62. To CoD November 10, 1782, FTWM 15:158–59.

63. Dean Mahomet says he landed at Madapallam, but he apparently mistook the name since that port was three hundred miles north of Madras.

THREE: DEAN MAHOMET IN IRELAND AND ENGLAND (1784–1851)

1. Cork Corporation, *Council Book* (1876); Charles Bernard Gibson, *History of the County* (1861), 2:217–18; *Volunteer Journal*, May 19, 1786; John Bernard Burke, *Burke's Irish Family Records* (1976), pp. 52–54.

2. "Index to Marriage Licence Bonds," Cashel and Emly Diocese, Godfrey Evan Baker and Margaret Massey, 1785, PRO Ireland. Rosemary Ffolliott, *Biographical Notices* (1980), "Baker."

3. "Index to Marriage Licence Bonds," Cork and Ross Diocese, Deane Mahomet and Jane Daly, 1786, PRO Ireland. Abu Talib Khan, "Masir Talibi," vol. 1, fols. 97–98. If we estimate a minimum age of fourteen at the time of her marriage, she would have been born in 1772. This would make her forty-seven when she bore her last surviving child in 1819, a late—but biologically possible—age. Jane gave herself several dates of birth: the 1841 census has 1791; her gravestone (St. Nicholas Church, Brighton) and obituaries say 1780. BG January 2, 1851; BH January 4, 1851. Neither of these dates is possible if she married Dean Mahomet in 1786. Obituaries of two descendants suggest that Dean Mahomet may have married a second time, to an Englishwoman from Bath, also named Jane. *Guy's Hospital Reports* (1885), 63:1–10; BH August 4, 1888. No conclusive evidence, however, has appeared to substantiate the existence of two different Jane Mahomets.

4. CG March 16, 1793.

5. Personal communication from Sister Mary Hourigan, Librarian, Ursuline Convent, Blackrock, September 15, 1994.

6. Bailie came from a landed Anglo-Irish family of county Down. After his return from India, he married the Honorable Elizabeth, second daughter of the First Viscount Doneraile, and settled on a sizable estate north of Cork city. In 1799, Bailie sold or let his Irish holdings and retired to Bath, England, where he later died. John Bernard Burke, *Burke's Irish Peerage* (1976), "Bailie;" HC August 29, 1799.

7. See Percy G. Adams, *Travel Literature* (1983).

8. Jemima (Mrs. Nathaniel Edward) Kindersley lived in Allahabad, 1767–68; two paragraphs in Dean Mahomet's Letter XIX paraphrase her *Letters*, pp. 251–53. Grose first published his *Voyage* in 1757, with expanded editions in 1766 and 1772; part appeared in John Knox, *New Collection* (1767), 2:474–96.

9. See *OED*, s.v. "Nabob"; James Mayer Holzman, *Nabobs* (1926); Lucy S. Sutherland, *East India Company* (1952); Marshall, *East Indian Fortunes*; HC June 15, 1786.

10. HC June 20, 1785; CG July 20, 1791, December 12, 1795.

11. HC November 20, 1788, March 24, 1796, February 11, 1799.

12. CG October 1, 1791; HC August 31, 1804; CA March 31, 1807.

13. Other plays and works of literature also contained similar themes. E.g., *A Voyage to India, An Operatic Performance*, announced in CA July 16, 1807 and selections from Edward Gibbon, *Decline and Fall* (1776–86), Chapter 50 on the Prophet Muhammad, republished in CG June 11, 1791.

14. CG August 17, 1791.

15. *Times* (London), April 20, 1813.

16. E.g., BPbC September 23, 1785.

17. Baker baptized her in Calcutta in 1785. "Baptisms in Calcutta" (1924), p. 199.

18. See Mark Bence-Jones, *Guide to Irish Country Houses* (1978); p. 126; Bengal Military Consultation Resolution December 7, 1795, FTWM 20:610–11; Richard Colt Hoare, *Journal* (1807), p. 84; Khan, "Masir Talibi," vol. 1, fols. 97–98, IOL.

19. NCEP April 22, 1799; CA July 20, 1799.

20. Khan, "Masir Talibi," vol. 1, fols. 97–98, IOL.

21. See Linda Colley, *Britons* (1992); Visram, *Ayahs, Lascars*; Guptara, *Black British*; and Fryer, *Staying Power*.

22. London newspapers contained advertisements from Europeans seeking Indian servants and Indian servants seeking employers. See William Hickey, *Memoirs* (1919–25), 3:150–51; J. Jean Hecht, *Continental and Colonial Servants* (1954).

23. Dean Mahomet never mentioned other Indians in print so we cannot know the extent to which he associated with them. He stated that he obtained spices, herbs, and oils from India but never revealed his source, perhaps Indian sailors.

24. E.g., [Thomas Broun], *Brighton* (1818), 1:232.

25. See also Harihar Das, "Early Indian Visitors" (1924), pp. 83–114; Digby, "Eighteenth Century Narrative."

26. Amelia (baptized June 11, 1809), Henry Edwin (baptized January 6, 1811), St. Marylebone Parish Register, GLRO. Hitherto, he had spelled his name Mahomet but in England, he often shifted the spelling to Mahomed. For consistency, I will continue to use the spelling Mahomet except in direct quotations.

Amelia's birth register has his name as William Dean Mahomed, apparently re-flecting his brief anglicization of his first name. From 1810, about when he turned fifty, he added the honorific "Sake" (*Shaikh*) meaning "venerable one"—an epi-thet often adopted by upwardly mobile Muslims in India.

27. Portman Square (constructed 1764–84) was rising to its peak by 1806. It contained mansions of no less than forty of the nobility and several wealthy Nabobs—topped by Cochrane's. E. B. Chancellor, *History of the Squares* (1907), pp. 262–75. Other former British officials of the Company lived in the area. E.g., William Collin Jackson, *Memoir* (1809).

28. Thomas Smith, *Topographical* (1833), pp. 197–98.

29. Basil Cochrane, *Improvement* (1809), pp. 1–2.

30. Horatio Mahomed, *Bath* (1843), pp. 31–35.

31. Cochrane, *Improvement*, Plates 3, 7.

32. E.g., Sir Arthur Clarke, *Essay* (1813); Edward Kentish, *Essay* (1809); Robert James Culverwell, *Practical Treatise* (1829), pp. 39–40. Eventually, over seventy medical men attested in print to the virtues of Cochrane's method.

33. In early-nineteenth-century London, the neighboring Old and New Hummums provided baths, coffee, food, and lodging. See *Epicure's Almanack* (1815) and other directories.

34. See Metcalf, *Ideologies*; David Arnold, personal communication, October 1994.

35. Dean Mahomet's later repeated assertions that he had been practicing shampooing his entire time in Britain may have referred to his practice on pa-trons or family in Ireland. Nevertheless, the first strong evidence of his having done shampooing comes from his work in Cochrane's vapor bath.

36. Lucius Annaeus Seneca, *Epistles*, Letter 66; Marcus Valarius Martial, *Epi-grams*, Book 3, Epigram 82.

37. Khan, *Seir*, 2:365.

38. Raymond in Khan, *Seir*, n188. See also James Forbes, *Oriental Memoirs* (1834), 1:156, 350.

39. See Michael Lambton Este, *Remarks on Baths* (1811); William Cleoburey, *Full Account* (1825); *Times* (London), January 29, 1813, September 29, 1813, March 21, 1814; [Mrs. Clermont], *Observations* (1814).

40. Rate Books for Marylebone, 1808–14, MPL. There were then some two thousand coffeehouses and five thousand public houses in greater London. John Feltham, *Picture of London* (1810), p. 397; Ralph Nevill, *London Clubs* (1911), p. 3; Ellis Aytoun, *Penny Universities* (1956), p. xiv; Bryant Lillywhite, *London* (1963).

41. Victualler's Licence 1810–12, GLRO; Marylebone Rate Book 1810–12, MPL; *Holden's Directory* (1811). Charles Street is built over, but a Japanese restaurant, Yumi, stands near the site of the old Hindostanee Coffee House.

42. The British Government identified public houses with both political unrest and morally licentious behavior, leading in 1753 to a tougher Licencing Act. 26 George II c 31, revising 5 and 6 Edward II c 25; Victualler's Licences, GLRO.

43. See *Epicure's Almanack*, pp. 123–24; Charles Stewart, a veteran of India, called it the "Hooka Club" in his 1814 (but not 1810) translation of Khan, *Travels*, 1:124.

44. *Times* (London), March 27, 1811.

45. 35 George Street, Marylebone Rate Book 1811, MPL.

46. *Epicure's Almanack*, pp. 123–24.

47. Lillywhite, *London*, pp. 330–35, 395–403.

48. *Epicure's Almanack*, p. 31; Lillywhite, *London*, pp. 289–94.

49. E.g., Sarah Shade, the widow of a Sergeant, had lived for half a dozen years in India and then cooked Indian dishes for a living in London. Sarah Shade, *Narrative* (1801), p. 27.

50. Victualler's Licence 1811, GLRO; Marylebone Rate Book 1812, MPL.

51. Docket Book (B.4.31): Docquet, March 18, 1812, case of Dean Mahomet, Tavern Keeper, George Street, PRO.

52. *Epicure's Almanack*, pp. 123–24.

53. The Hindostan Coffee House was licensed by George Spencer and Richard Burton only in 1812. Victualler's Licence (1812), GLRO. The *British Imperial Calendar* and Feltham, *Picture*, identified the Hindoostanee Coffee House as continuing there from 1812 to 1833. Lillywhite missed the early years of what he called the "Hindoostance [sic] Coffee House," dating it 1819–33. Lillywhite, *London*, p. 269.

54. William (1797–1833) had at least seven children. Parish Records, St. Leonard's (Shoreditch), St. Botolph-without-Aldergate, St. Bartholomew the Great; Census of 1841, 1851, PRO.

55. *Times* (London), April 20, 1813.

56. Richard Russell, *Dissertation* (1752). See also Anthony Relhan, *Short History* (1762; reprint, 1829).

57. John George Bishop, *Peep into the Past* (1892), pp. 225–26. Hot and cold baths were established in Margate by the 1760s, Scarborough by 1798, and Weymouth by 1785. Sue Farrant, *Georgian Brighton* (1980), p. 15.

58. In 1803, John Williams built a hot and cold bath institution near Awsiter's;

Nathan Smith established his "Air Pump Vapour Bath" at Artillery Place on Brighton's West Cliff by 1806. Ralph Blegborough, *Facts and Observations* (1803); John Feltham, *Guide* (1806), p. 85.

59. Edward Brayley in John Nash, *Illustrations* (1838), p. 1.

60. See Sue Farrant, "Physical Development of the Royal Pavilion" (1992); and Henry D. Roberts, *History* (1959).

61. Dean Mahomet's earliest testimonials are dated Brighton, September 1814. This bathhouse was apparently attached to the New Steyne Hotel run by W. R. Mott; see S. D. Mahomed, *Cases Cured* (1820), pp. 28–29. Mott's New Steyne Hotel featured baths until 1818; see Feltham, *Guide* (1815), pp. 117–18; Brighton Commissioners, Minute Books, February 4, 1818.

62. Newspaper advertisement (early 1815) in John Ackerson Erredge, *History* (1862, grangerized edition), 4:149.

63. S. D. Mahomed, *Shampooing* (1826), pp. viii, 17. For an inventory of Dean Mahomet's equipment, see Lord Chamberlain's Accounts, LC/11/49: October 10, 1825, January 5, 1828, PRO.

64. H. Mahomed, *Bath*, pp. 54–58.

65. See identical advertisements throughout April 1815 in SWA.

66. Advertisement (late 1815) in Erredge, *History* (grangerized edition), 4:149.

67. Baptized March 26, 1815, St. Nicholas Parish Records.

68. See H. R. Atree, *Atree's Topography* (1809), p. 62; and John Bruce, *History* (1833), pp. 43, 91; Brighton Commissioners, Minute Books, September 10, 1823; Board of Ordinance Minutes, WO 55/1578(7) February 17, 1827 PRO (Kew).

69. November 17, 1816, August 2, 1818, December 28, 1819, and January 7, 1818 respectively; St. Nicholas (Brighton) Parish Records, ESRO.

70. C. Wright, *Brighton Ambulator* (1818), pp. 137–39. Guides had praised Dean Mahomet's Devonshire Place Baths. E.g., Feltham, *Guide* (1815), p. 118.

71. Robert James Culverwell, *Life* (1852), pp. 26–38.

72. S. D. Mahomed, *Shampooing* (1822), Preface; *British Traveller* (London), 6 January 1823. These statements have led most later commentators who mention or discuss Dean Mahomet's life in Brighton to date his arrival there to 1784 or soon thereafter. E.g., D. Robert Elleray, *Brighton* (1987); Sir Evan Cotton, "'Sake Deen Mahomed' of Brighton" (1939); Farrant, *Georgian*, p. 18; Clifford Musgrove, *Life in Brighton* (1970), pp. 203–5; Frederick Harrison and James Sharp North, *Old Brighton* (1937), p. 111.

73. E.g., John Aldini, *General* (1819); John G. Coffin, *Discourses* (1818); M.

La Beaume, *Observations* (1818); Charles Gower, *Auxiliaries* (1819); Theodore Hart, *Treatise* (1819); William Scott, *Proposal* (1820); Andre Louis Gosse, *Account* (1820).

74. Dean Mahomet announced Mahomed's Baths as opened in February 1821 but must have temporarily shifted again to West Cliff late that year. See advertisement for his West Cliff establishment, BG December 27, 1821.

75. John Gloag, *Mr. Loudon's England* (1970), pp. 200–201.

76. Newspaper clipping (1821) in Erredge, *History* (grangerized edition), 4:148.

77. Brighton Commissioners, "Minute Books," March 19, 1823, April 2, 1823, November 11, 1829, ESRO.

78. The sources for my composite are: Letter to the Editor from A. Monsieur, Dieppe, May 12, 1826, BG June 1, 1826; A. B. Granville, *Spas* (1841), 2:562–64; Advertisements for auction, BH September 18–October 16, 1841, July 8–29, 1843, August 5–12, 1843, April 24–May 8, 1847; and BG September 16–October 14, 1841, August 2–9, 1843.

79. The plan comes from Cochrane's 1809 work on baths for Middlesex Hospital. The basement, pipes, and bathing arrangements seem to be similar to Mahomed's Baths, although the latter had two floors of baths, no consulting room, and no "Russian" style baths. Cochrane, *Improvement*, Plate 5.

80. Dean Mahomet was the legal proprietor and occupier of this house from 1822 until (the records end in) 1831. Brighton Land Tax Records, ESRO. From July 1839 onward, Dean Mahomet and Jane used 2 Black Lion Street as their address. The census of June 6, 1841, however, located them as having spent the previous night at King's Road. Perhaps they had recently moved back temporarily so as to install baths in their Black Lion Street home. In October 1841 and August 1843, other people were established in the King's Road house. From September 1844 until their deaths, however, Dean Mahomet and Jane lived consistently on Black Lion Street.

81. Review of *Shampooing* in *Gentleman's Magazine* (1823), p. 162. Since Dean Mahomet's second book, *Shampooing*, about medicine, received such notice, but his first book, *Travels*, did not, we must conclude that the place of publication, subject matter, genre, changing times and tastes, or a combination of these made his second book more attractive to British society than his first.

82. Decisive legislation to professionalize the medical profession did not pass in Parliament until 1858. See M[ildred] Jeanne Peterson, *Medical Profession* (1978).

83. S. D. Mahomed, *Shampooing* (1822), Preface. Popham died in 1821.

84. See F. B. Smith, *People's Health* (1979), pp. 333–45.

85. Letter of his grandson, G. S. Mahomed, BH August 11, 1888 (my thanks to Rozina Visram for this citation). Cotton cites this tradition in his interview with another grandson, Reverend James Dean Kerriman. Cotton, "'Sake Deen Mahomed.'" Dean Mahomet did not serve in the Twenty-Seventh Regiment, but Captain Hugh Cossart Baker, with whom Dean Mahomet lived in Cork, was an officer in the Twenty-Seventh Regiment of the Royal Army.

86. George S. Mahomed, "Sake Deen Mahomed" (1940).

87. S. D. Mahomed, *Shampooing* (1826), Preface.

88. S. D. Mahomed, *Shampooing* (1826), Preface.

89. S. D. Mahomed, *Shampooing* (1826), Preface.

90. E.g., Granville, *Spas*, 2:562–64.

91. Brighton Town Rate Books (1824, 1827), BRL; Brighton Rate Books (1826), ESRO.

92. E.g., BG June 14, 1821, January 10, 1822.

93. E.g., E. Wallis, *Brighton Townsman* (c. 1826), p. 61; and Charles Marsh, *Clubs of London* (1828), 1:168ff.

94. E.g., BG December 27, 1821, March 28, 1822, April 4, 1822.

95. BG January 10, 1822.

96. BG September 25, 1823. Competitors elsewhere in England also imitated Dean Mahomet's claims. E.g., Seaman's advertisements in *St. James Chronicle*, March 12–28, 1835.

97. BG December 27, 1821; S. D. Mahomed, *Shampooing* (1826), pp. 49, 55; (1838), pp. 138–39; Mrs. Meer Hasan Ali describes indigenous Indian "wet" and "dry cupping," using a buffalo horn. *Observations* (1832), 2:42–43.

98. For example, King William took eighteen shampooing and vapor baths in September 1830. BG September 8–10, 1830. Lord Chamberlain's Accounts, LC/11/69, October 10, 1830; LC/3/69, Warrants and Appointments, fol. 161a, September 20, 1830, PRO.

99. E.g., Lord Chamberlain's Accounts, LC/11/49, October 10, 1825, January 5, 1828, PRO.

100. E.g., Dean Mahomet's bill for 22 baths at 6 shillings to 4 members of the royal household staff. Lord Chamberlain's Accounts, LC/11/49, October 10, 1825. See also LC/11/49, January 5, 1828, PRO. The Duke of Wellington's set was well represented among his patients. Arthur Wellesley, *Prime Minister's Papers* (1975), 1:341, 343. Lady Bedingfeld (Woman of the Bedchamber to Queen

Adelaide) recorded the medical treatment of Princess Louise of Saxe-Weimar and herself by courses of Vapour Baths and "rubbing" in the Pavilion, September–November 1831. Lady Jerningham, *Jerningham Letters* (1896), 2:348–50. Lord Seaford reported his course of treatment and that of his peers, Lady Wharncliffe, *First Lady Wharncliffe* (1927), 1:315. See the long lists of nobility and gentry in Mahomed's Visitor's Books, BRL.

101. E.g., Deenshah Firamgee, probably a Parsi from Bombay. Mahomed's Visitor's Books (c. January 1827), BRL.

102. BG December 28, 1826, January 4, 1827. Musgrove mentions this but misdates it. *Life*, p. 171.

103. BG August 19, 1830. For example, while Dean Mahomet was a registered voter from 1841 on, he did not actually vote in Parliamentary elections until 1847. Poll Books: Brighton, 1835–59; East Sussex 1832–37; Sussex 1820–41; Westminster 1841–52.

104. BG September 9, 1830. See also BG August 17, 1826 and September 15, 1831.

105. BG October 7, 1837.

106. BG March 24, 1825, February 10, 1831, February 9, 1832, January 11, 1834.

107. BG December 7–28, 1833; January 18, 1834; February 15, 1834; *Brighton Guardian*, February 26, 1851.

108. Marsh, *Clubs*, 1:171–77.

109. Anthony Dale, *Brighton Town* (1976), p. 199; Brighton Commissioners, Minute Books, August 27, 1828, ESRO.

110. BH September 23, 1837; Brighton Commissioners, Minute Books, March 18, 1829, November 11, 1829, November 3, 1830, August 29, 1832, September 19, 1832, ESRO.

111. BH March 17, 1838.

112. [Isaac] Robert Cruikshank, *Brighton!!* (1830), p. 13; Charles Dickens, *Dombey and Son* (reprint, 1846–48), p. 101; Richard R. Madden, *Travels* (1829), 1:64–65; Marsh, *Clubs*, 1:168ff; Horace Smith, ed., *Comic Miscellanies* (1841), 1:330–33; George Augustus Sala, *Life and Adventures* (1895), 1:201–2; [Charles Malloy Wesmacott] Bernard Blackmantle, "Brighton Misnomers," BG April 27, 1826, and *English Spy* (1825), 1:345.

113. John Shaw, Letter, BG December 13, 1821; Poem of John Hills cited in S. D. Mahomed, *Shampooing*, (1838), pp. 124–27.

114. Horace Smith Letter (1828), Arthur H. Beavan, *James and Horace Smith* (1899), p. 280.

115. Granville, *Spas*, 2:562–64.

116. BG April 3, 1828–December 3, 1829; S. D. Mahomed, *Shampooing* (1838), pp. 138–39; Westminster Rate Books, 1830–35, WPL; St. James (Westminster) Parish Records, December 25, 1834, WPL.

117. Westminster Rate Books 1836, 1837, WPL.

118. BH June 30, 1838; S. D. Mahomed, *Shampooing* (1838), endmatter.

119. Horatio took over their operation almost entirely from about 1843 onward and remained there until 1858 when the Metropolitan Bath Company hired him as its "Resident Manager." In 1859, Horatio opened a small bath at his home in 42 Somerset Street near Portman Square where he remained until his death in 1873. Horatio Mahomed, *Bath*; and Horatio Mahomed, *Short Hints on Bathing* (1844). Westminster Rate Books, 1859–73, WPL.

120. Census figures in Henry Martin, *History* (1871), p. 26.

121. Brighton Valuation Registers 1846, 1848; Brighton Town Rate Book 1851, BRL.

122. BH October 5–19, 1844. Knight gave up this bath in 1848. An established swimming bath company, Brill, took possession and renamed it Brill's Shampooing Baths. In 1870, Markwell's hotel took over the site but was itself absorbed into the Queen's Hotel in 1908, which remains there today. In the 1970s, this hotel sought to market his name by installing a "Sake Dene Cocktail Lounge."

123. BH May 15, 1847.

124. BH September 28, 1844, October 5–18, 1844.

125. E.g., BH October 18, 1845; 1841 Census. Arthur ran this reduced bathing establishment there and later a few blocks away (64 West Street), apparently until his death in 1872. Advertisement (c. 1853) and Testimonial (October 30, 1854) in Mahomed's Visitor's Book, BRL.

126. *Brighton Guardian* February 26, 1851; BG February 27, 1851; *Gentleman's Magazine* April 1851, p. 444b; Willis, *Willis' Current Notes* (March 1851), pp. 22–23.

127. For discussion of "contact literatures," see Ron Carter, "A Question of Interpretation" (1986).

128. Said, *Culture and Imperialism*, p. 15.

129. Shampooing came to mean hair-wash only from the 1860s. For various

assertions about the British origins of the Turkish Bath, see Charles Bartholomew, *Turkish Bath* (1871); Richard Beamish, *Lecture* (1859); Robert James Culverwell, *Few Practical Observations* (n.d.); Diogenes [pseudonym], *Life in a Tub* (1858); Bartholomew de Dominiceti, *To the Public* (1764), and *Plan for Extending* (1771); John Gibney, *Treatise* (1825); Jonathan Green, *Short Illustration* (1825); James Lawrie, *Roman or Turkish Bath* (1864); Madden, *Travels*; Photophilus [pseudonym], *New Irish Bath* (1860); James Playfair, *Method of Construction* (1783); W. Gordon Stables, *Turkish and other Baths* (1882); John Symons, *Observations on Vapor-Bathing* (1766); David Urquhart, *Pillars of Hercules* (1850), *Turkish Bath* (1856), pp. 6, 27, and *Manual of the Turkish Bath* (1865); Henry Weekes, *Warm Water Remedy* (1844); Charles Whitlaw, *Scriptural Code of Health* (1838); John Wynter, *Of Bathing in the Hot-baths, at Bathe* (1728).

130. E.g., Edith Ohlson, Letter to the Editor, *Sussex County Magazine*, 9 (January–December 1935), p. 331.

131. Personal communication from J. Stewart Cameron, April 21, 1995. See his article with Jackie Hicks on Frederick Akbar Mahomed in *Kidney International* (1996).

132. See Visram, *Ayahs*, pp. 64–67; Guptara, *Black British*.

133. Dean Mahomet appears, for example, in a visual presentation at Liverpool's Trans-Atlantic Slave Trade Museum; he had no connection with the slave trade or the movement for its abolition.

134. Said, *Culture and Imperialism*, p. xx.

GLOSSARY

AREK [*Areca Catechu*]. The areca nut.

ARRACK [*araq*]. A palm tree liquor.

ASSAMMEE [*asami*]. A dealer or broker.*

AUMNOOZE [perhaps *amruda*]. The guava tree.

BAFFETY [*baft*]. A type of woven cloth.

BAHAREA [*bhari*]. A man who works as a carrier.

BANG. Cannabis extract.*

BANGALO. Bungalow, a Bengal-style house, usually single storied.

BANIAN [Ficus Indica]. The fig tree.

BANYAN [*baniya jati*]. A Hindu merchant caste.

BASLEEWALLA [*banri-wala*]. A flute player.

BAUDSHAW [*badshah*]. An Emperor.*

BAUDSHAWJODDI [*badshah-zadi*]. An Emperor's daughter.*

BELTON [bell-tent]. A bell-shaped military tent.

BESTIE [*bihishti*]. Water carrier.

BICE [*Vaishya varna*]. A merchant caste.

BOWBERCHEE [*bawar-chi*]. A cook.

BRAMA [*Brahma*]. The Hindu God of Creation.

BRAMIN, BRAHMIN [*Brahmin varna*]. The highest caste among Hindus.

BUCKSERRIA [*buxaria*]. A type of soldier recruited near Buxar.*

BUCKSHAW. Dried fish, a. k. a. "Bombay Duck."

BURKENDAWS [*barq-andaz*, lightning thrower]. A type of Indian infantryman.

BUXEY [*bakhshi*]. A paymaster.*

*This term also appears in Dean Mahomet's own glossary (Letter XVI).

CACHOONDA. An astringent.

CAFFRES [Kafir]. A non-Muslim African, originally a tribe's name.*

CARCANET. An ornamental necklace.

CATCHOO [*catechu*]. An astringent.

CAWN [*khan*]. A title or honorific, meaning Lord.

CEESOE [*siso*, Dalbergia Sisso]. A type of tree.

CHARWALLEY, CHERWALLEE [probably *charawaha jati*]. A grass/fodder cutter caste.

CHAUMNIE [*chhaoni*]. A thatched barracks.

CHEEQUE [*chiq*]. A bamboo screen.

CHEMARS [*Chamar jati*]. A leather-worker caste.

CHILM, HOOKA. Tobacco and the vessel in which it burns.

CHOKEEDAR [*chauki-dar*]. A watch-keeper.

CHOP [*chap*]. A personal seal.*

CHOPDAR [*chob-dar*]. A silver staff-bearer.

CHOUK [*chauk*]. A marketplace.

CHUNAM. Mineral lime.

CIRCAR [*sarkar*]. An Indian accountant.

CIRCARGA [perhaps *shikar-gah*]. A hunting park.

CODGI [*qazi*]. A Muslim judge.

COMEDAN [*komidan*]. An Indian Captain or Commandant.

CONSUMMA [*khan-saman*, master of supplies]. A majordomo.

COOLEY [coolie]. A manual laborer.

COSS [*kos*]. A measure of distance, about two miles.

COSSID [*kasid*]. A foot messenger.*

COWLE [*qaul*]. A surety or bond.*

DAWGAH [*darogha*]. A superintendent.*

DECOYT [*dakait*]. A gang robber.*

DERAWAN [*darwan*]. A doorkeeper.

DEWALLI [*Diwali*]. The Hindu festival of lights.

DIVAN, DIWAN [*diwan*]. A ruler's levee or audience hall.

DOMERAH [Dom *jati* or tribe]. A sweeper caste.

DOOLEY [*doli*]. A covered litter or sedan chair.*

DURBAR [*darbar*]. A ruler's court or throne room.

DUSTUK [*dastak*]. A permit or order.*

ENGLISH EAST INDIA COMPANY (1600–1858). Officially the United Company of the Merchants of England Trading to the East Indies; a joint stock corporation increasingly, after 1773, under the control of the British Parliament but also, from 1772, an officeholder in the Mughal Empire.

FAQUIR, FAQIR. Religious ascetic or mendicant, often a Muslim.

FILLIGRANE. Filigree work.

FOUZDAR [*faujdar*]. An Indian police commandant.

GAUT [*ghat*]. Waterfront steps.

GINANAH [*zenana*]. Women or women's quarters.*

GOOLDBUDTHEN [gul-budan, rose-bodied]. A type of cloth.

GOOLMORES, GOULMORES [gold *muhr*]. A coin worth Rupees 16.

GOUWARRAH [*gahawara*]. A Dhaka term for *taziya*, model tombs of Shiite martyrs.

GULLENDAS [*gol-andaz*, ball-thrower]. The artillery or an artilleryman.

GUSSEARA [*ghasiyara*]. A grass cutter.

HAJAM [*hajjam*]. A barber and surgeon.

HALCARAH, HALCORAH [*harkara*]. A man of all work, often a herald or messenger.

HANPACALLIE [hand-*pakhali*]. A water bag carried by a man instead of a bullock.

HARAM [*harem*]. Women's quarters, the wives of a man.

HOAKHA [*huqqa*]. A hooka, water pipe.

HOMALDAR [*amildar*, standard-bearer]. An Indian corporal, more commonly naik.

HOOKEBURDAR [*huqqa-bardar*]. A servant who tends a hooka.

HOTTEEWALLIE [*hathi-wala*]. An elephant keeper.

HOWALDAR [*havildar*]. An Indian sergeant.

HUMMUM [*hamam*]. An Indian or Turkish-style steam bath.

JAGGERNAUT [Jagan-nath, Lord of the World]. The Hindu God Krishna, whose major temple is at Puri, in Orissa.

JAGREE [*jagri*]. Palm-sap sugar.

JAIR [Jain]. A religious tradition advocating total nonviolence.

JANISSARIES. Turkish slave-soldiers.

JATI [birth]. Hindu caste.

JATS. A jati of agriculturalists.

JEMADAR, JEMMAUTDAR [*jam'dar*]. A leader of a body of men or Indian ensign.

JESSAMINE, JESSAMY. The jasmine plant and flower.

JOW [*juwar*]. An Indian millet.

KEEMCAUS [*kam-khab*]. Brocade cloth.

KILLEDAR [*qiladar*]. A fort-governor.*

KISTBUNDEE [*qistbandi*]. Assessed land revenue.*

KIZMUTGAUR [*khidmatgar*]. A serving man.

LACK [*lakh*]. A hundred thousand.

LASCAR [*lashkar*, army]. A camp worker or Indian sailor.

MAZIDE [*musjid*]. A mosque.

MEANAH [*mena*]. A curtained palanquin.

MOGREE [*mogra*]. Jasmine.

MOGUL. Mughal Empire, Muslim dynasty which ruled most of India (1526–1858), the final hundred and fifty years only nominally.

MOORIE [*muharrir*]. An Indian clerk.*

MORATTOES. Marathas, a jati of agriculturalists from west-central India who formed the core of an expansive state in the seventeenth and eighteenth centuries.

MUCHULCA [*mucalka*]. A bond.*

MULNA [*maulana*]. A Muslim cleric.

MUSSALCHEES [*mashal-chi*]. A torchbearer.

MUSSULMEN. Muslims, followers of Islam.

NABOB [*Nawab*]. A provincial governor or, derived from that, a rich, India-returned European.

NAKEEVE [*naqib*]. A herald.

OFFDAUR [*ab-dar*]. A water bearer.

OMRAH [*umara*]. A nobleman or high official.

PAISSAY [copper *paisa*]. A coin, sixty-four per Rupee.

PALANKEEN [*palki*]. A palanquin.

PATAMAR [*pattamar*]. A postman.*

PATAN [Pathan]. An Afghan ethnicity.

PELOU [*pulao*]. Pilaf, a rice dish cooked with meat.

PEON. A foot soldier or footman.

PERGANNAH [*pargana*]. A district.

PETTAH [*patta*]. A grant.*

PETTAH [*pettai*]. A village.

PIADA [*piyada*]. A foot messenger.

PONSWAY [*pansoi*]. A type of river vessel.*

PURDOE [*parda*]. A curtain, the seclusion of women.

RAFFTANNY [*raftani*]. Exports.*

RAJPUT. A warrior jati or caste.

ROHELLA. Rohilla, an Afghan ethnicity, with a polity in the upper Ganges plain.

ROUTEREN [*Rudra*]. Shiva, the Hindu God of Destruction.

ROYRAN [*rae rayan*, king of kings]. A revenue-collection official.*

SAHIES [*sais*]. A horse-groom.

SAIKS [Sikhs]. A religious community, based in Punjab.

SAKE [*shaikh*]. An honorific meaning "venerable one."

SAMSUNDAR [*sham sundar*, Dark Beauty]. A processional barge.

SEAPOY, SEPOY [*sipahi*]. An Indian infantryman, trained, dressed, and armed in a semi-European manner.

SEMIANA [*shamiyana*]. An awning.

SERAGLIO. Women's quarters.

SERAI [*sarai*]. A traveler's rest house.

SHAMPOOING [imperative of verb *champi*, to massage]. Therapeutic massage.

SIRPAH [*sar-o-pa*]. A head to foot honorific dress.*

SITTRI [*Kshatriya varna*]. The warrior caste.

SOTIBURDAR [*sonta-bardar*]. A mace bearer.

SOUBAH [*suba-dar*]. A provincial governor.

SUBIDAR, SUBEDAR [*suba-dar*]. An Indian lieutenant.

SUDDER [*Shudra varna*]. A servant and agriculturalist caste.

SURMA. Antimony.

TANKA, TUNKAH [*tankhwah*]. A revenue assignment.

TARGET. A round shield.

TELINGA. The region, and people from, the Deccan region of Central India.

TODDY [*tari*]. A palm tree and alcohol made from its sap; also the birds which frequent the tree.

TOMBOO [*tambu*]. Pavilion or canopy.

TOMBOURWALLA [*tambur-wala*]. An Indian drummer.

TOPASSI [*topasi*]. A type of soldier with mixed European and Indian traditions.*

TROOHEWALLA [*turhi-wala*]. An Indian trumpeter.

TUM-TUM [*tamtam*]. An Indian drum.

TURSACONNA [*toshak-khana*]. A wardrobe room.*

VAKEEL [*wakil*]. A trusted agent.*

VARNA [color]. A Hindu caste-grouping.

VIZERUT [*wazirat*]. Office of chief minister of state.*

WHISTNOW [Vishnu]. The Hindu God of Preservation.

WOOPTONG [*ubtan*]. Paste bath of meal and mustard oil.

ZEMINDAR [*zamin-dar*]. A landholder.

ZENANAH, ZANNANAH [*zenana*]. Women or women's quarters.

ABBREVIATIONS

BRL	Brighton Reference Library
CoD	Court of Directors of the English East India Company
ESRO	East Sussex Record Office
FTWM	Fort William-India House Correspondence
GLRO	Greater London Record Office
IOL	India Office Library, British Museum
MPL	Marylebone Public Library
PRO	Public Record Office of England (Chancery Lane)
PRO Ireland	Public Record Office of Ireland
PRO (Kew)	Public Record Office of England (Kew)
WPL	Westminster Public Library

BIBLIOGRAPHY

MANUSCRIPT SOURCES

BMC = Bengal Military Consultations, IOL.

BMCG = Bengal Military Consultations, General Department, NAI.

Board of Ordinance, Minutes, PRO (Kew).

BPbC = Bengal Public Consultations, IOL.

Brighton Commissioners, Minute Books, ESRO.

Brighton Land Tax Records, ESRO.

Brighton Rate Books, ESRO.

Brighton Town Rate Books, BRL.

Brighton Valuation Registers, BRL.

BSC = Bengal Secret Consultations, IOL.

BSMC = Bengal Secret and Military Consultations, IOL.

Docket Book (B.4.31), PRO.

Foreign Department Consultations, IOL.

Foreign Secret, Original Consultations, NAI.

GOCC = General Orders of the Commander-in-Chief, NAI.

Great Britain, Census 1841, 1851, 1861, 1871, 1881, 1891, PRO.

GRT = General Return of Troops, Fort William, NAI.

HMS = Home Miscellaneous Series, IOL.

Index to Marriage Licence Bonds, PRO Ireland.

Lord Chamberlain's Accounts, PRO.

Madras Military Consultations, IOL.

Mahomed's Visitor's Books, BRL.

Marylebone Parish Register, GLRO.

Military Consultations, NAI.

Minutes of the CoD, IOL.

Patna Factory Records, IOL.

Persian Correspondence, Translations of Issues, NAI.

Rate Books for Marylebone, MPL.

St. Bartholomew the Great Parish Records, Guildhall.

St. Botolph-without-Aldergate Parish Records, Guildhall.

St. James (Westminster) Parish Records, WPL.

St. Leonard's (Shoreditch) Parish Records, Guildhall.

St. Nicholas (Brighton) Parish Records, ESRO.

Victualler's Licence Register of all the Innkeepers' and Alehouse Keepers' Recognizances within the Division of Holborn taken at the General Meeting of the Justices, GLRO.

Westminster Rate Books, 1830–35, WPL.

PERIODICALS

BG = *Brighton Gazette*.

BH = *Brighton Herald*.

Brighton Guardian.

British Imperial Calendar.

British Medical Journal.

British Traveller (London).

CA = *Cork Advertizer*.

CG = *Cork Gazette*.

Guy's Hospital Reports.

HC = *Hibernian Chronicle*.

Holden's Directory.

Monthly Review.

NCEP = *New Cork Evening Post*.

St. James Chronicle.

Sussex County Magazine.

SWA = *Sussex Weekly Advertizer*.

Times (London).

Volunteer Journal.

BOOKS AND ARTICLES

Abul Fazl Allami. *Ain-i Akbari.* Translated by H. S. Jarrett, edited by Jadunath Sarkar. Reprint, New Delhi: Crown Publications, 1988.

Abu-Lughod, Ibrahim. *The Arab Rediscovery of Europe.* Princeton: Princeton University Press, 1963.

Achmet, Dr. *The Theory and Uses of Baths, Being an extract from the Essay on Waters by the late Charles Lucas, Esq., M.D. With Marginal Notes by Dr. Achmet.* Dublin: J. Potts, 1772.

———. "To the Committee of Physicians and Surgeons who were appointed by the whole faculty upon the 19th of August 1771." Broadsheet of proposed rules. Dublin: Achmet, 1773.

Adams, Percy G. *Travelers and Travel Liars, 1660–1800.* Berkeley: University of California Press, 1962.

———. *Travel Literature and the Evolution of the Novel.* Lexington, Ky.: University Press of Kentucky, 1983.

Alavi, Seema. *The Sepoys and the Company: Tradition and Transition in Northern India, 1770–1830.* Delhi: Oxford University Press, 1995.

Aldini, John. *General Views on the Application of Galvanism to Medical Purposes.* London: J. Callow, 1819.

Atree, H. R. *Atree's Topography of Brighton.* Brighton: The Author, 1809.

Aytoun, Ellis. *The Penny Universities: A History of the Coffee-Houses.* London: Secker and Warburg, 1956.

"Baptisms in Calcutta." *Bengal Past and Present* 28 (1924): 199.

Bartholomew, Charles. *The Turkish Bath . . . Evidence before the Doctors on the Prevention and Cure of Diseases by the Use of the Turkish, Oxygen, Ozone, and Electric Baths, and Medicated Atmospheres.* 6th edition. Bristol: The Author [1871].

Bayly, C. A. *Indian Society and the Making of the British Empire.* Cambridge: Cambridge University Press, 1988.

Beamish, Richard. *Lecture, Delivered at the Literary and Scientific Society of Cheltenham and Gloster, On the Functions of the Skin and the Value of the Bath, with special reference to the Improved Turkish Bath.* London: H. Bailliers, 1859.

Beavan, Arthur H. *James and Horace Smith.* London: Hurst and Blackett, 1899.

Beckett, J. C. *The Making of Modern Ireland, 1603–1923*. New York: Alfred A. Knopf, 1966.

Bence-Jones, Mark. *A Guide to Irish Country Houses*. London: Constable, 1978.

Berthou and Georges. *Album de Brighton*. Brighton: Berthou and Georges, 1838.

Bhabha, Homi. "Signs Taken for Wonders." In *"Race," Writing, and Difference*, edited by Henry Gates. Chicago: University of Chicago Press, 1985.

———. *The Location of Culture*. New York: Routledge, 1994.

Bickerstaff, Isaac. *The Sultan; or, a Peep into a Seraglio, A Farce, in Two Acts*. London: Theatre Royal, 1785.

Bishop, John George. *A Peep into the Past: Brighton in the Olden Time with Glances at the Present*. Brighton: J. G. Bishop, 1892.

Blackmantle, Bernard [Charles Malloy Wesmacott]. *The English Spy: An Original Work, Characteristic, Satirical, and Humerous*. 2 volumes. London: Sherwood, Jones, 1825.

Blegborough, Ralph. *Facts and Observations respecting the Air-Pump Vapour Bath in Gout . . . and other Diseases*. London: Lackington, Allen, 1803.

Broome, Arthur. *History of the Rise and Progress of the Bengal Army*. Volume 1. Calcutta: W. Thacker, 1850.

[Broun, Thomas]. *Brighton, or, They Steyne: A Satirical Novel*. 3 volumes. 2d edition. London: The Author, 1818.

Bruce, John. *The History of Brighton*. Brighton: John Bruce, 1833.

Burke, John Bernard. *Burke's Irish Family Records*. London: Burke's Peerage, 1976.

———. *Burke's Irish Peerage*. London: Burke's Peerage, 1976.

Callahan, Raymond. *The East India Company and Army Reform, 1783–1798*. Harvard Historical Monographs 67. Cambridge: Harvard University Press, 1972.

Cameron, J. Stewart, and Jackie Hicks. "Frederick Akbar Mahomed." *Kidney International* 49(1996): 1488–1506.

Caraccioli, Charles. *The Life of Robert, Lord Clive, Baron Plassey*. 4 volumes. London: T. Bell, 1775–77.

Carter, Ron. "A Question of Interpretation: An Overview of Some Recent Developments in Stylistics." In *Linguistics and the Study of Literature*, edited by Theo D'hean, 7–26. Amsterdam: Rodopi, 1986.

Chakrabarti, Shubhra. "Collaboration and Resistance: Bengal Merchants and the English East India Company, 1757–1833," *Studies in History* 10, 1 n.s. (1994): 105–29.

Chancellor, E. B. *History of the Squares of London*. London: K. Paul, Trench, and Trubner, 1907.

Clarke, Sir Arthur. *An Essay on Warm, Cold, and Vapour Bathing, with Practical Observations on Sea Bathing, Diseases of the Skin, Bilious, Liver Complaints, and Dropsy.* London: Henry Colburn, 1813.

Cleoburey, William. *A Full Account of the System of Friction: As Adopted and Pursued with the greatest success in cases of contracted joints and lameness from various causes.* 3d edition. Oxford: Munday and Slatter, 1825.

[Clermont, Mrs.]. *Observations on the Use of the Vapour, Tepid, and Other Baths.* London: The Author, 1814.

Cochrane, Basil. *An Improvement on the Mode of Administering the Vapour Bath, and the Apparatus Connected with It.* London: John Booth, 1809.

Coffin, John G. *Discourses on Cold and Warm Bathing.* Boston: John Eliot, 1818. Also published in 1826.

Colley, Linda. *Britons.* New Haven: Yale University Press, 1992.

Cork Corporation. *Council Book of the Corporation of the City of Cork, from 1609 to 1643, and from 1690 to 1800.* Cork: J. Billing and Sons, 1876.

Cotton, Sir Evan. "'Sake Deen Mahomed' of Brighton." *Sussex County Magazine* 13 (1939): 746–50.

Cruikshank, [Isaac] Robert. *Brighton!! A Comic Sketch.* London: William Kidd, 1830.

Culverwell, Robert James. *A Few Practical Observations on Warm, Vapour, Shampooing, Sulphur-Fumigating, and Medicated Bathing.* London: The Author, n.d.

———. *A Practical Treatise on Bathing; with Observations on Cold, Warm, Shampooing, Vapour, Sulfur, Harrowgate, and other Baths.* London: The Author, 1829.

———. *The Life of Dr. Culverwell, written by himself.* London: The Author, 1852.

Dale, Anthony. *Brighton Town and Brighton People.* London: Phillamore, 1976.

Dale, Stephen F., "Steppe Humanism." *International Journal of Middle East Studies* 22, no. 1 (February 1990): 37–58.

Daniell, Thomas and William. *Antiquities of India.* London: T. and W. Daniell, 1799.

———. *Oriental Scenery: One Hundred and Fifty Views.* London: T. and W. Daniell, 1816.

Das, Harihar. "The Early Indian Visitors to England." *Calcutta Review* 3d series 13 (1924): 83–114.

Dickens, Charles. *Dombey and Son.* Reprint, London: Bradbury and Evans, 1846–48.

Digby, Simon, "An Eighteenth Century Narrative of a Journey from Bengal to England: Munshi Isma'il's *New History*." In *Urdu and Muslim South Asia: Stud-*

ies in Honour of Ralph Russell, edited by Christopher Shackle, 49–65. London: School of Oriental and African Studies, University of London, 1989.

Diogenes [pseudonym]. *Life in a Tub, with a Description of the Turkish Bath.* 3d edition. Dublin: William McGee, 1858.

Dodwell, Henry. *Sepoy Recruitment in the Old Madras Army.* Calcutta: Superintendent Government Printing, 1922.

Dominiceti, Bartholomew de. *To the Public Tract expanding on an address of Doctor De Dominiceti of Chelsea to the Royal Society and the College of Physicians of London.* London: The Author, 1764.

———. *Plan for extending the use of Artificial Water Baths, Pumps, Vaporous and Dry Baths,, Fumigations, and Frictions by the mode and means invented and directed by Doctor Bartholomew de Dominiceti.* London: The Author, 1771.

Dyce Sombre, David Octerlony. *Dyce Sombre against Troup, Solaroli (Intervening) and Prinsep and the Hon. East India Company (also Intervening) in the Goods of David Octerlony Dyce Sombre, Esq., Deceased, In the Prerogative Court of Canterbury.* London: Henry Hansard, n.d.

———. *Refutation of the Charges of Lunacy in the Court of Chancery.* Paris: Dyce Sombre, 1849.

East India Company. *List of the Company's Civil Servants.* London: East India Company, 1771.

Elleray, D. Robert, A. L. A. *Brighton, A Pictorial History.* Chichester: Phillimore, 1987.

Epicure's Almanack; or, Calendar of Good Living Containing A Directory of the Taverns, Coffee-Houses, Inns, Eating houses, and Other Places of Alimentary Resort . . . A Review of Artists who administer to the Wants and Enjoyment of the Table. London: Longman, Hurst, Rees, Orme, and Brown, 1815.

Equiano, Olaudah. *The Interesting Narrative of the Life of Olaudah Equiano, or Gustavus Vassa, the African. Written by Himself.* Leeds: James Nichols, 1814.

Erredge, John Ackerson. *History of Brighthelmston: Brighton as I View it, and as Others Knew it.* Grangerized edition. Brighton: E. Lewis, 1862.

Este, Michael Lambton. *Remarks on baths: water, swimming, shampooing, heat, hot, cold, and vapor baths.* London: J. Ridgway, 1811. Also published in 1812, 1845.

Farrant, Sue. *Georgian Brighton, 1740–1820.* University of Sussex Centre for Continuing Education Occasional Papers 13. Lewes: University of Sussex, 1980.

———. "The Physical Development of the Royal Pavilion Estate and Its Influence on Brighton (E. Sussex) 1785–1823." *Sussex Archaelogical Collections* 130 (1992): 171–84.

Feldbaek, Ole. *India Trade under the Danish Flag, 1772–1808*. Copenhagen: Studentlitteratur, 1969.

Feltham, John. *Guide to All the Watering and Sea Bathing Places*. London: Longman, Hurst, Rees, Orme, and Brown, 1806–15.

———. *Picture of London*. London: Longman, Hurst, Rees, Orme, Browne and Green, 1806–32.

Ffolliott, Rosemary, compiler. *Biographical notices (primarily relating to counties Cork and Kerry) collected from newspapers, 1756–1827 with a few references 1749–1755*. Fethard, Tipperary: Glebe House, 1980.

Fisher, Michael H. *Politics of the British Annexation of India*. Delhi: Oxford University Press, 1993.

Fisher, Michael H., and Dean Mahomed. *The First Indian Author in English*. Delhi: Oxford University Press, 1996.

Forbes, James. *Oriental Memoirs; A Narrative of Seventeen Years Residence in India*. 2 volumes. London: Richard Bentley, 1834.

Fryer, Peter. *Staying Power: The History of Black People in Britain*. London: Pluto, 1992.

Gates, Henry Louis, Jr., ed. *The Classic Slave Narratives*. New York: Mentor, 1987.

———. "James Gronniosaw and the Trope of the Talking Book." In *Studies in Autobiography*, edited by James Olney, 51–72. New York: Oxford University Press, 1988.

Gibbon, Edward. *The Decline and Fall of the Roman Empire*. London: The Author, 1776–86.

Gibney, John. *A Treatise on the Properties and Medical Application of the Vapour Bath in Its Different Varieties, and their Effects*. London: Knight and Lacey, 1825.

Gibson, Charles Bernard. *The History of the County and City of Cork*. 2 volumes. London: T. C. Newby, 1861.

Gilbert, Arthur N. "Recruitment and Reform in the East India Company Army, 1760–1800," *Journal of British Studies* 15 (1975): 89–111.

Gloag, John. *Mr. Loudon's England; The Life and Work of John Claudius Loudon*. Newcastle: Oriel, 1970.

Gosse, Andre Louis. *Account of a Visit made to the Baths of St. Filippo in Tuscany*. Edinburgh: Printed for A. Constable, 1820.

Gower, Charles, M. D. *Auxiliaries to Medicine: In Four Tracts*. London: J. Hubbard, 1819.

Grace, Henry. *The Code of Military Standing Regulations of the Bengal Establishment*. Calcutta: Cooper and Upjohn, 1791.

Granville, A. B. *The Spas of England, and Principal Sea Bathing Places.* Volume 2. London: Henry Colburn, 1841.

Great Britain, Parliament. "An Account of the Number of Non-Commissioned Officers and Private Men sent to the East Indies from September 1762 to September 1772." *Eighth Report from the Committee of Secrecy.* 25 May 1773.

Green, Jonathan. *Short Illustration of the Advantages derived by the use of Sulphurous Fumigating, Hot Air and Vapour Baths in a variety of Obstinate Diseases.* London: The Author, 1825.

Grose, John Henry. *A Voyage to the East Indies with Observations.* London: S. Hooper and A. Morley, 1766. Also published in 1757, 1772.

Grunebaum, Gustav E. von. *Medieval Islam.* Chicago: University of Chicago Press, 1953.

Guha, Ranajit, et al., eds. *Subaltern Studies.* Volumes 1–8. Delhi: Oxford University Press, 1982–94.

Guptara, Prabhu. *Black British Literature: An Annotated Bibliography.* Sidney: Dangaroo Press, 1986.

Habib, Irfan. *The Agrarian System of Mughal India.* New York: Asia, 1963.

Harrison, Frederick, and James Sharp North. *Old Brighton, Old Preston, Old Hove.* 1937. Reprint, Hassocks, Sussex: Flare, 1974.

Hart, Theodore. *Treatise on the Dry Sulphuric Baths: with Observations on the Treatment and Cure of Psora.* London: George Taylor, 1819.

Hastings, Warren. *A Narrative of the Insurrection which happened in the Zemeedary of Banaris in the month of August 1781: and of the transactions of the Governor-General in that district; with an appendix of authentic papers and affidavits.* Calcutta: Governor General, 1782.

———. *Memoirs of the Life of the Right Hon. Warren Hastings, First Governor-General of Bengal, compiled from Original Papers,* edited by G. R Gleig. 3 volumes. London: Richard Bentley, 1841.

Hecht, J. Jean. *Continental and Colonial Servants in Eighteenth Century England.* Smith College Studies in History 40. Northampton: Smith College, 1954.

Hickey, William. *Memoirs of William Hickey.* 4 volumes. Edited by Alfred Spencer. 3d edition. London: Hurst and Blackett, 1919–25.

Hoare, Sir Richard Colt. *Journal of a Tour in Ireland, A.D. 1806.* London: W. Miller, 1807.

Holzman, James Mayer. *Nabobs in England, a Study of the Returned Anglo-Indian, 1760–1785.* New York: The Author, 1926.

Horsfield, Thomas Walker. *History, Antiquities, and Topography of the County of Sussex.* 2 volumes. Sussex: Lewes Press, 1835.

Jackson, William Collin. *Memoir of the Public Conduct and Services of William Collin Jackson, Senior Merchant on the Company's Madras Establishment.* London: The Author, 1809.

Jerningham, Lady. *The Jerningham Letters (1780–1843).* 2 volumes. Edited by Egerton Castle. London: Richard Bentley and Son, 1896.

Kakar, Sudhir. *The Inner World.* 2d edition. New York: Oxford University Press, 1981.

Kakar, Sudhir, ed. *Identity and Adulthood.* New York: Oxford University Press, 1992.

Kentish, Edward. *Essay on Warm and Vapour Bathing: With Hints for a new Mode of applying Heat and Cold, for the Cure of Diseases and the Preservation of Health, Illustrated by Cases.* 2d edition. London: Joseph Mawman, 1809. 3d edition 1813.

Khan, Abu Taleb. *Travels of Mirza Abu Taleb Khan in Asia, Africa, and Europe during the years 1799, 1800, 1801, 1802, and 1803; Written by Himself in the Persian Language.* 2 volumes. Translated by Charles Stewart. London: Longman, Hurst, Rees, and Orme, 1814. Also published in 1810.

Khan, Abu Talib. "Masir Talibi fi Bilad Afranji." 3 volumes. BM Add 8145–47, IOL.

Khan, Mirza Abul Hassan. *A Persian at the Court of King George, 1809–10.* Translated and edited by Margaret Morris Cloake. London: Barrie and Jenkins, 1988.

Khan, Sayid Ghulam Husain. *The Seir Mutaqherin.* 4 volumes. Translated by M. Raymond. Reprint, Calcutta: T. D. Chatterjee, 1902.

Kindersley, [Jemima]. *Letters from the Island of Teneriffe, Brazil, the Cape of Good Hope, and the East Indies.* London: Norse, 1777.

Knox, John. *A New Collection of Voyages, Discoveries and Travels.* London: John Knox, 1767.

Kolff, Dirk H. A. *Naukar, Rajput and Sepoy: The Ethnohistory of the Military Labour Market in Hindustan, 1450–1850.* Cambridge: Cambridge University Press, 1990.

La Beaume, M. *Observations on the Properties of the Air-Pump Vapour-Bath, pointing out their efficacy in the cure of Gout, Rheumatism, Palsy, etc. with cursory remarks on factitious airs, and on the improved state of Medical Electricity, in all its branches, particularly in that of Galvanism.* London: The Author, 1818.

Lawrie, James. *The Roman or Turkish Bath: Together with Barege, Medicated, Galvanic, and Hydropathic Baths.* Edinburgh: Maclachlan and Stewart, 1864.

Leigh, Samuel. *New Picture of London.* London: S. Leigh, 1824–34.

Lenman, Bruce P. "The Weapons of War in Eighteenth-Century India," *Journal of the Society for Army Historical Research* 36 (1968): 33–43.

Lillywhite, Bryant. *London Coffee Houses.* London: G. Allen and Unwin, 1963.

Long, Reverend J. *Selections from Unpublished Records of Government for the years 1748 to 1767 inclusive relating mainly to the Social Conditions of Bengal.* Volume 1. Calcutta: Superintendent Government Printing, 1869.

Lorimer, Douglas A. *Colour, Class and the Victorians; English Attitudes to the Negro in the mid-nineteenth Century.* Leicester: Leicester University Press, 1978.

Madden, Richard R. *Travels in Turkey, Egypt, Arabia, and Palestine in 1824, 1825, 1826, and 1827.* 2 volumes. London Whittaker and Treacher, 1829. 2d edition 1833.

Mahomed, George S. "Sake Deen Mahomed," *Sussex County Magazine* 14 (1940): 42.

Mahomed, Horatio. *The Bath: A Concise History of Bathing, As Practiced by the Nations of the Ancient and Modern World. Including a Brief Exposition of the Medical Efficacy and Salubrity of the Warm, Medicated, Vapour, Shampooing, Shower, and Douche Baths, with Remarks on the Moral and Sanative influence of Bathing.* London: Smith, Elder, 1843.

———. *Short Hints on Bathing, With Special Reference to the use of the Indian Medicated Vapour Bath, with the Operation of Shampooing, Being the Result of the Experience of the Author and his Father, Sake Deen Mahomet, During a Period of Fifty Years.* London: The Author, 1844.

Mahomed, S. D. *Cases Cured by Sake Deen Mahomed, Shampooing Surgeon, And Inventor of the Indian Medicated Vapour and Sea-Water Baths, Written by the Patients Themselves.* Brighton: The Author, 1820.

———. *Shampooing, or, Benefits resulting from the use of the Indian medicated vapour bath: as introduced into this country by S. D. Mahomed . . . containing a brief but comprehensive view of the effects produced by the use of the warm bath, in comparison with steam or vapour bathing.* Brighton: The Author, 1822, 1826, 1838.

Marsh, Charles. *Clubs of London: with anecdotes of their members, sketches of character, and conversations.* 2 volumes. London: H. Colburn, 1828.

Marshall, P. J. *East Indian Fortunes: the British in Bengal.* Oxford: Clarendon Press, 1976.

Martin, Henry. *The History of Brighton and Environs.* Brighton: John Beal, 1871.

Mason, Philip. *A Matter of Honour.* New York: Holt, Rinehart and Winston, 1974.

Meer Hassan Ali, Mrs. *Observations on the Mussulmauns of India.* 2 volumes. London: Parbury, Allen, 1832.

Metcalf, Thomas R. *Ideologies of the Raj.* Volume 3, part 4 of *New Cambridge History of India.* Cambridge: Cambridge University Press, 1995.

Miller, Susan Gilson. *Disorienting Encounters.* Berkeley: University of California Press, 1992.

Mir 'Abdul-Latif Khan Shustari. *Tuhfat al-'alam va zayl al-tuhfah.* Translated by Juan R. I. Cole, "Invisible Occidentalism: Eighteenth-Century Indo-Persian Constructions of the West," *Iranian Studies* 25, 3–4 (1992): 3–16.

Munro, Innes. *Narrative of Military Operations against the French, Dutch, and Hyder Ally Cawn, 1780–84.* London: The Author, 1789.

Musgrove, Clifford. *Life in Brighton.* London: Faber, 1970. Also published in 1981.

Nash, John. *Illustrations of Her Majesty's Palace at Brighton, Formerly the Pavilion, with a History of the Palace,* edited by Edward Wedlake Brayley. London: J. B. Nichols and Son, 1838.

National Archives of India. *Fort William-India House Correspondence.* 21 volumes. New Delhi: National Archives of India, 1949–85.

Ness, Gayl D., and William Stahl. "Western Imperialist Armies in Asia," *Comparative Studies in Society and History* 19 (1977): 2–29.

Nevill, Ralph Henry. *London Clubs, Their History and Treasures.* London: Chatto and Windus, 1911.

Obituary of Frederick Akbar Mahomed. *Guy's Hospital Reports,* 43 (1886): 1–10.

Peers, Douglas M. "War and Public Finance in Early Nineteenth-Century British India: The First Burma War," *International History Review* 11, 4 (November 1989): 628–47.

———. *Between Mars and Mammon.* London: I. B. Tauris, 1995.

Peterson, M[ildred] Jeanne. *The Medical Profession in Mid-Victorian London.* Berkeley: University of California Press, 1978.

Photophilus [pseudonym]. *The New Irish Bath versus the Old Turkish Bath; or Pure Air versus Vapour. Being an answer to the errors and mis-statements of Drs. Madden and Corrigan.* Dublin: William McGee, 1860.

Playfair, James. *A Method of Construction of Vapour Baths, so as to render them of small expence, and of commodious use in private families.* London: John Murray, 1783.

Poll Books: Brighton, 1835, 1841, 1847, 1852, 1857, 1859; East Sussex 1832, 1837; Sussex 1820, 1832, 1837, 1841; Westminster 1841, 1851–52.

Pratt, Mary Louise. *Imperial Eyes: Travel Writing and Transculturation*. London: Routledge, 1992.

Relhan, Anthony. *Short History of Brighthelmstone, with remarks on its Air, and an Analysis of its Waters*. 1761. Reprint, Brighton: Philanthropic Society, 1829.

Review of John Henry Grose, *Voyage, Monthly Review* 17 (1757): 301–6.

Review of *Shampooing, Gentleman's Magazine* 93, 2 (August 1823): 62.

Roberts, Henry D. *A History of the Royal Pavilion Brighton with an Account of its Original Furniture and Decoration*. London: Country Life, 1959.

Robinson, Ronald. "Non-European Foundations of European Imperialism." In *Imperialism*, edited by William Roger Louis, 128–51. New York: New Viewpoints, 1976.

Russell, Richard. *A Dissertation on the use of Sea-Water in the Diseases of the Glands. Particularly The Scurvey, Jaundice, King's Evil, Leprosy, and the Glandular Consumption. Translated from the Latin [1750] of Richard Russell, M.D. By an Eminent Physician*. London: The Translator, 1752.

Said, Edward W. *Orientalism*. New York: Vintage, 1979.

———. *Culture and Imperialism*. New York: Alfred Knopf, 1993.

Sala, George Augustus. *The Life and Adventures of George Augustus Sala written by himself*. 2 volumes. London: Cassell and Company, 1895.

Scott, William. *Proposal for Establishing in Edinburgh and other Towns a Newly Improved Apparatus for the application of the Vapour of Water, Sulphur, and other Medical Substances*. Edinburgh: Waugh and Innes, 1820.

Shade, Sarah. *A Narrative of the Life of Sarah Shade*. London: Knight and Compton, 1801.

Smith, F. B. *The People's Health, 1830–1910*. New York: Holmes and Meier, 1979.

Smith, Horace, ed. *Comic Miscellanies in Prose and Verse of the Late James Smith Esq*. 2 volumes. 2d edition. London: Henry Colburn, 1841.

Smith, Thomas. *A Topographical and Historical Account of the Parish of St. Mary-le-bone*. London: John Smith, 1833.

Spence, Jonathan D. *The Question of Hu*. New York: Vintage, 1988.

Stables, W. Gordon. *Turkish and other Baths: A Guide to Good Health*. London: The Author, 1882.

Sutherland, Lucy S. *The East India Company in Eighteenth Century Politics*. Oxford: Oxford University Press, 1952.

Symons, John. *Observations on Vapor-Bathing and its effects*. Bristol: n.p., 1766.

Urquhart, David. *Pillars of Hercules or, A Narrative of Travels in Spain and Morocco in 1848*. 2 volumes. London: Richard Bentley, 1850.

———. *The Turkish Bath with a View to its Introduction into the British Dominions.* London: David Bryce, 1856.

———. *Manual of the Turkish Bath. Heat a Mode of Cure and a Source of Strength for Man and Animals,* edited by Sir John Fife. London: John Churchill and Sons, 1865.

Visram, Rozina. *Ayahs, Lascars and Princes: Indians in Britain 1700–1947.* London: Pluto Press, 1986.

Voltaire, François. *Mahomet, The Impostor: A Tragedy.* Translated by Reverend James Miller. London: The Translator, 1778.

Wallis, E. *Brighton Townsman and Visitor's Directory.* Brighton: E. Wallis, c. 1826.

Weekes, Henry. *The Warm Water Remedy: A Treatise on the Warm, Vapour, and Medicated Baths, with directions for their use.* London: Edwards and Hughes, 1844.

Weintraub, Karl. "Autobiography," *Critical Inquiry* 1, 4 (June 1975): 821–48.

Wellesley, Arthur, Duke of Wellington. *The Prime Minister's Papers: Wellington Political Correspondence.* Volume 1. Edited by John Brooks and Julia Gardy. London: HMSO, 1975.

Wharncliffe, Lady. *The First Lady Wharncliffe and Her Family (1779–1856).* 2 volumes. Edited by Caroline Grosvenor and Charles Beilby. London: William Heineman, 1927.

Whitlaw, Charles. *The Scriptural Code of Health, with Observations on the Mosaic Prohibitions, and on the Principles and Benefits of the Medicated Vapour Bath.* London: The Author, 1838.

Williams, John. *Historical Account of the Rise and Progress of the Bengal Native Infantry, From its first Formation in 1757, to 1796.* 1817. Reprint, London: John Murray, 1970.

Williamson, Thomas. *The East Indian Vade Mecum.* London: Black, Parry, and Kingsbury, 1810.

Willis, G. *Willis' Current Notes.* Covent Garden: G. Willis, 1851.

Wright, C. *The Brighton Ambulator, containing Historical and Topographical Delineations of the Town from the earliest period to the Present Time.* London: C. Wright, 1818.

Wynter, John. *Of bathing in the hot-baths, at Bathe; chiefly with regard to the palsie, and some diseases in women.* London: W. Innys, 1728.

Yule, Henry, and A. C. Burnell. *Hobson-Jobson,* edited by William Crooke. 1903. Reprint, New Delhi: Munshiram Manoharlal, 1968.

INDEX

Adams, Captain, 35–36, 186
Adelaide, Queen of England (1830–37), 173
Afghans, 4, 21
Africans, xx, 5, 9, 76, 184, 185
Ahmed Shah, Mughal Emperor (1748–54), 91, 187
Ain-i Akbari, 83. *See also* Akbar
Akbar, Mughal Emperor (1556–1605), 79, 83, 91, 113
Allah, 64, 69–70
Allahabad, 21, 84–85, 117, 187–89
Ambaji Inglia, 112
Anglo-Indians, 135, 140, 142, 145, 180
Anglo-Maratha War, First (1775–82), 110–15
Anglo-Mysore War, Second (1780–84), 22, 113, 115
animal fighting, 93
annexation of Indian states, xv, xxii, 5, 11, 16, 179
Arabia, 2, 69–70
architectural styles: in India, 39–40, 43, 50–53, 58–60, 80, 84–85, 91, 97–101; in England, 146, 150–51, 157, 161–65; in Ireland, 40, 142
Arcot, 113

arek, 104, 139, 199
army. *See* Bengal Army; Mughal army
arrack, 57, 102, 199
artillery. *See* Bengal Army, artillery
Asaf al-Daula, Nawab of Awadh (1775–97), 21, 86–88, 94–96, 117
astrology and astronomy, 63, 80
audience for *Travels*, xvi–xvii, xxi, 138, 179
Aurangzeb, Mughal Emperor (1658–1707), 90
authorship of *Travels*, xix–xxiii, 138–40, 187, 189
Awadh, 3, 4, 11, 21, 24–25, 87–88, 117, 187. *See also specific rulers*
Awsiter, Doctor, 153, 193

Baharampur, 20–22, 57, 187
baharea, 61, 129, 199
Bailie, William Annesley, xx, 31, 89, 137, 189
Baillie, William A., 22, 113
Baker, Eleanor, 142, 190
Baker, Godfrey, 30, 135–36
Baker, Godfrey Evan: court-martialed, 22; death of, 136; in India, xv, 17–18, 21–29, 38–44, 47–49, 57, 114–15, 118–19, 122–24, 135; in Ireland,

Composition: Integrated Composition Systems
Text: 10/15 Janson
Display: Janson
Printing and binding: Thomson-Shore, Inc.